KOREAN CHURCH GROWTH EXPLOSION

Edited by

Ro Bong-Rin
and
Marlin L. Nelson

Publishers
Word of Life Press

Asia Theological Association

Cover Picture: Over one million people attended
the closing meeting of the 1973 Billy Graham
Crusade in Seoul. This was the largest Christian
gathering in the history of the church. (picture
used with permission of the Billy Graham
Evangelistic Association)

PREFACE

"Why is the Korean church growing so rapidly?" Many Christians around the world have asked this question. The rapid growth of the church in Korea has been reported in various Christian and secular magazines. Articles such as "Six New Churches Everyday," "Korea: Asia's First Christian Nation?" and "Church Growth Unlimited" have excited Christians around the world, particularly those who are involved in church growth studies.

According to the 1982 Gallup Research Institute's report, the Christian population in South Korea has increased to 20 percent including 4 percent Roman Catholics. Among the young adults (between ages 18 to 24), 30 percent, including 6 percent Roman Catholics, claim to be Christians.

The Korean church celebrates the Centennial Year of Protestant Missions in 1984. In 1884, 100 years ago, the first Presbyterian missionary from North America went to Korea to evangelize the people in this hermit nation. He was followed by the first Methodist missionary in 1885.

Although the missionaires and the Christians in Korea have gone through severe trials and persecutions, they have remained firm in their faith and have tirelessly proclaimed the gospel to the nation. The strength of the Korean church lies in the local churches. Under the leadership of their pastors, the local churches have trained the laity for their ministries in evangelism, missions, the Christian home, teaching, and social service.

The contributors to this book have analyzed various factors in the church and in Korean culture which have contributed to the rapid growth of the church in Korea. Some of these factors are more cultural, such as Korea's religious traditions, history, politics, and socio-economic situation. Other factors are more spiritual, such as the church's emphasis on prayer, evangelism, missions, Christian education, Bible study, and stewardship. Each contributor was requested to deal with one or more specific factors which have contributed to the growth of the church in Korea. The writers are well-known pastors, para-church leaders, and theologians who are authorities in the areas in which they write. They present the strengths, weaknesses, and dangers of rapid church growth in Korea. This provides a balanced view of both the positive and negative dynamics of rapid church growth and how to cope with them.

We pray that this book will be used as a textbook for church growth in theological schools and that it will inspire and stimulate many pastors and lay leaders to adapt any principles which may be useful to their own situations.

We want to recognize a number of people who have helped produce this book. Dr. Ruth Eshenaur, textbook production coordinator for the Asia Theological Association, and Rev. and Mrs. George Blackstone who were on the staff of the Asian Center for Theological Studies and Mission in Seoul, Korea, helped type and edit the book. Several articles were written in the Korean language and needed to be translated into English because all of the writers except two missionaries are Korean. Dr. Eshenaur and Rev. and Mrs. Blackstone have spent much time and effort making English more clear and checking the accuracy of some of the statements. The Chinese staff of the Asia Theological Association have also spent a great deal of time and effort typing and retyping the manuscripts. All of the ideas in this book do not necessarily represent the viewpoint of the authors or the publishers but are presented here for your thoughtful consideration.

Ro Bong-Rin
Marlin L. Nelson

TABLE OF CONTENTS

Women's class in the Central Presbyterian Church of P'yongyang with Pastor S.A. Moffett. This picture was taken about the time of the great P'yongyang Religious Revival.

Early missionaries experienced much suffering. Rev. Chase A. Sawtell (left) died after two years of service. Other missionary is unidentified.

Students doing personal evangelism.

Baptism of Korean soldiers.

Christians caring for abandoned children.

The 1973 Billy Graham Crusade in Seoul.

Explo '74 sponsored by Campus Crusade For Christ.

Student evangelism opportunities are numerous.

High school students praying during a Crusade.

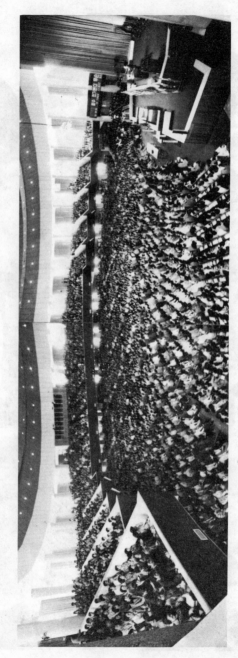

Interior of Yoido Full Gospel Central Church.

PART ONE

EVANGELISM AND
FOREIGN MISSIONS

Dr. Kim Joon-Gon, National Director of Korea Campus Crusade for Christ and Director of Affairs, C. C. C. Int. East Asia Area, graduated from the Chosun University, did graduate studies at Fuller Theological Seminary (U. S. A.) and received an honorary Doctor of Literature degree from the Chun Buk University. An ordained Presbyterian minister. chaplain and principal of the Soongsil High School in Kwangju (1951-55) he received a variety of experiences equipping him to serve as Executive Chairman for both Explo '74 and 80 World Evangelization Crusade.

The Korean Christians are zealously concerned about winning their family and friends to Christ. Some are active in personal evangelism, others bring unbelievers to church. Crusades with an unbelievable attendance of two million have also been conducted in Seoul making an impact upon the entire nation. Dr. Kim Joon-Gon relates his personal struggles of|faith and how to live a Spirit-filled life. Your faith and commitment will be challenged anew as you read this chapter.

I KOREA'S TOTAL EVANGELIZATION MOVEMENT

by Kim Joon-Gon

The first drop of water splashed to earth. More drops of water fell until they became rain. The rain formed a small brook; gathering momentum, it became a stream. The stream became a river. The rain continued to pour down, causing the river to swell and overflow its banks. As the flood surged across the land, it influenced everything with which it came into contact.

It seems that the national evangelization movement of Korea began like the rain. And it is our urgent prayer that it will so continue. The movement had no organized beginning; it sprang up sporadically, beginning in churches, prayer houses, and group meetings. The total evangelization of Korea has become the common vision of Korean Christians. All who are fully committed to the Lord are conscious of this goal and are seriously trying to evangelize the nation. Thus, thousands of small brooks are running into the widening river--and the river is beginning to flood across the land.

My Personal Vision for Korea

Together with the Korea Campus Crusade for Christ staff, I am one of these small brooks. My personal vision for the national evangelization movement was born many years ago. Reared in a strict Confucian home, I first heard about Jesus Christ as a third-grade student in primary school. During my teenage years, I became interested in Christianity and sought out a Christian church to attend. It was there that I committed my life to Christ and became active in the church. This interest lasted throughout my school days and early married life.

However, the starting point of my real Christian life began when I later faced persecution and death. To escape the Japanese domination, I took refuge in Manchuria for nine months. While hiding there, I prayed for national liberation from Japan.

Then came the Korean War. While on Chido I was under the domination of the Communists for three months. One night my family, including my wife and father, were murdered before my eyes. I was beaten repeatedly with a club until I lost consciousness. I was then left for dead, but somehow in the night I revived and went to search for my small daughter. During those months I narrowly escaped death twenty-one times. Out of a population of 20,000 in my area, 2,000 people were murdered. I almost died physically and at times could not move to help my little girl who was also dying from hunger and longing for her mother. My consciousness came and went for days at a time. I had already died psychologically because I had no hope. I saw no way of escape.

But the most serious part was my spiritual condition. I had stopped praying or expecting God to answer; I even had no desire for eternal life. I lost sight of God, and within my soul I was complaining and trying to cut myself off from Him. I experienced the total despair and darkness of spiritual death, feeling completely separated from God.

Then a strange thing happened. Suddenly, I realized that my lips had begun to move in prayer to God. That prayer was begun on my lips by the Holy Spirit, and it ended in my heart. At that moment I passed from death to life. As I turned to my Savior, great peace and joy sprang up within my heart like a river.

Out of this valley of death, the Lord called me to witness to the very Communist who had murdered my family. As I began to pray for this man whom I hated, my strength was restored. I experienced a new freedom from fear, hatred, and death. I went to this Communist to express my love to him and to tell him about the love of God and the forgiveness of sin through Jesus Christ. The Communist leader, startled that I was still alive and overwhelmed that I would come to him in love, wept in repentance for his sins and became a new man in Christ. Today, he is an elder in a Korean church, and we continue to pray for one another everyday.

While I was in the United States of America in 1957, I met Dr. Bill Bright, president of Campus Crusade for Christ. Dr. Bright inspired me to return to Korea and start the Korea Campus Crusade for Christ.

Twenty-three years ago the Korea Campus Crusade staff and I dedicated ourselves to taking our part in the total evangelization of Korea. In 1960 following a week-long staff conference, we were greatly burdened to pray for the spiritual destiny of our nation. Eight staff members and I climbed to the top of Samgak mountain which overlooks both North and South Korea. We prayed throughout the night in a cave in 16 degrees below zero weather. That night a plan for the total Christianization of Korea was given to us. We agreed together that *every Korean must have the opportunity to become a Christian.* To this task we dedicated ourselves.

We then asked ourselves five questions. The first question was, "Is this vision given by God? and is this vision the will of God?" The second question was, "Since God is willing, is He able; can He do this task?" Third, since both questions were answered positively--God is both willing and able to accomplish the task--our next question was, "When and where do we start this movement?" The answer was "Here and now." "How do we accomplish this task?" was our fourth question. Zechariah 4:6 gave us our answer, "Not by might, nor by power, but by my Spirit..." The task would be accomplished through prayer and faith and the Holy Spirit's power. Finally our fifth question was, "Who is responsible?" The answer from Isaiah 6:8 was clear, " Here am I. Send me!" In other words, we were responsible.

When our five questions were examined, we knew we were responsible. We were called to be sent. Through the Holy Spirit's power, we felt responsible for the\Christianization of Korea.

Without a Vision the People Perish

If we are to accomplish the total evangelization of Korea, we must have a vision of what God desires us to do. What is God's deepest desire for our beloved countrymen living in this beautiful land? What is His command? What is the most urgent task of the Korean church during the centennial celebration of Protestant missions?

The will of God is that the people of this land should

repent, believe in Christ, and become God's children. To complete this task, every believer must witness faithfully for Christ because every non-believer must hear His message in order to believe. "Faith comes by hearing" (Romans 10:17). Presently, no nation on earth is completely Christianized. Before the coming of the last days of earth, surely it is possible that one people--just one--could be totally given to God so that all they have is at His disposal. I believe that we in Korea are facing just this miraculous possibility.

In order to perform great miracles, God often plants dreams in the hearts of His servants. He causes His servants to see what others cannot see, to believe tremendous things that others find incredible, to believe the impossible and make it possible through faith and prayer.

What will occur when our prayers are answered and our vision is realized? In every field and village praise will pour forth from the women at the well and the men at their work. Without compulsion the Word of God will be taught and eagerly studied in every classroom. Every child will be cradled in prayer and nurtured in faith. National leaders will reverently seek the mind of God in all national affairs. Korea will become a godly nation; a light in the Far East. According to His unchanging purpose and promise, God will prosper this land under His blessing. He who makes all things new will make Korea a nation rooted in righteousness and grounded in truth, flourishing under God's blessing.

What is the Korea National Evangelization Movement?

With the above background, I would like to give you my personal, subjective definition of what the Korea National Evangelization Movement includes. Over the past twenty years I have developed criteria necessitating the following characteristics:

Evangelization. Every Korean must have the opportunity to hear and respond to the message of Christ.

Discipleship training. Every Christian must become an effective witness. And in order for him to become an effective witness, he must be trained in how to do personal evangelism.

Maximize Christian influence and impact. The full influence and impact of Christ will stem from Christian homes, Christian businesses, Christian education, Christian culture, Christian politics, a Christian army--Christ's rule in our nation.

A combination of evangelism plus national consciousness (a positive form of spiritual nationalism). God has chosen the nation of Korea to be a holy nation to serve other nations and to evangelize with the love and gospel of Jesus Christ.

A sense of the Kingdom of God (God ruling). Jesus Christ is Lord of all, changing the times, changing the seasons, removing kings and setting them up (Daniel 2:21), closing doors and opening doors, ruling over our nation and everything in this land.

Social salvation and reform. Evanglism is the most effective way to bring about social reform because a good quality of faith and a large number of Christians with faith create a spiritual group dynamic which will change the whole social structure.

A sense of eschatological crisis. The hour is urgent; Christ is coming again soon.

A unique opportunity and openness. Within a few years Korea will be evangelized while it is still day before the night comes when it is too late, because God has uniquely opened our hearts to His message.

All Christian resources organized in order to generate energy and power. This would provide a spiritual-economic community to serve as an economic base, benefiting and serving the entire nation.

Were the above characteristics embodied in the nation, they would provide a political movement not based on revolution theology, political theology, or liberation theology, but a spiritual movement based on biblical evangelism. The end result will not be a utopia. The earth will not enjoy utopia until Jesus comes again and Satan is bound and defeated. However, I do envision these concepts to be necessary for the total evangelization of Korea. They cover pre-evangelism, evangelization, discipleship, socialization, and the total Christianization of this nation. When they are realized, the amazing blessing promised in Deuteronomy 28:1-4 will apply to us. In Christ all things will be made new.

Steps to National Evangelization

Several strategies have been implemented and major thrusts have occurred in recent years. These have all served as stepping stones to the overall goal of total evangelization of this nation.

Training. Training in evangelism and discipleship is one of the most important aspects of any strategy. In my opinion several traits characterize effective evangelistic and discipleship training. It must utilize a standardized curriculum which has been tested and proven to have good results. The standardized training curriculum must include simple "how to's" such as "how to become a Christian," "how to be filled with the Holy Spirit by faith," and "how to pray." The training must be intensive and thorough, clear and simple, and easy to learn and teach. It must be put into practice, not simply taught in a classroom. The training must infect the trainee with a vision for national evangelization.

Through this training a special group dynamic, or spiritual atmosphere, will be created. In our Korea Campus Crusade for Christ training we have developed a unique communication situation. Small group dynamics are utilized in the cell group, or what we call *Soon* [a sprout or branch] (See Isaiah 11:1).

Our basic training takes from ten to fourteen hours. The full training course requires about 100 hours involving four nights and five days. We eat together, sleep together, learn together, and pray together. The effectiveness of the course depends on the leader. He must be thoroughly trained and have a spiritual temperature of 100 degrees boiling point. Then, we can put thirty degree or sixty degree or even below zero degree people with him.

When the leader is placed together with approximately ten trainees, he becomes their shepherd, spiritual parent, teacher, and superintendent for twenty-four hours every day for 100 hours. The schedule is very tight with no time to talk or think about other things. This program provides an excellent communication situation. According to our experience, 98 percent of our trainees have a life-changing experience while in this group. They are either transformed by being born again or by becoming Spirit-filled.

We have personally used this type of training with our students and have had phenomenal results. In August 1971 one of our major training conferences was held in Taejon for more than 10,600 registered trainees. Following the training, many of them echoed the comments of a church elder, "Now I know the true meaning of\the passage, 'Love your neighbor as yourself.' The greatest way that I can show love for others is to tell them about Jesus Christ." More than 16,300 persons indicated that they had prayed to receive Christ that week through the witness of these trainees. As a result of this training conference, seventy-two additional county and city-wide institiutes were held during the remaining weeks of August. that year for students across the country.

Churches have also benefited from the same style of training. One example of church growth is the Soong Hee Methodist Church in Inchon pastored by Rev. Lee Ho-Moon. Eight years ago this church had 250 members. Now, after repeating this type of training more than ten times the church has over 4,000 adult members.

There are many illustrations of how this training atmosphere can be created. On a large scale, EXPLO '74 is an example of training designed around the same type of strategy. On a smaller scale, examples include small groups meeting in classrooms, tearooms, private homes, military units, offices, prisons, factories, public parks, or wherever there is a committed leader. The location of the *Soon* group is the leader himself.

Also involved in training particularly in Korea is the use of the *sarang bang* (love room). The rural culture of Korea is sometimes referred to as the *sarang bang* culture. The *sarang bang* is like a coffee shop or the legendary one-room school house in the United States. Many different activities are carried on in the *sarang bang*. Sometimes it is used as a factory where items such as straw rope are made. At other times it serves as the social center of the community where marriages are arranged by the matchmaker; business transactions are conducted; politics and news are discussed; rumors are spread. In other words, it is the news center of the community and where people reconcile disputes--or gamble away their money or where someone might recite a love story or read aloud. At other times the *sarang bang* becomes the village school with about ten students and a tutor. At times the Chinese classics (*seudang*) are studied there. For many years, the Buddhist schools used this *sarang bang* system.

Realizing the need for rural evangelization within the *sarang bang*, from 1971 to 1973 we trained over 14,000 school teachers and village leaders to establish such groups within their villages. The *sarang bang* was used for informal Bible studies and for Sunday school classes. As a result, this training gave birth to many churches.

Our experience revolutionized the concept of church planting. Before, Korean church leaders thought of church planting in terms of erecting buildings and supporting seminary graduates. However, we have now discovered that if we train village leaders, they, themselves, will establish a church.

A new church planting concept, revolving around this type of training was launched in the Hap-Tong Presbyterian denomination. It was called the 10,000 New Church Planting Project. According to a report in the November 7, 1978, issue of *Christian Weekly,* the Hap-Tong Presbyterian Church established 1,200 new churches in two years. By January 1976 they had 2,484 churches. As of November 1978 they had 3,884. The church's membership has almost doubled over this period of time, increasing from 680,000 to 1,000,000. Korea Campus Crusade for Christ assisted in the program spiritually, financially, and technically.

Cooperative evangelism. Several large cooperative evangelistic events have strongly promoted national evangelism. The first of these was the Billy Graham Crusade in 1973. Over one million people gathered each evening for this five-day crusade held on Yoido Plaza in Seoul.

The second was the mammoth training conference, EXPLO '74, held in August 1974. This conference, designed to train one-tenth of Korea's Christian population, which at that time ·was three million, drew more than 300,000 trainees.

Humanly speaking, EXPLO '74 was impossible. In August 1973, a year before EXPLO '74, seventy staff members met for a retreat both to pray and to plan. No one dared to contribute any positive ideas because the size of the training program appeared to them like a Goliath or enormous problem. Feeding, lodging, transportation, finances, training, mobilization, promotion--every single item seemed impossible. At this retreat we posted large sheets of paper on the walls, and I encouraged everyone to speak- out and name the problems. We listed all the anticipated difficulties and problems. When we were finished, we had listed seventy-four "Goliaths" on the sheets of paper. The plan seemed to collapse completely.

It was a critical moment because seventy-four Goliaths threatened seventy Davids. I was utterly discouraged. But the Holy Spirit took the initiative to overcome our lack of faith. I posed the same questions we had asked regarding national evangelization to my staff members. "Do you believe that God is willing for us to train 300,000 Christians?" They an - swered positively, "Yes!" I continued to ask questions. "Since training is God's will, is He able? Do we really believe that if we ask anything according to His will, He hears us?" For awhile we meditated on God's will, faith, prayer, and the power of the Holy Spirit. We then repented of our unbelief.

The seventy staff members were assigned to take one Goliath each and to pray and fight for its defeat. During EXPLO '74, seventy-two of the seventy-four giants were overcome. Regarding the other two, we had prayed for clear weather, but it rained one night very heavily, and we had prayed for a stable political situation, but Madam Park was assassinated on August 15, 1974.

The results of EXPLO '74 went far beyond our highest expection. Out of the audience of 1.3 million people on the first night, it is estimated that 70 percent received assurance of their salvation by faith as a result of the message which explained how they could receive Christ and know that He was in their lives. Thousands more received Him as the 323,400 trainees from seventy-eight countries shared the gospel with individuals on the streets of Seoul that week. The impact was felt across our nation, and in many other countries as well through the 3,000 foreign delegates who returned home as fire seeds to ignite spiritual flames in their own nations.

The impact did not stop with the one week in August 1974, but was felt in churches throughout Korea during the following years. In July 1974 one month before EXPLO '74, one thousand students were sent to one thousand churches in various cities in Korea to collect randomly one thousand church bulletins. One year after EXPLO '74 in July 1975, another one thousand bulletins were collected. The comparison shows a 33 percent increase in church attendance and a 64 percent increase in church offerings. This means that the Korean church increased by one million people one year after EXPLO '74. Four years later we had seven million Christians, so the church increased by 33 percent in the next four years. Many factors contributed to this growth, but training helped make the difference.

Another great united witness stirred the nation in the summer of 1977. Outstanding Korean evangelists conducted large evangelistic crusades which were further used to unite Christians and increase vision for the total evengelization of Korea. At that time the vision for a 1980 evangelization crusade was born. After eighteen months of preparation, this group of well-known Korean evangelists requested that I serve as the executive chairman of the '80 World Evangelization Crusade. This was the most recent cooperative mass crusade held in Korea and was used of God in a phenomenal way.

1980 World Evangelization Crusade
"Here's Life, Korea"

Organization. The basic unit of organization for the '80 World Evangelization Crusade was the local church. Each cooperating church appointed individuals to coordinate training, prayer, and activities. Thirty-seven committees were formed according to classifications such as teachers, college students, women, children, lawyers, doctors, elders, high school students, etc.

Number of people participating in '80 WEC--Here's Life, Korea

Meeting	Total Attendance
Yoido rally	10,500,000
All night of prayer	5,200,000
Morning sessions	250,000
50 Church conferences	240,000
12 Major conferences	160,000
Total	16,350,000 *

* Prayed to be filled with the Holy Spirit: 1,800,000
* Received Christ as Savior: 1,000,000
* Missionary Pledge: 1,000,000

Over 90 percent of Korea's 18,000 churches were involved. And 411 executive committees of which 203 were in Seoul City coordinated the churches' involvement. In Seoul each of the 203 committees represented ten strategically located churches.

Weekly committee meetings were held in each district and the 203 committees met collectively once each month. The largest committee was the Seoul Womens' Prayer Committee, consisting of 290 leaders.

Promotion. Momentum for the crusade was gathered through various forms of promotion. First, a twenty-five minute audio-visual slide presentation was prepared for use by 230 mediated training units. The plan was designed to impart vision and to challenge every Christian to become involved in the '80 World Evangelization Crusade--"Here's Life, Korea." Then, 178 well-known revival speakers were commissioned to speak in each district in order to encourage nationwide revival and promote involvement in the crusade. Committee prayer meetings were held in each district once a month. In eighteen months, 13,434 prayer meetings were held, the size varying in each district. Christians received evangelistic and follow-up training across the country. Korea Campus Crusade staff alone trained 224,200 people. Actively involved almost full time were 680 of our graduate students, known as Nazareth Brothers. They trained 481,000 people and an additional 283,000 people were trained through the use of our mediated training units. A total 988,600 Christian workers received evangelistic and discipleship training.

Throughout the year, radio spots were used to promote the crusade. Far East Broadcasting Company broadcasted 227 radio spots. From December 1, 1979, through August 14, 1980, CBS, a Christian radio station, broadcasted 274 radio spots of sixty seconds each. Six stations were used and a total of 970 radio spots were aired during the first part of the year. These announcements were used as a spiritual challenge to become involved in the crusade. Later, during the "Here's Life, Korea" media campaign they were changed to "I Found It!" spots which created a curiosity similar to that recorded in Acts 2:7. People all across the country were amazed and marveled because of the suspense generated by announcements of "I Found It. You Can Find It Too!" A responsive climate of warm associations was created resulting in many people finding new life in Jesus Christ.

Television was used extensively. The Lord gave us a special blessing in this regard. Appoximately fifty Christian employees working for the government television station had formed a *Soon* Bible study. These employees served as one committee for the crusade and made it possible for us to buy time from the government television station. This had not been done before because of government regulations that (1) only worthwhile nationwide activities could be promoted and (2) these could be for thirty seconds only. However, we were given forty-and sometimes fifty-second spots. Our total time equaled 150 twenty-second spots over a one-month period of time. In addition, two commercial stations, NBC (nationwide), and TBC (Seoul and Pusan), were used. The total number of television spots was 236.

Beginning in September 1979 our two largest daily newspapers carried a Christian column which contained both spiritual food and '80 World Evangelization Crusade promotional information. Normally these columns would cost $ 800,000 but we paid only around $ 200,000 which was pledged entirely by students. This discount was given because officials were aware of the Christian influence in Korea, and they felt the Christian column would increase their current circulation of one million readers each. It is estimated that one paper's circulation increased by 70,000 readers, and I was given an award by the newspaper company for the promotion.

Prayer. Prayer was the strongest emphasis of the crusade. A forty-day national prayer and fasting campaign was held from February 10 to March 20, 1980, due to the critical political situation across the country. It centered on personal repentance and commitment and called for the seven million Christians of Korea to claim from God a nationwide moral and spiritual awakening. The climax of preparation for the crusade was a three-day prayer and fasting rally at the Hanul Mountain Prayer Retreat Center from February 28 to March 1. More than 30,000 people gathered at this mountain retreat. However, 10,000 were turned away for lack of space. Because the building could hold only 10,000, the people had to change places every two hours. Since it was very cold outside, 10,000 would come inside for two hours of prayer; then they would exchange places with the 10,000 who were praying outside on the mountainside.

During the forty-day period, each church was challenged to set aside a three-minute break during the Sunday morning worship service for personal repentance. Every Christian was encouraged to fast for at least one meal per week. Every church received a large fasting offering by its members, which was used for the needs of that church.

Personal prayer was strongly emphasized during the entire promotional and preparation phases of the crusade: Every Christian was given one of eighty-seven different prayer cards listing five prayer items: (1) the name of a North Korean village, (2) the name of one of the provinces in mainland China, (3) the name of one of the countries of the world (every nation was prayed for during this time), (4) the doubling of their own church membership, (5) their own personal "womb" Christian (the person in their area of influence to whom they would witness and bring to Yoido Plaza during the crusade). In addition, they prayed for one of eighty-seven specific '80 World Evangelization Crusade prayer items. Altogether, five million cards were distributed across the country.

For seventeen months groups of 300 students each rotated daily to keep the fires of fasting and prayer burning continually (see Leviticus 6:13).

Motivation to Participate. Several events were used to motivate participation in the '80 World Evangelization Crusade--"Here's Life, Korea." First of all, God used the political uneasiness to motivate non-Christians because they felt insecure and sensed a crisis. Secondly, the people were very curious because the air was very warm spiritually from the prayer and extensive mass media coverage; they wanted to know what deserved so much attention.

Concerning the churches, the long-range effect of the crusade was their primary interest. The crusade satisfied their concern in several ways, First, we assured them of "absolutely doubled attendance" if they participated fully. When we assured them that their attendance would double, they were very motivated to attend.

Also attractive to the churches was the fact that this crusade was a tangible test of church growth. The growth of their church could be measured. I knew the growth of the church would be determined by the degree of enthusiastic participation of each church. If they were 100-percent enthusiastically involved, they would get 100-percent growth; if not, their church attendance would not increase.

The "womb" Christian concept in which each Christian prayed for, encouraged, and became involved with a non-Christian was very effective. Every local Christian was to be responsible for bringing one non-Christian to Yoido Plaza. Christians in Seoul City were to invite their non-Christian relatives in the rural areas. Thus, Seoul was full of Christians involved with non-Christians all week long.

Other motivational factors were the impact of the media coverage which was unprecedented in our country. Also, the organizational structure was comprehensive. Never before had 80,000 Christians been organized so extensively. Everyone wanted to be involved and to do his part.

Climax. From August 12-15, 1980, the '80 World Evangelization Crusade--"Here's Life, Korea," coordinated four days of seminars, rallies, and prayer meetings. For four hours each day, twelve major seminars and fifty area church conferences were held across Seoul. Approximately 60,000 people attended the fifty church conferences. Attendance at the twelve major seminars was as follows:

Conference/Attendance		Conference/Attendance	
Youth	2,500	Professionals	200
College students	10,000	Sunday school teachers	2,000
High school students	8,000	Theologion/evolution	1,200
Women's prayer		seminar	
congress (Korean)	2,500	Pastors (Korean)	1,500
Women's prayer		Pastors (Foreign)	3,200
congress (foreign)	300	Theologians	200
Women evangelists	3,000		

Each evening, over two million people gathered on the Yoido Plaza for rallies where internationally-known leaders spoke. The goal of two million people attending was reached by assigning one million Christians to bring one million non-Christians. Here, through the messages of some of God's choice servants of the present generation, these unbelievers were given the opportunity to hear how they could accept Christ in a personal way and grow in their Christian lives.

Also, each evening 1,500,000 Christians remained all night on Yoido Plaza to pray for national evangelization. The 12:00 to 4:00 a. m. martial law curfew was lifted on the Yoido Plaza area specifically so that these people could remain outside to pray.

Results. The results of the '80 World Evangelization Crusade have been unprecedented. Many segments of society have been touched. The church has grown. In March 1979 our students counted 2,050 churches in Seoul. As of August 1981 the Korean Christian press and government agencies, such as the Ministry of Culture and Information, have published that 4,700 churches in Seoul have been located. This indicates that the number of churches has doubled during the past two years.

In January 1981 we surveyed sixty-four of the churches which had been active in the '80 Crusade, and we found very encouraging results. Three churches had increased more then 100 percent in the six months following the crusade. Twenty churches had increased 40 percent. There was an average of 30 percent increase in church attendance among the sixty-four churches. The actual growth depended on how intensely the church was involved, Everywhere in Korea the fields are ready for harvest so growth depends on the attitude of the laborers.

Another result of the crusade is a tremendous spiritual openness across the country. Because 80 percent of the population was aware of and thrilled with the campaign, everyone is challenged to become involved with the majority. The populace can see the moving power of God. Churches are now praying for five to ten times increased membership. Their plans are bigger. Their vision to win non-Christians has increased.

The '80 World Evangelization Crusade was a spiritual turning point in our nation. No one can deny the impact of the crusade; it is having an influence in many areas of society and the church as a whole.

Called to be sent. During the final rally of the '80 World Evangelization Crusade, over one million volunteered when the missionary-sending challenge was given. This was a three-fold challenge: to pray for and finance the missionary-sending project; for parents to surrender their children to go overseas for one year; and for the volunteer to pledge one year of missionary service overseas.

It is estimated that 300,000 of the people stood in response to the challenge to invest one year of their lives overseas as missionaries. We have now launched a program to send 100,000 missionaries and volunteers overseas during the next ten years.

Since that challenge was given, every day in our office we receive telephone calls and letters from persons requesting information on how they can prepare to go overseas and where they can go. People on the street inquire about how they can fulfill this commitment. Already we have registered over 30,000 names and addresses of people willing to go. The utilization of this vast source of manpower will be one of our greatest challenges during the next few years. We must seriously think through the follow-up and implementation of this missionary-sending project.

As a result of these volunteers committing one year of their lives to serve overseas, we have thousands upon thousands of nurses, doctors, teachers, pastors, businessmen, and others desiring to go. Pastors are talking of taking their sabbatical leave, supported by their church, and going overseas. Forty thousand pastors are willing to go as one-year missionaries any place we can send them. Professors of Theology also want to go. Students desire to go to Muslim countries to study. The attitude of thousands of Christians is, "Here am I. Send me!"

God will honor this willingness and eagerness of His people to share His love and forgiveness around the world. He is uniquely answering the prayers for the total evangelization of this nation. He will also answer our prayer to be His light in the Far East.

Total Evangelization Crusade Committed to the Task

"Blessed is the nation whose God is the Lord" (Psalm 33:12). "Behold, I will do a new thing" (Isaiah 43:19). "You shall be unto me a kingdom of priests, and an holy nation" (Exodus 19:6).

Romans 4:13-16 reveals to us that the concept of Israel is not so much a nation of the promised by blood, as it is of a nation by faith. Although there will be no utopia on earth until His second coming, God would be pleased to have a nation won for Christ to serve as a model. That nation would be used uniquely by God as a witness for Christ to all nations of the world. Korea can be that nation! The National Evangelization Movement is committed to this vision and task.

I am personally convinced that Korea will be able to supply through prayer the finances and manpower to support one hundred thousand (100,000) Christian volunteers and missionaries within the next ten years.

Dr. Bradley, the founder of International Center for Learning, has suggested that Christians should "Go forth as seeing the invisible, believing the incredible, and doing the impossible." It has also been said that "You don't test the resources of God until you attempt the impossible so that, unless God is in it, it is doomed to failure."

With the eyes of faith, we can see it--a dream becoming reality. The light springtime showers have passed and already the rain is falling heavily. Small brooks are turning into giant rivers. The rivers are overflowing their banks soon to flood the entire nation. Christ is being planted in every Korean heart! The season of Christ is coming to this land!

The Relation of the Holy Spirit to Spiritual Explosion

Many precious treasures are hidden because of man's indifference, ignorance, misunderstanding, or unbelief. The Messiah was hidden from the Israelites due to their ignorance and unbelief.

One of the largest oil pools in the world lay hidden under the field of a poor farmer in Texas. For many years this man lived in poverty because of his ignorance. When an oil company drilled a test well, they struck a huge oil reserve. This poor farmer had owned it all. He could have been a multi-millionaire, but he had been living in poverty because he didn't know the oil was there!

Atomic power was hidden from man until just a few years ago. Before then, man was ignorant of its existence and its potential use. How much other precious knowledge exists of which we are utterly unaware?

Even though they believed in Jesus, the Christians in Ephesus said, "We have not so much as heard that there is a Holy Spirit" (Acts 19:2). What ignorance was theirs not to know the fullness of the Holy Spirit.

Yet, many of us are like this today. We hear much talk about the filling of the Holy Spirit, but we must seriously and honestly examine ourselves. Are we experiencing the fullness of the Holy Spirit? Or does His power remain hidden from us?

Ephesians 5:18 tells us, "Be filled with the Spirit." The fullness of the Spirit is a simple, practical discovery. It is this precious hidden treasure that I want to explain. The Scripture gives us valuable insight into who the Holy Spirit is, why He came, and how we can personally experience His fullness.

Who Is the Holy Spirit?

The Holy Spirit is not the spirit of the universe. He is not some universal principle. He is not a vague, impersonal force. He is not an "it." He is a person. He is God, the third person of the Trinity. He is co-equal with God the Father and God the Son. He possesses all the attributes of God Himself.

Why Did the Holy Spirit Come and What is His Work?

The work of the Holy Spirit has two aspects. First is the general aspect and second is the special, redemptive aspect of His work.

Genesis 1:2 tells us, "And the world was without form ...and darkness was upon the face of the deep and the Spirit of God moved upon the face of the earth." The Holy Spirit was involved in the creation. He is the God of creation.

In Exodus 31:1-12 the Holy Spirit is described as giving wisdom, knowledge, and creative ability. This ability or workmanship included guiding, designing, and building of the tabernacle. Nothing happens without the Holy Spirit's work. A good illustration of His redemptive work is a symphony in which the Holy Spirit can be compared with the conductor. The composer of the symphony is God. The subject of the symphony is the redemption of Jesus Christ. The musical notes are the Bible. The musicians are Christians, and the audience is non-Christians. As the conductor, the Holy Spirit works for and assists in the work of redemption according to the musical score, the Bible.

Summing up the work of the Holy Spirit, He is the spirit of missions. He is the Spirit of Christ who came to glorify Christ. He came to convict sinners and draw them to Christ, to illuminate the truth of Christ, and to conform the Christian to the image of Christ.

He also came to bear the fruit of Christ--inner character fruit and soul fruit--both of which are the the fruit of the Holy Spirit. Thus, He reproduces the life of Christ in believers.

The Filling of the Holy Spirit

To be filled with the Holy Spirit means to be controlled by the Holy Spirit. An opposite analogy to being filled with the Holy Spirit is to be filled with hatred or to be drunk with wine. Hatred or drunkenness can control those who hate or drink. When wind fills a sail, the boat will move because the wind controls it.

The filling of the Holy Spirit mentioned in Ephesians 5:18 is not a one-time experience. It is continual. It is an experience which must be repeated. It means we must keep on being filled. We must let the Holy Spirit dominate our lives and control us. The Spirit-controlled life is a life yielded to God.

In the New Testament the filling of the Holy Spirit is mentioned fourteen times. In the book of Luke it is mentioned four times, in the book of Acts nine times, and once in Ephesians 5:18.

We are told that John the Baptist and his parents were filled with the Holy Spirit. These three persons, Zacharias, Elizabeth, and their son, John the Baptist, were witnesses of Christ. So the purpose and result of being filled with the Holy Spirit involves witnessing for Christ.

The book of Acts mentions the filling of the Holy Spirit nine times. At Pentecost 120 people were all filled with the Holy Spirit. When Peter was filled with the Holy Spirit, 3,000 people were converted by his preaching.

Being filled with the Holy Spirit and witnessing for Christ is the New Testament pattern. The following nine references from Acts show us that being filled with the Holy Spirit resulted in witnessing for Christ. The first reference in *Acts 4:31* tells us that after the disciples were filled with the Holy Spirit, they spoke the Word of God with boldness.

Acts 4:8 tells us that Peter was filled with the Holy Spirit and witnessed for Christ before the Sanhedrin. *Acts 6:3* records that seven deacons were full of the Holy Spirit and wisdom. The head representative, a Spirit-filled man named Stephen, preached Christ and was killed for his witness. All seven deacons preached Christ. *Acts 7:55* tells us that Stephen, "being full of the Holy Spirit saw the glory of God and Jesus standing on the right hand of God."

Acts 9:17-18 informs us that at the beginning of his Christian life, Paul was filled with the Holy Spirit and began preaching Christ. *Acts 11:24* explains that Barnabas, who was full of faith and the Holy Spirit, became a Christian witness.

Acts 13:7-8 tells us that Paul was filled with the Holy Spirit while he was speaking to the proconsul, Sergius Paulus, and the magician, Elymar. Paul was filled with the Holy Spirit in order that he could share Christ with them.

Acts 13:52 states, "The disciples were continually filled with joy and with the Holy Spirit." And *Acts 14:1* says that the disciples spoke of Christ in the synagogue in Iconium where there were many Jews and Greeks. As they spoke, many believed in Christ. This was a natural result of being filled with the Holy Spirit. So, we can see that in all nine references the filling of the Holy Spirit brought joy, wisdom, and faith which caused these men to share Christ with great boldness.

What We Need to Know to be Filled
With the Holy Spirit

First, we must know the value of being filled with the Holy Spirit. This is a precious discovery—like finding a a precious jewel. The Spirit-filled life is of tremendous value. When we realize this value, we will make every sacrifice to obtain it.

Second, God commands the Spirit-filled life. It is not optional. It is a must. We must obey God's command to be filled with the Holy Spirit.

Third, there is no true Christian life apart from the Spirit-filled life. The normal Christian life is the Spirit-filled life.

Actually, the world has three kinds of people. The natural man, the carnal man, and the spiritual man. 1 Corinthians 3:1 tells us, "And I, brethren, could not speak unto you as unto spiritual, but as unto carnal, even as unto babes." The natural man is the man without Christ. He has not yet been born again. The spiritual man knows Christ and allows His Spirit to control his life. The carnal man has received Christ but is not Spirit-filled. The spiritual man is living the normal Christian life.

The *fourth* fact we need to know is that we are filled with the Holy Spirit by faith. This important point is often misunderstood. I was filled with the Holy Spirit when I was on Chido Island after my family was murdered by the Communists. For several months after this experience, I was filled with a sense of joy and release. But somehow I lost that experience, and I began to seek it again. For ten or fifteen days at a time I fasted. Many times I did this. I didn't mention my search to many people, but deep in my heart my desire was to restore that experience.

But the experience of the filling of the Spirit came and went. I would have it for a few hours. Then I would lose it again. So my Christian life was full of despair. A few years later I became very stable in the Lord with no more up and down experiences. Why? What gave me stability?

I heard Dr. Bill Bright, president of Campus Crusade for Christ International, explain that we are filled with the Holy Spirit by faith. This was a new biblical truth for me. This was what my Christian life lacked. I was then filled by faith. Now my experience is very stable and without doubts. Regardless of my feelings, I am filled with the Holy Spirit by faith. No longer do I have up and down experiences, because I do not depend on my feelings.

So, do not depend on your feelings. Place your faith in the trustworthiness of God and His Word. By faith we are saved. By faith we receive the Holy Spirit. And by faith we keep on being filled with the Holy Spirit.

The *fifth* thing we need to know is that the filling of the Holy Spirit is easy to obtain. Do not expect to become a perfect man. It is wrong to think that you cannot be filled with the Holy Spirit until you become a perfect, holy person. We must depend on God in order to be holy. Right now we can be filled, and God wants us to be filled with the Holy Spirit.

The *sixth* fact is the small amount of time it takes to be filled by faith. How long does it take to wash away our sins? Do we need to cry for several hours, fast for forty days? How long does it take?

The Buddhists practice an eternal washing process for the remission of sins to obtain forgiveness. They have to pay every penalty for sins by their own efforts. It takes an eternity. How long does it take God to forgive sins? An eternity? How long does it take us to accept Christ? Billy Graham extends an invitation and right away decisions are made. The gospel is presented and someone accepts Christ and becomes a Christian. It takes an instant. How long does it take to change directions in a car? If you are going south, how long does it take to go east?

None of these these things take much time. The issue is not the amount of time but heart attitude. Likewise, we can be filled with the Holy Spirit right now by faith. By faith we receive eternal life. By faith we will be resurrected. Without faith it is impossible to please God. What is not of faith is sin. We live by faith, not by sight.

In Galatians 3:2 Paul asks: "Have you received the Holy Spirit by works or by faith?" And he continues by referring to Abraham's blessing. In 3:14, he says that "We might receive the promise of the Holy Spirit through faith." Through faith, we can right now receive the Holy Spirit promised to Abraham. It is not a matter of time.

The *seventh* thing we need to know is that the filling of the Holy Spirit is in proportion to the degree of the maturity of the Christian. An example is the pistons in an engine. Both a two-piston engine and an eight-piston engine can run at full speed. Like an engine, a Christian can be 100 percent Spirit-filled according to his maturity and capacity.

Both a small and a large vessel can be filled. So every believer from a child to a pastor can be filled with the Holy Spirit. A new Christian or a mature Christian can both be filled with the Holy Spirit. The new Christian will run like a two-piston engine. The more mature Christian will run like an eight-piston engine. But both will be running to their full capacity when they are filled with the Holy Spirit by faith.

Eighth, when we are filled with the Holy Spirit, we will always produce two kinds of fruit. One kind is the inner fruits of character mentioned in Galatians 5:22-23. We will bear these nine spiritual fruits. The other kind is soul fruit. The lost will come to know Christ personally, and we will produce the fruit of serving the Lord and His people. Inner character fruit and outer soul fruit are the result of being filled with the Holy Spirit by faith.

And *finally,* we should know that we are filled by the Holy Spirit by grace, not by law. We have the tendency to think that our heart must be pure, like crystal clear water. So we try to become perfect with no sin nature. This is similar to Buddhist thinking in trying to attain enlightenment and perfectionism.

This kind of thinking hinders our understanding and application of the Spirit-filled life because no human can be perfect. We are imperfect during our entire life. We are progressively sanctified and made more like Christ until our death. We are like a small child beginning to walk who falls down and gets up many times. We should not be discouraged when we fall. Even though we strive for perfection and conformity to the image of Christ, we still live by grace. We have no human resources to live the Spirit-filled life and so must depend on His grace completely.

How to be Filled with the Holy Spirit

The most important part of this subject is how to be filled with the Spirit by faith. Since my own personal discovery, that we are filled with the Spirit by faith, I have shared the concept with thousands of individuals and groups. Several years ago, I shared this concept with 200 Korean evangelists who had never heard it before. The majority of their lives were revolutionized by this teaching, just as mine had been. Today, they preach this same message across Korea. The key is to discover how to use faith in order to be filled with the Holy Spirit.

First, recognize the Spirit's indwelling as a person. Recognize His personhood. Realize that "He, not it, now dwells in my heart." He is closer than my father, closer than my wife, closer than myself. We are in relationship with an intimate, loving person. Recognize that person within you.

Second, long for and thirst after Him. Hunger for Him. "If any man thirst, let him come unto me and drink." "He that believes on me, as the Scripture has said, out of his heart shall flow rivers of living water." Long for and desire to be filled with the Holy Spirit.

Third, confess your sin. 1 John 1:9 tells us, "If we confess our sins, He is faithful and just to forgive our sins and to cleanse us from all unrighteousness." "Confess" means to agree with God. We must agree with God concerning three things.

First of all, agree that at the cross the Lord removes all your sin: past, present, and future. He died for all sin. *Second,* agree with God's conviction that sin is wrong. And *third,* agree with the fact that if we confess our sin, God cleanses and forgives us. He will give us the power to overcome sin.

The *fourth* thing we need to know is that we must ask to be filled. Because the Spirit is a person, we can invite Him to forgive our sins and control our lives.

How do we know He will hear our prayer? Because of the promises of His Word. 1 John 5:14 and 15 says, "And this is the confidence that we have in him, that, if we ask any thing according to his will, he heareth us; And if we know that he hear us, whatever we ask, we know that we have the petitions that we desired of him."

Luke 11:13 tells us that a father gives his son best gifts. "If you then, being evil, know how to give good gifts to your children, how much more shall your heavenly father give the Holy Spirit to them that ask Him?" This is very important. How much more will your heavenly Father give the fullness of the Holy Spirit to them that ask him? Sincerely invite the Holy Spirit to control you, and you can be sure He will.

Fifth, when you pray to invite the Holy Spirit to take control of your life, you must believe that He answered. Prayer is 50 percent and believing is the other necessary 50 percent. Prayer and believing put together make 100 percent. Without believing, prayer is just half of what is necessary.

If you ask for filling but do not believe, you are putting out the Spirit's fire (1 Thess. 5:19), because without faith it is impossible to please God. After you confess your sin and invite the Spirit through prayer to control you, then believe that He is controlling your life. Again, I want to stress that we are not filled with the Holy Spirit because of our great desire or because we confess our sins or do something else. We are filled by faith. Our desire and our confession of sin are factors which prepare our hearts for the filling of the Spirit by faith.

Sixth, to express your faith, you should thank and praise God often that you are filled with the Holy Spirit. Giving thanks makes the fact real in your experience.

"A bell is not a bell until it is rung.
A song is not a song until it is sung.
Love is not love until it is expressed."

In the same way, the filling of the Holy Spirit does not become real to you until you thank and praise Him for it.

Seventh, the filling of the Holy Spirit involves your willingness to commit your life to Him. You must yield your life to God and let Him control you. This commitment is like married life. If there is something wrong, both people know it. Suppose the husband is giving 90 percent of himself but holds back 10 percent from the relationship. No matter how much they try to harmonize, it is impossible until they both abide by their original commitment. The original commitment is his 100 percent and her 100 percent. Marriage must remain a 100 percent commitment of both parties throughout life.

The same is true of the Spirit-filled life. If you reserve 10 percent or even 2 percent, you will not experience His fullness. Something will be missing. Until this unreserved commitment is made, you cannot be filled with the Holy Spirit. Even though you may pray some nice- sounding words asking the Spirit to fill you, they are a lie. We must give Him 100 percent commitment. This is the commitment spoken of in Romans 12:1: "Present your bodies a living sacrifice..."

How to Continue the Spirit-Filled Life

Once we are filled with the Spirit, how do we continue living the Spirit-filled life? What happens when we sin again and take control of our own life? When we sin, our fellowship with the Lord is broken. To restore our fellowship, we need to practice spiritual breathing. By faith we can continue to experience God's cleansing and filling.

If you are aware of an area of your life that is displeasing to the Lord, breathe spiritually. This is just like physical breathing. It involves exhaling the impure and inhaling the pure.

When we *exhale,* we confess our sin. We agree with God concerning our sin. And we thank Him for His forgiveness. Then we *inhale* by surrendering the control of our life to Christ and by receiving the fullness of the Holy Spirit by faith. Trust that He controls and fills you. He commands in Ephesians 5:18: "Be filled with the Spirit." And He promises in 1 John 5:14, 15 that "If we ask anything according to His will, He will hear and answer our prayer." We can, therefore, be sure He will anwer our prayer to be filled by faith.

Through practicing this simple concept of spiritual breathing, we can cease being defeated, fleshly Christians. We can begin living the joyful, victorious life of a Spirit-filled Christian.

Why are we filled? Just like those in the book of Acts, the main reason we are filled by the Holy Spirit is to make us witnesses. The life we live and the words we speak should be a witness for Christ.

The final words of Jesus to His disciples were: "You shall receive power after the Holy Spirit is come upon you: you shall be witnesses unto me both in Jerusalem, and in all Judea and Samaria, and unto the uttermost part of the earth" (Acts 1:8). The power of the Holy Spirit turned a wicked Roman Empire upside down. Today, through believing, obedient Christians, His power can be released to turn our world upside down. He can cause a spiritual explosion in your church and nation.

Unchangeable Pattern for Spiritual Explosion

Pentecost, as described in the Book of Acts, gives us the unchangeable pattern for spiritual explosion. Pentecost was the birthplace of the church. Pentecost is also an example for all churches and Christians down through the ages. This example includes six unchangeable steps for us to follow.

First, the disciples of Christ obeyed the Lord's Great

Commission. Second, they anxiously expected and waited for the power of the Holy Spirit. The Greek word for dynamite (dunamis) is used. They were expecting and waiting for the dynamic power of the Holy Spirit to come on them.

Third, they were involved in desperate, united prayer. The fourth step is a result of the Holy Spirit's coming. When He came upon these believers, all differences of race, nation, culture, religion, and ideology were broken through. This means that through the power of the Holy Spirit, they were able to communicate the gospel. Fifth, they were united in the love of God.

And sixth, they spread the gospel everywhere. Christians were being added to the church daily. Starting in Jerusalem, their vision extended to the uttermost parts of the earth.

Evangelism. Evangelism involves world vision and adding to the church daily. Just as fire exists by burning, the church keeps her vitality through evangelism. When evangelism dies, all dynamism dies. When evangelism dies, prayer dies. When evangelism dies, unity and love die.

The flames of the Holy Spirit, evangelism, prayer, love, and unity are inseparably related to one another. If these flames are not kept burning, all other vital aspects of the church will die.

Another negative result in the church when evangelism dies is destructive controversy and dissent. For example, in the fifteenth century, the Muslims had surrounded Constantinople. It was a critical hour. Constantinople was the second Rome then, a holy, Christian city.

During this desperate hour, one of the assemblies of the clergy was discussing three controversial topics. The first topic of discussion was the color of the virgin Mary's eyes. Were they black or were they blue? Another disputed subject was the sex of angels. Are angels male or female? The third subject was holy water. If a fly dies in the holy water, is the holy water polluted by the fly or is the fly sanctified by the holy water?

Instead of desperately praying for their city, these church leaders were arguing about these trivial questions. While they wasted time discussing unimportant subjects, Constantinople was captured and ever since that time has remained a Muslim city. Church history records many similar illustrations of what happens when evangelism dies. Irrelevant subjects gain top priority in our thinking and our golden opportunities to advance Christ's kingdom are lost. Spiritual explosion will not happen unless the flame of evangelism is kept burning.

Praying. I also want to stress the importance of prayer in relation to spiritual explosion. The man of God must be deeply burdened for the spiritual condition of his nation. He must have compassion for lost people and be willing to pray and work for their salvation and for revival in the church.

Down through history prayer has preceeded every great movement of God-not ordinary prayer, but desperate, urgent prayer. History yields no exceptions.

It is common knowledge that the Korean church is a praying church. It has kept the fire of prayer burning in our nation. Korea is open in an unprecedented way to evangelism because across the nation we have prayed desperately, without ceasing. Thousands of men and women of God have prayed and fasted. This is the key which has opened Korea's doors to evangelism.

Through prayer we can open and close doors. Paul asks us to pray for evangelism's door to open. Jesus knocks at the door in Revelation 3:20. This refers to both the door of the heart of an individual and a nation. Prayer is absolutely essential to opening a nation's door to the gospel. As you pray, God will bring a spiritual explosion to your nation, too.

Dr. Han Chul-Ha is president and professor of systematic theology at ACTS (Asian Center for Theological Studies and Mission) which was established in 1974. Dr. Han graduated from the Seoul National University (B. A. and M. A.), Westminster Theological Seminary (Th. M.), and Union Theological Seminary in Virginia (Th. D.) Dr. Han is author of A Study on Ancient Christianity *and has published numerous articles on theology and mission.*

Few systematic theologians have a vision, strategy, and zeal for the evangelization of Asia, a continent where over 95 percent do not yet follow Christ. Dr. Han combines his experiences as pastor, scholar, and administrator to challenge Christians to evangelize and to develop their own nations. Biblical aspects of Korea church growth are presented which can be practiced in other Asian countries. Missiologists will be especially interested in the significance attributed to the role of foreign missionaries.

2 INVOLVEMENT OF THE KOREAN CHURCH IN THE EVANGELIZATION OF ASIA

by Han Chul-Ha

The Korean Church is a Praying Church

The Korean church is well known as a praying church. The church commonly practices early morning prayer meetings, all-night prayer meetings, and fasting and praying for several days at a time at a prayer mountain.

Every deep mountain valley has prayer houses where some men and women pray and fast for as many as forty days at one time. Nowhere else in the world are early morning prayer meetings commonly practiced. Of course, not all Korean Christians participate daily in these meetings, but we can say that prayer is a dynamic factor in the Korean church. Pastors are equipped spiritually through their daily morning prayer meetings, surrounded by a group of men and women of prayer who take upon themselves the responsibility for the spiritual care of their congregations. Furthermore, the number of churches practicing all-night Friday prayer meetings is increasing. Even Korean congregations in New York, U.S.A., encourage this practice.

Because of the fervent prayer life of Christians, several characteristics are evident in the Korean church. Korean Christianity emphasizes the experiential more than the intellectual side of faith. The real presence of God is experienced in prayer. Often the Korean church is accused of being influenced by its Shamanistic cultural background. The zeal, dedication, and enthusiasm of Korean Christians are very similar to extreme Shamanistic practices. The Scriptures reveal that God's people throughout the ages demonstrated a similar devotion. The God of Israel introduces Himself as a jealous God who does not tolerate any idolatry. The zeal of Phinehas turned aside God's wrath from the adulterous children of Israel (Numbers 25 : 7). Isaiah prophesied that the zeal of the Lord of hosts will fulfill His Messianic prophecy (Isaiah 9 : 7). The risen Lord prefers that we be cold or hot rather than lukewarm. Because the Laodiceans were lukewarm and neither cold nor hot, He said He would spue them out of His mouth (Revelation 3 : 16).

The primary attribute of God in the mind of Korean Christians is His power. God is experienced primarily as power exercised through the working of the Holy Spirit. The healing power of the Spirit is manifested as Korean believers seek the provision of every need from the Almighty God. God is Giver of everything good since He has already given to us His Son (Romans 8 : 32). They depend upon God for blessings, material as well as spiritual. In short, biblical Christianity is experiential. The God who has been saving the world in a mighty way through the gospel of Jesus Christ from the beginning of history is manifesting His mighty and divine power beyond measure in these days in Korea. As it is written, "They shall not hurt nor destroy in all my holy mountain: for the earth shall be full of the knowledge of the LORD, as the waters cover the sea" (Isaiah 11 : 9). So Korea is full of the knowledge of the Lord and this knowledge shall spread throughout the continent of Asia.

God, who chose His people as His instrument for self revelation, and who manifested His power particularly through His Son, is now working through His Spirit among the believers as He has been doing throughout the ages. God cannot be comprehended without prayer and meditation because He is Spirit. Since prayer is the chief exercise of faith, He manifests His power particularly among praying people. If Korea is blessed, it is a result of the earnest and devoted prayer life and zeal of believers. It is also because of this zeal that God can use the Korean church and this nation for the evangelization of Asia. God's desire is the evangelization of not only Korea but of the entire continent in which it is located. God has raised up the Korean nation as His people for Asian evangelism through the gracious working of His Spirit.

A Praying Church Is a Missionary Church

In the beginning of the New Testament era, Jesus commanded His disciples to assemble for the coming of the Holy Spirit, a new means of saving the world. Previously His redemptive operation was limited to one nation, but with the gospel made complete through Jesus Christ, the entire world was about to be saved. Since God is a Spirit, He wanted to manifest Himself to the hundred and twenty disciples, the Spirit-seeking community which continued with one accord in prayer and supplication. It was to this united praying community that God descended in the Spirit and began the work of redemption through Christ's shed blood. These men and women became the children of God, the new beings of God, by faith in the resurrected Jesus Christ. It was these men and women of prayer who started to manifest the transforming power of Jesus Christ. If the evangelization of Asia is expected through the Korean church, it will only be accomplished through her continual prayer for Asia's evangelization. Whenever God is recognized as Lord, He gives what we request. God will establish His reign in Asia only when He is recognized as the Sovereign Ruler of heaven and earth through His Son Jesus Christ. How can anyone know Him without praying and meditating upon Him? Prayer must be continued even though we have received the Holy Spirit.

The apostolic church continued steadfastly in prayer (Acts 2:42). As the work of the Church expanded, the apostles delegated the work of service to the deacons but retained the work of prayer and preaching for themselves: "But we will give ourselves continually to prayer, and to the ministry of the word" (Acts 6 : 4).

One congregation near my house had a pastor who was critical of the Christian faith although he stressed ethical attitudes. As long as he maintained this attitude, the church did not grow. Later his thinking and attitude changed to encourage faith and prayer, and a revival resulted in the church in direct correlation with the degree of change in the pastor's attitude. After his resignation a young pastor, indeed a totally devoted man of God, came to the congregation. Immediately the spiritual atmosphere changed and it became a praying community. The church attendance increased daily. During a midnight service at the beginning of the new year, the pastor prayed that the members of the congregation would abide in Christ throughout the entire year. Now God and Christ are real to the congregation and the presence of the Spirit is being experienced.

A praying church cannot refrain from becoming a witnessing community. The Lord promised, "But ye shall receive power, after that the Holy Ghost is come upon you: and ye shall be witnesses unto me both in Jerusalem, and in all Judea, and in Samaria, and unto the uttermost part of the earth" (Acts 1:8). After receiving the Holy Spirit, Peter, immediately witnessed to God's power through the crucifixion of His eternal Son, Jesus Christ, by proclaiming repentance and regeneration for all who believe. God's saving work was not limited to the 120 disciples in the Upper Room. Because God is the God of the universe, salvation is for the whole world. Every creature must be obedient to the gospel. Thus, the preaching of the gospel must not be confined to any particular nation or locality; it should be directed to the whole earth as Isaiah prayed, "Let the earth hear, and all that is therein" (Isaiah 34:1), and "... unto the uttermost part of the earth" as the Lord declared (Acts 1:8). All creatures must become obedient to their Creator and renewed in Jesus Christ.

The Korean church is now becoming a missionary church. The largest church in Taegu, the Su-Moon Presbyterian Church, completed its sanctuary and is now reaching out for overseas mission work. Ten percent of the total annual budget is set aside for missionary purposes and the mission committee members were sent to ACTS to explore various possibilities for mission work.

Large congregations in Seoul, such as Sung-Do Presbyterian Church, Shin-Il Presbyterian Church, Dong-An, Ung-Am, and many others have taken a similar course of action and are turning their attention to foreign missions. Being invited to participate in church-planting projects in Indonesia (100 new churches), in the Philippines (50), and in Thailand (30), a response greater than the need came from participating churches. A praying church will become a missionary church.

A Praying Church Is a Growing Church

A praying church cannot help but become a growing church. As a church prays, it grows, because God comes and works through the church. When the Holy Spirit came upon the Jerusalem church, there was tremendous growth. Three thousand souls were added by Peter's preaching, and others were saved daily. The numerical growth of the believers corresponded directly with the preaching of the Word of God (Acts 6:7; 9:31; 12:24; 16:5; 19:20). Before the Antiochian church became a missionary church, it became first of all a growing church. Through the missionary engagements of those who were scattered because of persecution, a great number believed and turned to the Lord because the hand of the Lord was with them (Acts 11:21). Then, through Barnabas, a man full of the Holy Spirit and of faith, many people were added unto the Lord (Acts 11:24). Later, Barnabas and Paul brought together a greater multitude of people at Antioch (Acts 11:26). We see here that a praying church will become a preaching church by receiving the Holy Spirit, and a praying church will become a growing church, and a growing church will become a missionary church. If a church does not follow the dynamic leading of God to launch out to conquer the whole world, the Spirit will depart from the congregation.

The Korean church is a growing church. No one can explain exactly the reason for the tremendous growth. At the end of World War II, the total number of believers was about 300,000. Since that time, the number has doubled every ten years: about 600,000 in 1955, about 1,200,000 in 1965, about 2,400,000 in 1975. The 1980 statistics from the government show 7,180,627 Protestant Christians. If the number of Roman Catholics is included, the number will become over 8,500,000. This rapid increase of Christian believers is not the result of the so-called people's movement because there has not been a mass conversion but rather many became believers through individual evangelism- one by one. Sunday after Sunday every church is adding to its numbers.

There are more than 20,000 congregations in Korea. Suppose each congregation added one new member every Sunday; that means that there would be 20,000 new Christians every Sunday or one million new believers each year. I have observed that most churches have a time for introducing newcomers each Sunday and generally there are new persons to be introduced. This numerical growth indicates that it is the working of the Holy Spirit and not a people's movement influenced by culture or society. Rather individuals are turning to God and away from the world after being disappointed by all other helps.

Only a growing congregation aspires to become a missionary church. Some small congregations are barely self-supporting and could hardly be expected to help others beyond the boundaries of the country. The growing congregations in Korea, with their power and energy, are growing in missionary interest. Of course, the starting point of any missionary work is the Great Commission of our Lord Jesus Christ. It is His will to make all nations disciples. Therefore, it is in obedience to His will and commission that any believer makes any missions attempt. Because of the Great Commission, every Christian is compelled to pray for world evangelization so as to bring the world to obedience to Jesus Christ, the crucified and risen Lord of the universe, whom God has appointed as the ultimate and eternal judge of all. Every nation and every person must be saved and be brought into the Kingdom of the Lord.

Despite the Great Commission, many believers and churches have not dared to think about overseas mission work because of inexperience in working abroad. Today, the situation is changing radically. Millions of people are moving around the world. Tens of thousands go abroad annually even from Korea for business, migration, or tourist purposes. If traveling abroad is so common for secular purposes, how can Christians neglect the Great Commission? A growing community cannot escape from obeying the Great Commission.

Evangelizing Asia Through Nationals
Evangelizing Each Country

The task of evangelizing each Asian country falls primarily upon the shoulders of the national church. Only in exceptional cases is a country strong without strong national churches. Even in Nepal and Bangladesh strong national churches have been established although Christians are still a small minority. In most countries more than one percent of the population is Christian. In these countries we can safely say that the evangelization of the country will be carried out by the national church. Strong national churches have been established in Japan, Taiwan, Hong Kong, China, the Philippines, Indonesia, Singapore, Malaysia, Thailand, Sri Lanka, India, Bangladesh, and Pakistan; theological seminaries have been established for the education of the national pastors in these countries.

The most important matter for the church as a whole today in view of national evangelization is the strengthening of the national church. More effort and attention should be given to the training of leadership for the national churches rather than the sending of missionaries into those countries. Of course, I do not say that foreign missionaries are not necessary. Foreign missionaries are needed to assist and encourage the national churches in their effort to evangelize the nation. But foreign missionaries should not do their own work of evangelization independent of the national churches. If we borrow Ralph Winter's terminology, we must depend upon persons of the same culture for the evangelization of Asia (E-1) rather than upon persons from a similar culture (E-2) or by persons from an entirely different culture (E-3).

From a cultural viewpoint, there is no such thing as a homogeneous unit in Asia. These days there is a tendency for each cultural tradition to try to preserve its own cultural heritage. Despite cultural nationalism or traditionalism, there is no pure cultural unit which can successfully prevent the intrusion of various heterogeneous cultural influences. No traditional culture can isolate itself from radical secularization. Industrialization, modern scientific education, and the establishment of modern political states are radically transforming the minds and lives of Asian people today. In fact, because Christianity itself has been contributing to the modernization and education of each of the nations, we should pay more attention to the upbuilding of national churches and national evangelization.

An American missionary does not need to cross the cultural boundaries of China or India and attempt to become Chinese or Indian. However, if he is successful in crossing the cultural boundaries and identifying with the national culture, it is beautiful. But the missionary must first be a good American, and then he must do his best to assist Chinese Christians or Indian Christians. National church growth is the supreme matter. Regrettably, Western missiology in many instances has been too concerned with crossing cultural barriers to the neglect of the responsibilities of the national church.

The gospel has never been associated with nationalism except in modern Asia. The history of the gospel of Jesus Christ almost from the beginning has been concerned with international interests. It is true that God chose the Hebrew nation as a particular instrument for self-revelation and redemption. In a sense, a theocracy existed from Abraham to Christ, but since the coming of Christ, the cosmic Savior, the national boundaries of salvation history were broken when the eleven Jews were sent to all nations.

At Pentecost representatives of all nations under heaven gathered together as witnesses of wonderful works of God. On that day human languages were brought together as one intelligible language to remedy the human tragedy at Babel - the confusion of human languages. Thus, the gospel is closely linked with internationalism. All those who believe in the gospel of Jesus Christ will be saved without respect of persons, whether Jews or Gentiles, Helenes or barbarians.

In Western history, the development of nationalism went along with the secularization of the West. Martin Luther appealed to the German nobilities with territorialism although it was not truly related to the essence of the gospel. Nationalism in the West has always been something shameful. It is, in the last analysis, rooted in an egotistical and devisive spirit, breaking the common heritage of Christendom. When nationalism took the form of fanatical Nazism and Facism in Germany, it was an intolerable demonic spirit. Many Christian people like Dietrich Bonhoeffer sacrificed their lives to fight against German nationalism.

In Asia nationalism has a different history from that of the West. In Korea it was the missionaries who taught Koreans patriotism. In the early period of modern Korean history, it was in churches that the national anthem was sung and the national flag was raised during various national occasions. When Queen Min-Bi was assassinated and King Kojong was in danger, the missionaries slept in the room next to the King's with pistols while the missionary wives provided food. When Bertrand Russell traveled to Peking in the early 1920's, he found Korean Christian bomb throwers. In Korea, Christian love took the form of patriotism in the midst of Western colonialism. In this Asian situation Christianity can provide the best spiritual principle of national integration. When I met Dr. Chandran, the principal of the United Theological College in Bangalore, India, I asked about his Christian viewpoint of India. He immediately enumerated three facts: First, economic development; second, national integration; and third, bridging the gap between the church and Indian culture.

In theory, by national evangelization, I mean the establishment of a Christocracy in the midst of national life. Christ must be present in every individual's heart and then His spiritual and personal rule must be established at every level of national life. Of course, it is clear that such a thing is not possible now and can only be hoped for at the second coming of our Lord Jesus Christ. If Asia is going to be evangelized, national evangelization must come first. However, international relationships are something quite different. Even evangelized nations will not always come together for international peace. Christian international relations must be patiently developed. The evangelization of nations and true international peace will be realized perfectly when the Lord Himself returns to reign.

From the Asian viewpoint, culture refers not to the matter of crossing cultural boundaries; it is a question of Christian ethics. A traditional culture must be seen first of all in its religious aspect so that the idolatrous elements may be judged and the true object of worship may be sought after. Then the values inherent to the culture must be re-evaluated from the viewpoint of Christian ethics. These questions have nothing to do with the matter of crossing cultural boundaries.

We must view all these questions concerning the evangelization of Asia from within this continent as well as from within each nation rather than from the perspective of Western missionaries who consider the crossing of cultural boundaries the primary concern.

In summary, my conviction is that the primary agent for the evangelization of Asia is the national church within each country. Although Christians may constitute only a minority in most countries, they must aspire to evangelize their own nation. God may not grant the total evangelization of a nation on this earth. Indeed, a hostile spirit prevails throughout the world and mankind's ignorance, slothfulness, and fickleness of nature keeps us from the glory of the kingdom. Consequently, we should never expect the fulfilment of the perfect kingdom of God on the earth, even in a small area. Even in the midst of prayer, we rarely come into the real presence of the Divine Majesty. The power of salvation may be manifested only among a small minority within our nations; yet, we know that evangelization is the only true way of national integration.

Who can be a true patriot except one who is willing to sacrifice his own life for others? Consequently, we believe that the followers of Jesus Christ are the truest patriots. The early missionaries in Korea were thoroughly dedicated to this poor nation. It was they who taught this nation patriotism. The first ordained Presbyterian missionary, Horace G. Underwood, lamented the fact that the darkness of ignorance covered the entire nation. This concern was communicated in his weekly newspaper. The first page had news of government decrees; the second page had articles about agricultural and industrial development; only the third page was dedicated to Sunday school materials. The first Methodist missionary, Henry G. Appenzeller, also published a Christian weekly newspaper which emphasized firstly, loyalty to the King, then patriotism, and finally, love for the people. On one occasion the paper lamented the fact that Korea celebrated the national holidays of China rather than its own.

Today, many Christians live in every nation. They should be the ones to speak to their fellow citizens about the best future for their own nation. The Christian church must be the source of the national spirit by which a nation is led in the right direction. We must expect Christian nations to arise and we may hope for Christian international relations among nations.

The Korean Church as a "Second Israel"

Korean people are often called a "second Israel" or a "chosen people of God." But until large numbers become Christian, that association remains only idealistic. It is one thing to say that Christianity is the best spiritual principle for this nation; it is quite another thing to say that Korea is a Christian nation or that it even aspires to become a Christian nation.

As far as I know, the first person in Korea who dared to aspire for national evangelization was the Rev. Kim Chi-Sun. Rev. Kim, pastor of Namdaemoon Presbyterian Church, proposed a "Three Million Evangelization Movement" at the time of liberation in 1945. At that time., the total Christian community numbered about 300,000. Why did he propose an evangelistic movement ten times the number of Christians? Actually, 3,000,000 represented a tithe of the total population of 30,000,000. Behind his proposal we can discover a spirit of national evangelization.

In the early 1960's the General Assembly of the Presbyterian Church made a resolution to plant a new church in every *myun*, the second smallest administrative unit of the government. Through this effort, the Christian people caught a vision for the evangelization of the whole country. In 1965 Rev. Han Kyung-Chik and Dr. Helen Kim developed a Korean evangelization movement with the catch phrase "Thirty Million to Christ." The Billy Graham Crusade of 1973 was, to that date, the largest mass rally in Korea. A million believers assembled at the Yoido plaza during the crusade. Although the vision of national evangelization was not stressed, Dr. Graham praised this nation as having the strongest Christian church in the whole world. The clearcut expression of national evangelization was the vision and conviction presented at Explo '74 which was led by Rev. Kim Joon-Gon of Campus Crusade for Christ. The theme of the movement was "Let the Season of the Holy Spirit Come upon This Nation." In 1977, however, the strong conviction of this spirit was expressed at "The Holy Assembly of the Nation," the largest gathering of Christians Korea had known. This assembly was led by prominent evangelists and represented by Rev. Shin Hyun-Kyun, who prepared himself through a forty-day period of fasting and prayer.

The Protestant Christian population is about seven million (20 percent) out of a population of thirty-five million. If the growth rate does not drop, by the end of the 80's half of the entire nation of South Korea will be Christian. This projection means that Christians will then be able to lead this nation with Christian principles of life. When we look at Korean people living abroad, it is most fascinating to see that the Korean church is already the center of ethnic life. Indeed Diaspora Koreans today maintain their national identity only by means of the gospel.

The Jews kept their national identity through their religion for thousands of years. Their faith as a chosen nation, that is, their elite consciousness, was the ground for their national identity. We Christians also share with them the conviction that they were indeed a chosen nation because the redemptive revelation of God was given through them. They were the instrument of God to bless and redeem humanity and the created universe. The handmaid was chosen by God from among them to give birth to the Messiah. Now the gospel of Jesus Christ needs to be preached to all nations on the earth and whoever accepts and believes will be saved.

A countless number of Korean people have been saved by the gospel; they have dedicated their lives as living sacrifices to God; they serve God for the sake of the gospel. Consequently, the number of Christians is increasing daily. Now, if these children of God have determined to dedicate the whole nation to God in every important aspect of their national life, can we not say that the kingdom is near to this nation? As God was gracious to His children as individuals, so He may choose a people as His servant nation at the national level.

Now a Messianic nation should not require other nations to serve her, but rather she must sacrifice herself for the service of other nations. Previously Korea had almost nothing but a strong spirit. Our people went through all kinds of adversity, poverty, frequent foreign invasions, and hardly an opportunity for peaceful settlement. Korea is still divided into two parts with split families and millions uprooted from their homeland. If such a shattered nation could be established as a saved nation through the gospel, she should be particularly thankful to be so blessed. When either an individual or a nation is saved by God, he or the nation most certainly are thankful for Christ's love and will immediatedly attempt to witness and proclaim this love to others. Also, one must begin to pray that God's kingdom may come on earth as perfectly as His will is done in heaven. The apostle Paul explains how this gospel must be preached: "We preach not ourselves, but Christ Jesus the Lord; and ourselves your servants for Jesus' sake" (2 Corinthians 4:5). If any nation is going to witness of salvation by Jesus Christ and preach Him to the world, she must become a servant nation for Jesus' sake.

This blessing as a chosen nation is prepared for all nations. Isaiah prophesied: "In that day shall Israel be the third with Egypt and with Assyria, even a blessing in the midst of the land: whom the LORD of hosts shall bless, saying, Blessed be Egypt my people, and Assyria the work of my hands, and Israel mine inheritance" (Isaiah 19:24-25). Actually every nation on earth needs to recognize its Maker and worship Him, the true source of all blessings and to acknowledge in the arena of national events that Jesus Christ is the Son of God, the Savior of their nation. Every nation needs to aspire after the fulfillment of Christ's reign, the day of exaltation of the lowly, the weak, and the poor. If these things happen, we certainly will have to recognize such a nation to be God's chosen nation. In the Isaiah passage, Egypt and Assyria come under the chosen nationhood together with Israel. Both nations were adverse to the people of God and put Israel under captivity and exploitation. We can then conclude that the way to this salvation is open to all other nations.

We must notice that the eschatological passages in the Old Testament in regard to the nations of this world are not only for the evangelization of individual nations, but are more related to international peace. Assyria and Egypt came under the divine dominion together with Israel. Actually the entire world has the possibility of coming under the blessing of the Lord of Hosts. Isaiah 2 : 2-4 prophesies international peace and that the word of the Lord shall judge over the nations. Consequently, any nation which has been so blessed as to welcome Christ can look forward to the eschatological future of international peace and must launch out to become a missionary nation to other nations. She must pray for the kingdom for God sent His Son to earth out of love for mankind.

The Asian Center for Theological Studies and Mission as an "Upper Room" for the Evangelization of Asia

The work of world evangelism began on the day of Pentecost when God poured out His Spirit upon the disciples as recorded in chapter two of the book of Acts. Jews and devout men out of every nation under heaven had gathered in Jerusalem. Every man was amazed to hear the disciples speaking in his own native tongue the wonderful works of God. At the Asian Center for Theological Studies and Mission (ACTS), as in Jerusalem, all nations in Asia are brought together. Because ACTS is only a small institution it must not presume such a cosmopolitan role as that which the Jerusalem Upper Room played in world evangelization; yet, there is certainly a parallel.

ACTS was established for the evangelization of Asia. Although it is located in Korea, ACTS has been dedicated for an international ministry. It is the visible expression of faith in the gospel by numerous believers both at home and abroad. It came into being and grew to its present status solely by the power of God who has broken through numerous impossibilities. In a word, the impossible has been made possible by God's grace. No one could overcome the many obstacles except a Higher Power.

How will this center function for the great task of

the evangelization of Asia? The work of evangelization is nothing but the work of the Holy Spirit. God Himself shall manifest His power of salvation by the Spirit according to His pleasure; otherwise, it will not be God's saving work. ACTS will only function as God intended when the Spirit of God descends upon all faculty members as they engage in prayer aided by theology and are empowered to speak the Word of God with boldness. ACTS will only function according to the will of God when the students with great sincerity engage in daily prayer and are aided by the Spirit in their study of the Word of God. ACTS will only function as it should when the students are enriched in the knowledge of the invisible world and firmly determine at any cost to proclaim the glorious message of the Lord to their own people. Then the knowledge of the Lord will spread from ACTS to all the countries of this continent, which is at present full of misery, transforming it to one filled with the saving knowledge of the Lord Jesus Christ. We read in Isaiah 11:9, "They shall be full of the knowledge of the LORD, as the waters cover the sea."

It was to a praying community on the Day of Pentecost that the power from above descended and the movement of witness began. It is only through prayer that God manifests His power because, as Calvin stated, "Prayer is the chief exercise of faith." Faith is the only way by which union and communion with Christ takes place. ACTS is a theological center, but theology is only an aid to prayer . Therefore, ACTS, as a theological center, must be a prayer center if it is to be blessed and used as an instrument for the evangelization of Asia. This is the mountain where the "... root of Jesse ... shall stand for an ensign of the people; to it shall the Gentiles seek! and his rest shall be glorious" (Isaiah 11: 10).

And in this mountain shall the LORD of hosts
make unto all people a feast of fat things, a feast

of wines on the lees, of fat things full of marrow, of wines on the lees well refined. And he will destroy in this mountain the face of the covering cast over all people and the veil that is spread over all nations. He will swallow up death in victory; and the Lord GOD will wipe away tears from off all faces; and the rebuke of his people shall he take away from off all the earth. (Isaiah 25: 6-8).

At this place many pastors and believers shall be called together to participate in the mighty work for the evangelization of Asia, particularly through their prayers. They shall receive reports of the work of the Lord from many parts of Asia so that they may be encouraged and comforted. They may participate in the grace of the Lord, that is, suffering for His sake in various countries on this continent.

We envisage an international prayer movement spreading from one country to another. An international prayer congress may be the chief organ through which God will come to establish the kingdom of His Son upon one nation after another.

Indeed, this day is a day of good tidings (2 Kings 7 : 9). This is a God-given time of salvation, as the apostle Paul declared: "... Behold, now is the accepted time; behold, now is the day of salvation" (2 Corinthians 6 : 2). If His work of evangelism progresses in Korea and if ACTS is used by Him to promote the evangelization of Asia, these are only small ensigns of God's mighty power to make a new heaven and a new earth. To Him, the eternal Triune God of our salvation, be praise and worship. Amen!

Dr. Lee Jong-Yun is professor of New Testament theology, director of the D. Min. program at ACTS and director of the Research Institute for the Evangelization of Communist Areas. Dr. Lee studied at Yonsei University (B. Th., Th. M.). Westminster Theological Seminary (M. Div.), the University of St. Andrews (Ph. D.), Scotland, and at Tubingen and Temple Universities. He has published articles and books on reaching Marxists as well as New Testament studies.

In a western TV program "Mission Impossible," the hero always succeeds due to ingenuity and careful planning. Christianity was initially stronger in North Korea, but now this country is virtually isolated from the world community and Christianity is illegal. But many Christians in South Korea left family members and friends in the North as they fled during the Communist War (1950-53). For 30 years they have prayed for their kinsmen in the North. Is God deaf to their prayers? Is Kim Il-Sung more powerful than God? Dr. Lee's research is informative and shocking, urging continued concern for these unreached people.

33 NORTH KOREA: MISSION POSSIBLE?

by Lee Jong-Yun

Religious Life in North Korea Since 1954

Communism to the North Korean people was not a homegrown product; it was imported from Russia just after the Allied victory in 1945 when Korea was liberated from Japanese colonial rule. The Communist system was very alien to the long established way of life and system of values in North Korea. Communism's conflict with traditional values inevitably caused a great deal of internal resistance and revolt. The Russian and North Korean Communists wanted to impose their system at any cost.

The Koreans' initial political resistence to this imposition of foreign ideology was counteracted by the Communists resorting to political coercion, thought control, and massive use of dictatorial power. Religious persecution became an inevitable feature of the North Korean community.

The early Protestant missionaries emphasized work in North Korea because there was a greater response there than in the South. But the present situation in North Korea is completely different. Against this historical background, we will analyze the peculiarities of the North Korean social system that has developed over the past thirty years.

The first is the enshrinement of Kim Il-Sung monism as the only basis of political ideology superseding all other ideologies, both indigenous and foreign.

The second is the enforcement of the Kim Il-Sung ideology which has enormously strengthened the one-man dictatorship of Kim Il-Sung. The end result of this ideology is a system of total nepotism and geneological political power wielded by Kim's family which is akin to monarchic practices.

The third is the fact that North Korea politically, economically, and socially is a closed society. No one knows the way of life in North Korea except through propaganda released by the government.

North Korea society has no concept of human basic rights such as property rights of individuals, the right to freely choose one's occupation, freedom of faith, and the equality of individuals before the law. Article 49 of the North Korean Constitution stipulates the principle that the individual exists only for the benefit of the collective whole. This makes the concept of individual rights and duties a mockery because it is said to be derived from that collectivistic principle.

From 1945 to 1950 the North Korean religious policy

sought to limit freedom. In 1946 the Labor Party enacted the land reform law. All religious groups, including the Buddhists, lost their land. This was followed by the nationalization of all properties in 1948 when the government confiscated all church buildings, temples, and monasteries and used them as warehouses for collective farms, public day-care centers, or retreat centers for the party members.

From 1950 to 1955 the religious policy of North Korea changed to *persecution* of Christians. The government in the South, which was freely elected under the supervision of the United Nations in 1948, faced an extreme test when the North Korean Communists invaded South Korea, on Sunday, June 25, 1950. The intervention of the United Nations representing twenty-one countries preserved freedom in the South. But the United Nations had heavy casualties--over 74,000 killed, 250,000 wounded, and 83,000 missing or captured. Over 400,000 civilians were killed and millions fled to the South for refuge, including many Christians. Following the war the North Korean government placed religious people in the same category as the politicians and the rich, all of whom were blamed for the military defeat and were severely persecuted.

From 1955 to the present time, the *destruction* of religions has been the policy of the government. Whenever a religious person is found, he is killed. In 1959 the Labor Party declared its opposition to religion as an enemy of science and development, supposedly hindering the conscious struggle for self-understanding. Religion, as the root of this non-scientific and superstitious thought, must be eliminated. In 1971 the North Korean Labor Party sent letters to each regional party office ordering an analysis and classification of all the population into three categories. In 1977 the Labor Party reported 25 percent as hard-core Communists, 35 percent as "shakey," and 40 percent as reactionaries who would be sympathetic with South Korea in case of a future war. Most people who had followed a traditional religion were placed in this third category. Surviving ministers and monks and their families and relatives were further labeled as "complicated folks" in the classification of social classes and were denied even the marginal freedoms that workers had.

In December 1972 North Korea adopted a new constitution. Article 54 gives people freedom for faith and freedom for anti-religion [sic]. In 1975 the Communist party, in an attempt to enhance diplomatic relations with other countries, formed a pro-government religious group as a tool that was also used to discover members of the underground church.

In January 1975 the North Korean Communist Party sent three representatives from the Chosun Christian Corporation to attend the Asian Christian Peace Conference in India. An attempt was made in July 1976 to send representatives to the Fourth Asian Buddhist Peace Conference held in Japan, but entry visas were refused.

The Idolization of Kim Il-Sung

The key to understanding the life-style imposed upon the people in North Korea, especially those thirty years of age and younger, is the Kim Il Sung personality cult. Kim's cult has far surpassed the cults of Stalin and Mao both in intensity and scope. The promotion of the personality cult of Kim Il-Sung has recently been expanded to deify and glorify Kim and his family members.

Kim Il-Sung has been depicted as a great thinker, the philosopher of monism. At the Fourth Party Congress in December 1967 the term "monisn" was first introduced. Monism has no logical basis or philosophical foundation and is a complete sham. In North Korea today whatever Kim says is claimed to be in total harmony with Marxist Leninism. Anyone who dares to question Kim's speeches or teachings is considered a "revisionist" who is challenging monism. Kim Il-Sung is the supreme theoretician--absolutely beyond criticism. Ordinary people in North Korea are forced to recite his lectures and theories by memory.

Even the genealogy of Kim Il-Sung has become an object of idolization. He and his entire family are depicted as heroic revolutionaries who contributed greatly to Korea's liberation. All publications including newspapers, magazines, textbooks, and academic works are used as propaganda to promote the cult. A 745-page political dictionary published in October 1970 includes 2,604 references glorifying Kim Il-Sung. The intensity of the personality cult becomes obvious upon examining textbooks for elementary students. Altogether, 35 percent of the subject matter of these books deals with class struggles and 65 percent with the cult of Kim Il-Sung. Most of the materials in class lectures are concerned with the idolization of Kim. In lectures on moral virtue, for example, the ratio of moral virtue compared to the idolization of Kim is 42 percent to 58 percent; in mathematics-30 percent to 70 percent; in drawing and writing-50 percent each; and in music-33 percent to 67 percent.

Kim Il-Sung's birthday on April 15 is the most important national holiday. Academic seminars, debates, movie festivals, artistic performances, sports competitions, memorial tree planting awards, memorial editorials, and beautification campaigns are undertaken on or around Kim's birthday. The cult is also promoted by artistic and cultural activities in exhibition halls, museums, and other public places. Furthermore Kim receives many gifts from various places. This day is comparable to Christmas for Christians.

Kim is viewed as the father of society and all good things result from his favor. This philosophy is repeated frequently and related to every aspect of daily life. His goal is the establishment of a classless utopian society. Any action which helps to achieve this revolution is of value. The government evaluates people according to their loyalty to Kim's teachings.

These ideas are not from some fiction book but are being zealously taught by the North Korea Communist leaders who have isolated themselves from the free world. Their worship of Kim is comparable to the veneration of the Japanese for Emperor Hirohito and the dedication of the Germans to Adolf Hitler.

Are There Any Christians in North Korea?

Officially no Christians exist in North Korea, but is there any evidence of a secret Christian movement? Those who do research on North Korea answer in the affirmative. In 1968 a Rev. Park was arrested in Pyung Won-Gun. In 1973 an anti-Communist movement occurred in the Gae Po-ong area, probably led by Christians according to their own report. In 1974 Kim Il-Sung's car was overturned in front of the Shinpo railroad station. The government blamed the Christians in the underground for this accident. In retaliation the deification worship of Kim Il-Sung continued to intensify. In 1974 the Labor Party's newspaper reported that all religious "miscellaneous spirit and thought" must be destroyed, so the persecution of Christians was increased even more. Surely the presence of Christians in North Korea prompted these actions.

Strategy for the Evangelization of North Korea

Many Christians in South Korea have a deep evangelistic burden for the North and an undying love for the Christians in North Korea. But before the country can be evangelized, it is necessary to understand its value system and strong anti-religious political and social conditioning.

We must remember God's commission to Jonah: "Arise, go to Nineveh, that great city, and cry against it; for their wickedness has come up before Me" (Jonah 1:2, KJV). Jonah's reaction showed his disregard of God's command and the needs of people. Today we face the same problem--indifference to God's commission and to the needs of a wicked world. Yet, despite Satan's grip over North Korea, the Spirit of God is untiringly moving among the people.

We shall consider two kinds of strategy, direct and indirect, for the evangelization of North Korea. Subpoints are listed under each strategy.

Direct Strategy

1. Broadcasting through Christian radio stations HLAZ, HLKX, and HLKY in South Korea and through radio stations in other Asian countries. In 1970 the Fifth Congress of North Korea passed a bill whereby every home in the country was to have a radio. Such a move has made it easier to propagate Communism, but at the same time the gospel is entering these same homes via radio.

2. Sending Bibles and tracts with persons traveling to North Korea who can legally enter the country.

3. Contacting North Koreans serving as diplomats, students, technical advisors, and in other capacities in Third World countries.

4. Mobilizing Christians who can enter North Korea from countries that have diplomatic relations such as Japan, China, Indonesia, India, Canada, and Norway.

5. Constructing a hospital in Manchuria by Koreans living in the United States.

Indirect Strategy to Support These Activities

1. Pray for the secret believers, for a change in the attitude and policy of the government leaders, and for God's Word entering via literature and radio.

2. Pray that the Holy Spirit will prepare hearts to receive the truth of the gospel of the Immortal God.

3. Awaken the worldwide body of Jesus Christ to the need and lay upon believers a prayer burden for the extension of the Kingdom in North Korea.

4. Continue research on the value systems and all other aspects of life in North Korea.

5. Alert by all means possible the North Koreans to the falsehood and danger of worshiping a mortal man.

We have received reports of changes in the economic, military, and political situations in North Korea. The unexpected can happen there as in other Communist countries. The Christians of South Korea have been praying for their friends and relatives in the North for thirty years. Someday the King of Kings will open a wide door of witness to the people of the North. Let us continue to prepare for that day and trust that it will come in the near future.

Dr. Chun Chae-Ok is associate professor, department of Christian Studies, College of Liberal Arts and director of International Co-ed Summer School in Asian Studies at Ewha Womans University. A graduate of Ewha University (B. A.) University of London (Dip. Th.) and Fuller Theological Seminary (Th. M. and D. Miss.) she did student evangelism in Pakistan from 1961 to 1974. She has translated and printed two books, "Esther" and "By Searching."

Over half of the Christians in Korea are women. What were the "felt-needs" fulfilled by Christianity? What training and opportunities have Korean women received and what new role can they expect during the next century? Dr. Chun cites the importance of women in the ministry of Jesus, and offers stimulating and constructive ideas for mission today.

4 KOREAN PROTESTANT WOMEN IN MISSION

by Chun Chae-Ok

A Korean Christian Woman's Perspective In Mission

Mission was a primary concern of the Korean Protestant women during the last century. It was their loving and persistant persuasion in the work of the gospel work which has had an uncomparable contribution to the growth of the Korean church and missions. It was their sun-type approach by which people from a non-Christian background yielded to Christ. In order to understand something of the Korean protestant women in mission, I would like to begin with a biblical view of women from Jesus' perspective and then look at a traditonal picture of Korean women in the Yi dynasty prior to surveying the early, current and future aspects.

Biblical View of Women From
Jesus' Perspective

1) Jesus' contadictory understanding of women from His Jewish contemporaries: Jesus sometimes contrasted His own teachings with those of the Jewish leaders of His day. But, He did not counteract so much with the Jewish leaders when it came to the subject of women in His time, and in His society. Jesus did not clash with His contemporaries regarding women's place and role as He did with some other issues such as keeping the Sabbath. Nevertheless, He was a revolutionary in regard to women's place and women's contributon in His mission. It was not so much what He said about them but rather how He actually related Himself to them during His earthly life and work. His attitude toward women was different from His Jewish people. He saw women as God's creation equal to men in every aspect. And that is why He could draw women for the work of His mission.

2) Women disciples of Jesus: In Jesus' presence women were accepted without discrimination. He broke the barriers of tradition and custom related to women. In His early ministry, a group of women disciples accompanied Him on His preaching missions along with His twelve disciples. Among these women followers were Mary Magdalene, Joanne, the wife of Herod's steward, Susanna and many others. Some of them had means to provide toward His ministry (Lk 8:1-3). These women, married or single, followed Jesus wherever He went for preaching, teaching and healing, and remained faithful through the time of His crucifixion. His male disciples left Him: one even betrayed Him, and another denied Him three times when He needed His friends most. But the women

who had followed Him, Mary Magdalene, Mary the mother of James, Salome and many others (Mk 15:40, 41) stayed near the cross even risking their own lives. But by contrast, as soon as Jesus was arrested, His other disciples all left Him and fled (Matt. 26:56).

3) Jesus and Women in Mission: There were other women who did not follow Him from place to place and evidently there were family duties and prevailing customs which kept them from following Him all the way. But, they certainly contibuted toward the mission of Jesus. The two sisters-Mary and Martha (Lk 10:38-42) are outstanding examples. Martha received Jesus and Mary sat at His feet to hear Him teach. Martha complained that her sister was not helping her, but Jesus said Mary has chosen the good part that shall not be taken away from her. What Jesus did in this case must have been very unusual to them. For they would never normally think of a man entering a house where two unmarried women lived. Moreover they would dare not converse with Him concerning spiritual things. In this circumstance, Jesus shows utter disregard for the custom of His day in order that He might do His mission.

In a like manner, He fellowshiped with the women who were His disciples even as He fellowshiped with men disciples. He showed the freedom and respect to the women as God's children. In the Gospel of John, the disciple whom Jesus loved, writes that Jesus loved Martha, her sister and Lazarus and vistied their home before His crucifixion. Women became His disciples from all classes and stations of life. Some of them were from well to do families like Joanna, the wife of Herod's steward (Lk 8:3) and some from a low and poor background, like the unnamed sinner in a village of Galilee (Lk 7:37).

The woman who discourses with Jesus in John 4 was not only a woman, not only a woman of poor reputation, but a Samaritan woman. Regardless of the custom of the day when they would never think of passing through the area of Samaria, Jesus asked her to give Him water to drink. It was such a surprising event for her. Not only was she amazed, but the disciples were also astonished when they saw Him speaking to a woman. In the chapter, we read that the woman eventually becomes an active witness to Jesus in her region. It was because Jesus, disregarding the custom and His disciples' surprise, led her to realize who she is.

He heals women. His teaching on parables often focuses on women. At His greatest suffering hour of crucifixion, He shows concern for women. Some of the faithful women, who followed Him to the cross-Mary Magdalene, Mary the mother of James and Salome (Mk 16:1) were the first to whom the risen Lord appeared (Mt 28:9, 10).

Traditional Role of Korean Women

1) Women as subordinate to men: Korean women were legally subordinate to men according to Confucian ethics. The Yi dynasty encouraged women to achieve Confucian virtues. To be a woman of Confucian virtues, women had to stay at home and be submissive to men. Their role was only to keep the household and to raise a family. Girls had to obey their parents totally and they were not consulted even in the matter of choosing their life partner. Parents decided for them whom they would marry and after their marriage they had to listen to their husbands. A widow could not ever marry again even if she were very young.

Until the early period of the Yi dynasty, women enjoyed outdoor time, but the Yi rulers prohibited them and systematic control and subjugation of women started with the promulgation of Kyongguk Taejon in the 15th century which was a complete code of laws of the time. It forbade women of upper class from enjoying outdoor games and feasts. If they were to break the rule they were to be punished with lashes. Women's social life in the Yi dynasty was limited to special groups and occasions, especially for upper class women. They did not use their names because they were identified by their position relative to men. When they were with their parents, they were known as so and so's daughter. After marriage, so and so's wife, and in her old age, so and so's mother. It was evident that women traditionally were subordinate to men in every aspect of life.

2) Women as wife and mother at home: One of the words for wife was "anae," meaning "inside person." It meant that she was expected to stay within her house. Her separation from the outside world was also evident in the design and structure of the houses which were divided into two sections as "sarang chae and anchae." In "sarang chae," men stayed and in "anchae," women stayed.

Although the upper class wife had material and social advantages in comparison with the common woman, she had nevertheless equally heavy duty for the household. Since a large family with three and sometimes four generations lived together, she had complicated family relationships to manage and to serve. Since a large number of family members lived together in the same house she had the primary responsibility of preparing food, clothing and other matters. She had the purse for the family and decided how the money should be spent. Although she had to stay in the house and never had a chance to go out for a long time, she was not a slave in the house but rather she was the queen of the house. It can be said that this kind of background of managing the household enabled Korean Christian women to be so active in serving churches and also to be involved in raising church funds.

3) Limited vocation for woman: Only common women who had to work had jobs as seamstresses or laundresses. In villages, farm women took part in farm labor. However, for upper class women there were women of the court, queen

consorts and royal secondary wives. They were women from the highest social status in the Yi dynasty. There were also women of influence from a low-class background. They were shamans, folk healers and women entertainers.

According to some studies, a system of training medicine women was first started in the 15th century because many sick women were dying due to the problem of consulting male doctors. Women of high class would rather die than receive cures from male doctors. So, it was necessary to train women to take charge of female patients. Girls who worked in special jobs and skills were almost all from low-class families. It was considered undesirable, even unthinkable, for girls from upper-class families to work outside their home.

4) Women with no formal and public education:Women had education only at home. There was no formal and public schooling for them. The Confucian concept of observing strict segregation between the sexes made it necessary for girls and boys to be separated in learning. Boys learned at *So-dang,* then went to *Hyanggo.* Afterwards, they proceded to *Songgyungwan.* Women were not encouraged to have systematic learning. It was understood that women needed to learn how to keep domestic life in good order. Both politicians and literali of the time considered it fruitless to educate women in academic subjects. Women were encouraged to develop feminine virtues based on Confucian doctrine. They thought that reading and writing had nothing to do with women. An 18th century scholar depicted an ideal woman as one who cultivated diligence and chastity. If a woman disobeyed Confucian virtues, she was a disgrace to her family. So, family upbringing was considered sufficient education for women. Thus, women's education in the Yi dynasty meant family centered, informal education received at home.

Early Korean Protestant
Women in Mission

1) Effect of Mission on Korean Women: Korean women's reaction against her role in the Confucian social order began with Catholicism which spread rapidly during the second half of the 18th century. It drew many women believers from the upper and low classes. It introduced equality of men and women in the eyes of God and man. When leaders in the hierarchical Confucian order realized the threat of Catholicism, they tried to suppress its influence. However, women believers would give their lives rather than give up their faith in the new found values of Catholicism. Two thirds of the Catholic martyrs of 1839 were women. Their fearless martyrdom opened the way for a change in the status of women is society. Formal and public education started in 1886 for women. Ewha Hakdang was opened for girls by an American missionary woman, Mary E. Scranton and later became the largest woman's university in Korea.

2) Single women pioneers: When there were no career women in the traditional Korea except that of the career as court women, shamans, medicine women and women entertainers, some Korean women who received Christianity became women evangelists. In the beginning they were language teachers and assistants to missionaries. In the pioneering work of evangelism during the Yi dynasty, it was necessary to have women evangelists in order to reach women. Since married women who had to care for their families could not travel outside of their home, single women were called to this work. However, young single women were not able to take the role of itinerary mission work because they had to think of marriage and home making. Thus, widows who were not so young were the ideal persons for such ministry. They could be received with respect because of their age.

In 1907, when churches were growing rapidly, there

was a shortage of church leaders and teachers. And moreover, two thirds of the congregations were women and churches needed women evangelists to teach them. Therefore, the early church emphasized training women evangelists. Also, Korean women evangelists were easily welcomed as counselors and teachers as functional substitutes for Korean shamans. They worked diligently as leaders of local churches. In a church, two women evangelists reached 2,450 women in a year and someone, not known by name, contacted 6,912 women in a year.

As they labored in this new career, it was evident that there was a need for systematic training for such women. So, Women Bible Institutes were started. The Methodist church started one in 1917 which was the first of its kind. The Presbyterian church followed in 1923. The Korean Methodist church started ordaining women in 1930. Some women in the 1920's and 30's went to Japan to study theology.

3) Changing role of women in mission: From 1884 to 1910, the first period of the Korean Protestant church, women evangelists or church women had three distinctive roles to play: 1) assistance to missionaries, 2) personal evangelism, and 3) teaching *Sakyung Hoe* (Bible conventions). The next significant period for women in mission was between 1920-1930. It could be said that this period was a high light for church women evangelists as they had very effective leadership. They worked toward an enlightenment program for women in general, such as literacy work and campaigned against alchohol and smoking. They worked to uplift the status of women and were welcomed as counselors. At the same time, they had an effective teaching ministry as well as personal evangelism. Margaret Mead, while visiting Korea, commented that there could be such a strong and effective leadership among the Korean Christian women because traditional women had training and experience in managing the household and family relationships. It is observed that there is no such comparison in other Asian

countries where women have been so effectively involved in church leadership.

4) Narrowed function of church women: Today, the function of women in mission as leaders is weakened. With the exception of about 40 ordained women ministers, all other women evangelists do only house to house visitation.

What are possible reasons for such a change? A Presbyterian woman professor commented that it might be due to Japanese pressure on women. They pressed women to accept only the roles of wife and mother at home. The Japanese rule reenforced the Yi dynasty tradition. So, in suppression, women evangelists began to lose their dynamic leadership and gradually they have been unable to stand up to their rightful position and responsibility even to this day. In 1910 men and women had to sit in separate places in churches, yet women exercised their leadership and had opportunities to preach in pulpits. But today they rarely have an opportunity to preach. In 1920 and 1930 women evangelists were Bible teachers, social workers and independent movement pioneers. They were revolutionaries and reformers. But today, the function of women evangelists is attenuated as helping hands to ministers.

Yet, we should not be pessimistic. There are united efforts among protestant women in and through structures such as United Missions of the Korea Presbyterian women, and the United Missions of Korea Methodist women. These two main line denominational missions have been laboring for decades within the country and are now reaching to culturally remote areas as well. The Association of Korea Church Women is another effort in mission venture. Beginning in 1979 The Women Theological Association was formed in Seoul and has been active in bringing together Korean women leaders. Within and without these groups, there are significant individuals who have been so ardent and faithful for the growth of the Korean church.

The Decade of the 1980's

1) Experiencing freedom: Korea as a country has been making big steps toward development for a better economic standard and a better political situation. Since the Korean War, society has been under many pressures. yet in the midst of it all, the Korean church has been growing rapidly. In endless efforts for church growth, the women's role has been invaluable. However, there is further need for freedom for women both inwardly and outwardly. Inwardly they need to learn true Christian freedom from materialism and superficialism, and outwardly they need to experience freedom to serve the church on equal basis with men in decision making. Women should exercise freedom of simplicity in the midst of rich churches in a few big cities in Korea so that they may truly be leaders for women of all walks of life. And they must also learn to exercise their gifts from God where these are needed regardless of custom and tradition.

2) Balance between evangelism and social work: All areas of ministry should be open for Korean Christian women. There is continuous need for personal evangelism and cooperative evangelism as it has been a strong point in the church in Korea. But along with it, there should be more careful study by Christian women to learn where they can serve the people in truly needy situations. They need to be bold to find hidden places and people so that can bring them to the church's attention and learn to keep balance between evangelism and such social needy work.

3) Men and women as partners in mission: During a century church women were responsible for a major share of the evangelism and social work that brought to birth many churches. Two-thirds of the Korean Christians are women, and church women should know that they are not only assisting their ministers and their ministry, but that they

are in reality the active means for church growth and missionary outreach. Ministers need to have that reali- zation. They are co-workers and partners in the mission of Christ. Christian women are not to work just among women and children. They have an important role in the growth of the church.

Arthur Glasser who visited mainland China in 1981 stated that the believers were being ministered to by women leaders in house churches. He said that 85% of the leadership in Christian churches are women in the People's Republic of China.

4) Formation of a world missionary committee of Ko- rean church women: There will be an increase in the number of Korean missionaries. Young Christians will dedicate their lives for the cause of missionary work wherever they are led. Therefore, there is a need for emerging mission societies and denominational mission departments to come together, to think together, and to pray together to avail their organiza- tions for increasing candidates for missionary work. The formation of a world missionary committee of Korean church women is imperative to meet the needs of missionary volun- teers both for Korea as well as for other countries during the decade of the 1980's.

Marlin L. Nelson graduated from the University of Minnesota (B. A., 1952) and from Fuller Theological Seminary in Pasadena, California (M. Div., 1955). He went to Korea in 1956. He served as director of World Vision of Korea until 1973 when he was seconded to ACTS (Asian Center for Theological Studies and Mission). He is now associate professor and director of mission relations. Dr. Nelson received the D. Miss. from the Fuller Theological Seminary School of World Mission in 1976. He has authored **The How and Why of Third World Missions: An Asian Case Study,** and has edited **Readings in Third World Missions: A Collection of Essential Documents** (both published by William Carey Library). Dr. Nelson is also associate director of the Asia Church Growth Institute and has published in Korean **Principles of Church Growth.**

Though many may think that the primary emphasis of church growth advocates is simply more Christians and bigger churches, the author enlarges this concept to include missions also. This valid emphasis is worthy of careful thought, especially by those responsible for developing missionary strategies. This article may please some readers while it may provoke others.

5 KOREAN CHURCH MISSION GROWTH

by Marlin L. Nelson

The purpose of this book is to consider various aspects of Korean church growth. I believe *quality* growth is important with particular emphasis on maturity in Christ by learning God's Word, praying, worshiping, serving others, giving tithes and offerings, etc.

If there is quality growth, there must also be *quantity* growth. As Christians become more like Christ and have compassion for others which leads to witnessing to family members and neighbors, new believers will join the church and we may joyfully see an increase in membership.

A third kind of church growth is *extension* growth which refers to planting branch or daughter churches. Most new churches are now established by existing national churches rather than by foreign missionaries.

A fourth aspect of church growth is *mission* growth. This refers to evangelism and church planting among people of a *different* language and culture. In this way mission growth is distinguished from quality, quantity and extension growth.

People usually think of missionaries as people who go to other countries. Although this is true, it is not limited to geographical or political boundaries. It may refer to foreign groups within one's own country, such as Chinese, Japanese, Americans, etc., living in Korea. A Korean witnessing to a Japanese living in Seoul is doing *missionary* work. Mission work is thus distinguished from evangelism which occurs when a Korean witnesses to another Korean within the same culture.

The Korean translation of the Great Commission in Matthew 28:19-20 is better than the English translation. We are to "go and make disciples of all nations..." Nations emphasize groups of people rather than a group of people living within a political or geographical boundary. If this principle is correctly understood, we would see the importance of *mission* organizations working *within* such countries as the Philippines, Indonesia, and India, where many different groups live within the same country.

Dr. C. Peter Wagner, professor of church growth at the Fuller Theological Seminary School of World Mission and a former missionary to Bolivia, has written an interesting article, "Full Circle: Third World Mission."[1] He mentions that mission societies send out missionaries who win people

---

1. C. Peter Wagner, *Stop the World I Want to Get on,* (Regal Books Division, G / L Publications, Glendale, CA, 1974), pp. 101–113.

to Christ (90°). The mission establishes a church (180°) and then the church becomes indigenous (270°). But the mission- ary seldom challenges this church to form its own mission society and send out its own missionaries (360°). When this occurs, the church has come "full circle." How we sincerely thank God for the growth and maturity of the Korean chur- ch which sent its first missionary in 1907 and is now send- ing many missionaries.

According to my survey of Korean missionaries (May, 1982), there are 47 mission organizations sending 323 mission- aries to 37 different countries. The majority of these, 249 missionaries, are sent by 8 mission societies, and 31 mission societies are supporting and promoting activities in various ways but are not presently sending out missionaries.

Although Korean church leaders usually count only the husband as a missionary, I am following the internation- ally recognized system of counting both husband and wife as missionaries. However, this total does not include the University Bible Fellowship staff of 101 Korean and national workers serving as "tent makers" (self- supporting lay-mission- aries) in eleven countries excluding the U. S. A. and Canada.

According' to my research, there are 180 diaspora missionaries and 143 cross-cultural missionaries. Although all missionaries are witnesses of Jesus Christ, their primary work is not evangelism and church planting. Some are in- volved in the nurture of Christians as a pastor, and teacher. Others do service as a doctor, nurse, secretary, etc. Some are directly involved in some form of evangelism, such as church plánting and literacy evangelism. I have attempted to indicate the *primary* activity of each missionary by using letters E (evangelism), N (nurture), and S (service). Obviously some are involved in all three, but this emphasizes their main activity which is summarized as follows: Evangelism 120; Nurture 195; Service 8.

Some people ask, "Why should the church send missionaries to evangelize other people when their own people are not yet all evangelized?" There is a mission principle clearly stated in Acts 1:8. The apostles were told to be witnesses in Jerusalem AND Judea AND Samaria AND to the ends of the earth. The Bible does not say Jerusalem and then Samaria. The Bible does not say Jerusalem or Samaria. These three aspects of witnessing are to be simultaneous.

Paul did not wait until all of the Jews repented before going to the Gentiles. Peter and Paul preached to both, although Peter emphasized evangelism to Jews (same language and culture) and Paul emphasized missions to Gentiles (a different culture).

If the apostolic church had waited until all people had been evangelized in the Middle East, they would not have sent missionaries to Asia, Africa, or Europe. If churches in Europe and America had waited until all of their people were evangelized, no missionaries would have been sent to Korea.

The Great Commission was given not only to the apostolic or Western churches, but to all Christians. Surely the Korean church will not fail to accept the responsibility and privilege of preaching the gospel, making disciples and serving people of other nations for whom Christ died. In order for the remaining 95% in Asia to hear the gospel, Christians in both Western and non-Western countries need to mobilize their financial resources and train and send both men and women as evangelists (to their own people) and as missionaries (to people of another culture).

Following the International Congress on World Evangelization held in Lausanne, Switzerland, in 1974, there has been an increasing awareness of cross-cultural mission work. "Reaching the Unreached People Groups" was emphasized at the Consultation on World Evangelization (COWE) at Pattaya, Thailand, in 1980. People became more aware of unevangelized people groups through careful research.

Three aspects of world evangelization were clearly

defined as follows:

NATURE: The nature of evangelization is the communication of the good news.

PURPOSE: The purpose of evangelization is to give individuals and groups a valid opportunity to accept Jesus Christ.

GOAL: The measurable goal of evangelization is to persuade men and women to accept Jesus Christ as Lord and Savior and serve Him in the fellowship of His church. [2]

Although the emphasis on unreached people groups is important, some weaknesses in the exclusive use of this mission strategy may be identified:

1. "An unreached people is a group that is less than 20 percent *practicing* Christian." [3] It is difficult to determine when nominal Catholics and nominal Protestants are "practicing Christians." Even in many Western "Christian" nations, a small percent regularly attend church. Are they less "reached" than Taiwan (R. O. C.) or Korea? There is a need to emphasize the evangelization of *each* generation.

2. Are Korea and Iran equally unreached? Obviously not. Therefore, the Lausanne Committee for World Evangelization now gives some percentages of being reached. If there are no practicing Christians among a group of people, they are referred to as "hidden people." This definition is

....

2. Edward R. Dayton, *That Everyone May Hear Reaching the Unreached,* (Missions Advanced Research and Communication Center, Monrovia, CA, 1979), p. 14.

3. Ibid., p. 27.

very clear. These people groups must be evangelized by *missionaries* from the East or the West. They may be citizens of the same nation, yet be quite different culturally from other Christians who may be nearby. The Committee uses other categories "initially reached, minimally reached, and possibly reached" to describe people groups with from 1% to 20% Christians.[3]

3. The use of missionaries for evangelizing a people's group is emphasized until 20% become Christians. Data on 2914 unreached people groups indicates the presence of some Christians in most groups.[5] The strategic question is not how the Asian or Western missionary can do evangelism and plant churches, but rather how to stimulate those indigenous Christians to win more of their own people.

Some Korean church leaders say, "Don't send out our own missionaries but multiply God's work." This statement can easily be misunderstood. The goal of the church and mission societies is to multiply God's work. But "work" needs to be clearly defined. As stated earlier, activities of missionaries can be described as evangelism, nurture, and service.

As there is a shortage of Christian workers in most countries, the church will often assign the missionary to work in the church. If the church is actively involved in various types of evangelism and church planting, this may be a good strategy for evangelism. But if the church is concerned only about improving the quality of the present church members, there will be no quantity, extension, or mission growth. Wagner calls this attitude the "church develop-

4. Edward R. Dayton & David A. Fraser, *Planning Strategies for World Evangelization,* (Eerdmans, Grand Rapids, MI, 1980), pp. 97-98.

5. C. Peter Wagner and Edward R. Dayton, editors, *Unreached Peoples* '81, (Cook Publishing Co., Elgin, Il, 1981), pp. 239-306.

ment syndrome."[6] We need to realize that all indigenous churches are not growing churches. The significant question that church and mission leaders should ask is how can the presence of a foreigner, and the interest of Christians in other countries help stimulate the outreach of the national church. ACTS (Asian Center For Theological Studies and Mission) encourages missionaries to have the role of "liaison" between churches and denominations in two different countries.

What then is the mission philosophy emphasized at ACTS? Although every aspect cannot be mentioned in detail, a few observations will be made:

1. We sincerely thank God that the Christian witness is now worldwide and that churches have been established in most countries and among the major groups of people. The Bible or portions of the Bible have been translated into 1,710 languages.[7] Even though probably 3,000 to 3,500 languages representing 200 million people still await translation, some of these people can hear the gospel through a "trade language" (a common language in their area). The number of speakers of each language is less than 100 to more than seven million. The average is between 5,000 and 10,000. National governments are becoming increasingly resistant to special attention given to tribal groups as they desire more national unity with a common national language.

2. We believe that the national Christians are usually the most effective witnesses and are primarily responsible for the evangelization of their own people. Although God has a sense of humor, usually God's wisdom could be described

....

6. C. Peter Wagner, *Frontiers in Missionary Strategy*, (Moody Press, Chicago, 1971), p. 169.

7. Hyatt Moore, ed., "Jubilee," (Vol. 7, No. 6, Summer 1981, Wycliffe Bible Translators, Inc., Huntington Beach, CA), p. 13.

as "common sense." For example, men can walk awhile upside-down on their hands, but they usually walk on their feet. There are instances when God sends someone to a distant place to witness in a completely different country, but usually Christians are expected to witness to their family members and friends.

The principle of self-propagation emphasized by Henry Venn, Rufus Anderson, John Nevius, and Roland Allen are essential for mission strategy. The growth of the Korean church is an example of this important policy. Usually Christians of the same race, same language, and same culture are the most effective in reaching their own people at home or abroad. There are special cases when class prejudice or tribal conflicts make communication of the gospel difficult or impossible, but these are exceptions to this policy.

3. We hasten to add, though, that the Korean church has a responsibility to evangelize and train people of other cultures also. This can be done in several ways.

a. With increasing political barriers hindering travel of Western and non-Western missionaries, ACTS desires to bring to Korea young Christian leaders from other nations for study and observation. They can discern the dynamic life of Korean Christians as they zealously serve and worship God with their prayers, offerings, and disciplined lives. As God was glorified when other nations observed blessings upon the people of Israel, people from other nations marvel to see God's power and grace in Korea.

b. New believers should become active members of local churches. Being convinced of this important biblical teaching, the number of Protestant churches has inceased from 5,302 with 1,324,659 Christians in 1956/57[8] to 19,637

----

8. Kenneth J. Foreman, ed., *Prayer Calendar of Christian Missions in Korea and General Directory,* (The Christian Literature Society of Korea, Seoul, 1959), Statistics for 1956 / 57 from KNCC.

churches with 6,349,201 Christians in 1981.[9] In 1980 the Asia Evangelistic Commission (AEC) was organized to encourage church planting in other countries. Korean churches, World Vision International, and denominational and church leaders in Indonesia, Philippines, and Thailand are now cooperating to establish new churches. Thus far, 100 new churches have been planted in Indonesia, 50 in the Philippines, and 17 in Thailand. Plans are being made to extend this program to Pakistan also. The director of the Barengay Church Planting Program in the Philippines reports that "six church buildings have already been constructed. There is a total of 1294 members in these congregations (Jan. '83) and 1586 new believers (April '83)." Although it is impossible to measure statistically spiritual work accomplished, yet these figures indicate that the work of God has progressed during the last two years. Any mission organization, Asian or Western, would be pleased if their missionaries could accomplish this work within a two-year period.

c. Several Korean churches have formed their own mission society to emphasize missions. Although some may proudly or selfishly speak of "my missionaries," most of these churches cooperate with their own denominational mission program. Therefore, it may be better to consider these organizations as a missions committee rather than as a mission society. However, the idea of having their own society may cause more people to become actively involved in missions.

Some of these church mission societies send money regularly to ACTS alumni (nationals in other countries) for a specific ministry. For example, a student from Thailand returns home and is thought of as a missionary sent by a lo-

---

9. W. Ransom Rice, Jr., ed., *Prayer Calender of Christian Missions in Korea and General Directory,* (The Christian Literature Society of Korea, Seoul, 1982), p. 250. Statistics were compiled early in 1981 by ROK Ministry of Culture and Information.

cal Korean church. Although the church leaders consider this a good example of partnership and wise stewardship of money, this policy may discourage sacrifical stewardship of Christians in other countries. "Our missionaries" (from the viewpoint of the Korean church) may be viewed by people in other nations as "employees of foreign Christians," whether the money comes from Western or non-Western churches. It is important for the Korean church to send a contribution toward the worker's salary or special project rather than to pay the entire amount.

Churches also contribute money to construct church buildings in other countries. The Korean Evangelical Church, in cooperation with OMS International, has helped build over 100 churches in India for their sister denomination, and are now helping with support of some rural pastors.

d. We also need to remember that Jesus commanded us to *go* and make disciples of all nations. This requires the personal sacrifice of individuals and families who are willing to leave home in order to live or die among other people for the witness of the gospel. The presence of foreigners and their perspective can add a wholesome dimension to the quality of the church. Sometimes foreigners can see and do things which others might neglect. The "good Samaritan" was a foreigner and not a Jewish priest.

e. Korean missionaries are needed in the task of the evangelization of the world. But where will they go and what will they do? Some Western missionaries in Korea are very dedicated, yet it is difficult to see a significant contribution by their work. Korean missionaries may have a similar experience. What work remains after the missionary leaves?

Some early Western missionaries to Africa experienced painful toothaches due to the lack of Western-trained dentists. Some mission societies decided to remove all the teeth of missionaries and give them dentures before sending them to work in the interior regions of Africa. Perhaps that was a good policy then, but no longer necessary in 1983.

Most countries now have a few cities where good medical care is available.

Let us apply this principle to mission activities. The early missionaries often needed to prepare dictionaries, translate the Scriptures, establish schools, teach literacy, and train church leaders. Many missionary men, wives, and children died during those days as modern medicine had not yet been developed. But does the Korean missionary need to repeat the work of the pioneer missionaries? No. We can thank God for modern medicine, modern transportation, and mass communications. The Korean missionary can use the translated Bible for preaching and teaching, in churches, hospitals, schools, etc. When the Korean missionary arrives, he is usually greeted by Christians instead of by people opposed to the gospel. Let us praise God for the extension of the church during the last two centuries.

What then does the missionary do? He may begin a seminary with Korean teachers or become the pastor of people in one village or town. And there are hundreds of cities and towns in Asia where there is no Christian church. But is this the best use of his life in a foreign country?

I suggest that the person selected to become a missionary be a "specialist" in some field. This is not to make him proud, but so he can become an example to stimulate people with new ideas and actions.

The Korean missionary may preach the gospel as a member of a international team composed of Western and non-Western Christians. People will be attracted by the witness of Christians from different countries. There will be much interest as the Korean missionary tells about the persecution, prayer life, zeal, and sacrificial service of Korean Christians. This team may also conduct seminars to teach and inspire other Christian leaders.

Many countries have people who are able to witness more effectively than any foreigner. These countries, however, may still lack teachers in Bible schools and seminaries.

The Korean people are well educated and there are many well-trained Christian teachers. If the international language of English is learned, the Korean missionary could immediately teach in Bible schools and seminaries in Asia, Africa, and Latin America.

Others may be specialists, such as doctors, dentists, pharmacists, and social workers. These professional Christians can go to other countries and serve God in institutions that are already established but where there are few qualified Christians. They may encourage clinical work in nearby villages and help the witness of the local church through a healing ministry.

Korea's literacy rate of 92% is among the highest in the world. Contrast this with the report to President Reagan by the National Reading Council in America that "18. 5% of all Americans over 16 years of age are functionally illiterate." Illiteracy is not only a problem in America, but affects the development of non-Western countries and the growth of the church.

Literacy and Evangelism International was organized by Robert Rice, a former Presbyterian missionary in Korea. Many countries have invited his workers to come and teach the people to read. Some of these countries do not give visas to missionaries, but literacy is taught by using biblical materials. Korean missioniares are now working with this organization in the Philippines and in India. But you ask, "Can't the nationals teach their own people to read?" Yes, they can if they want. They need the stimulation of an outsider, a specialist trained in literacy, to help them with this important work.

There is also a need for "tent-making missionaries," especially in countries closed to the traditional missionary. These are Christians who go as professional workers, students, etc., with the primary purpose of giving a witness. Much training is needed before these people enter Islamic countries.

The Korean mission movement is developing as a fire

in the church. But for a fire to burn, many sticks need to be placed together. How can this flame be increased?

I suggest that every church organize a *missions committee*. There are already committees for evangelism, music, education, and visitation. The missions committee is a group of people primarily interested in missions who report to the church. They will write to missionaries already working in these countries and learn how to' pray more effectively. As the pastor and church members become more aware of needs in other countries, young people will volunteer to go and the church will be willing to give support. We need one another to keep alive the fire of mission interest.

Likewise, the Korean missionaries need one another. Some denominations send ten families to ten different countries and give the impression that each country will be evangelized by their workers. But this can become false pride. Instead, we need to send teams of workers to each country, so they can encourage one another. If there is only one Korean missionary family, often they must become part of an international community and lose their own Korean identity. Their children attend expensive international schools and may not even want to return to Korea. Because of the problem of education, many dedicated missionaries are unable to return to their field for a second or third term of service. There is a need for several families to work together and to include school teachers also as members of their *team*. Later a Korean school may be established in Asia and Africa where the children may attend.

Most Korean missionaries lack adequate supervision of their work. Who can advise them to make proper goals and to regularly evaluate the effectiveness of their work? The independent faith missionary has freedom to work as he thinks the Spirit of God is leading him. Yet, most of us need the discipline of being responsible to someone else. Most countries have a group of evangelicals who are ready to cooperate. Regardless of the group, denomination, or church with which the missionary works, it is essential that clear goals are established and mutually understood and agreed upon. Will his primary activity be evangelism, nurture, or service? If he is to teach in a Bible school, the home church should not expect glowing reports of evangelistic activities and establishment of new churches.

There is also an urgent need for a clear financial policy. Does the missionary live by faith, making his needs known only to God, following the policy of the Overseas Missionary Fellowship (formerly China Inland Mission) established by Hudson Taylor? Does the missionary have an agreed upon salary that is adequate for transportation, living, housing, education, medical care, and retirement? Is the amount of salary reviewed regularly to meet the increasing costs of inflation? Is this salary sent regularly or is a minimum salary given, requiring the missionary to write letters directly to friends and churches asking for money to purchase a car, conduct an evangelistic crusade, build a school, or to pay medical expenses? There is a need for wise, adequate, and honest reporting of finances by the missionary and the mission society.

There are mission societies, churches, and Christians especially concerned about witnessing to North Koreans and to others in Communist countries. There is worldwide interest in The People's Republic of China and many foreign Christians would quickly enter if they had permission. But what would they do? How effective would the witness of a "foreigner" be among these people who have suffered so much?

It was recently reported that though there were only about one million Protestant Christians in China in 1949 when most missionaries had to leave, there is now an estimated 25 to 50 million Christians in Mainland China. This is almost unbelievable. This represents 2.5-5% of the population of the largest nation in the world with over one billion people. Surely they need more Bibles, Christian literature, and hymnals, but is this not an excellent illustration of people winning their own even in the midst of persecution?

There is a Korean proverb that it is often the darkest under the candle. Many Korean missionaries want to go to Mainland China but cannot. However, it is possible to go to Taiwan (R. O. C.), but few want this. Why? The population of Taiwan is 18 million and only about 3% are Protestant Christians. Surely these Christians could be helped by the partnership of some Korean missionaries who are specialists in some aspect of Christian work. I suggest sending several teams of Korean missionaries to work in nearby Taiwan.

Japan has nearly five million university students, more than any other Asian country. Recognizing the unfriendly relationship that existed for many years between Korea and Japan, this may now be an opportunity to show Christian love to our neighbor. Although it is not easy to get a visa to do missionary work in Japan, it is not impossible. Many Japanese church leaders have visited Korea to learn about the church. Although the Japanese church is weak, it has 39 mission societies* sending out 154 missionaries (including wives) working primarily among non-Japanese people. Perhaps the day is coming when Asian countries will seek further cooperation not only for economic, political, and military reasons, but for the evangelization of Asia.

The words of Jesus recorded in Matthew 9:37, 38 are still appropriate today. "The harvest is plentiful, but the laborers are few; pray therefore the Lord of the harvest to send out laborers into his harvest."

These are great days for spiritual harvest. But there is still a shortage of laborers. By God's grace, each of us can in some way become laborers with Jesus Christ. Let us thank God for this and remember that "thine is the kingdom and the power and the glory." "Not by might, nor by power, but by my Spirit, says the LORD of hosts" (Zechariah 4:6).

----

* 25 denominational; 12 interdenominational; 2 independent.

Rev. Cho Dong-Jin (David), Founder and General Director of the Korea International Mission, President of the East-West Center for Missions Research and Development, and General Secretary of the Asia Missions Association, graduated from the Presbyterian Theological Seminary in Seoul, the Asbury Theological Seminary ,(Th. M.) and received the Lit. D. from the International Academy in Mexico and the D. D. degree from the Belhaven Presbyterian College and from Asbury Theological Seminary. Dr. Cho gives frequent lectures and has written and translated several books.

Dr. David Cho has been a forerunner of Third World Missions for more than a decade. Goals, obstacles and accomplishments are described in this chapter which will inspire church and mission leaders in other non-Western countries. The uniqueness of the Korean Christian is again recognized as a gift from God for the evangelization of the world.

6   THE GROWTH OF KOREAN MISSIONS AND ITS CONTRIBUTION TO WORLD EVANGELIZATION

by David J. Cho

Understanding Korea

Uniqueness of environment.--Although it is the smallest in size among the major nations of Asia, Korea is one of the most densely populated. This tiny peninsula is cramped among the three superpowers--Russia to the north, China to the west and Japan toward the east. The Korean peninsula stands as a scared hare picked on from all three sides by the bear which is Russia, the lion which is China, and Japan symbolized as the ferocious crocodile with its mouth agape toward its southern borders.

A most wondrous thing about this nation is the fact that throughout its long history of almost 5,000 years of perpetual harassment from its neighbors, it has nonetheless stood its ground and has never been completely lost to any one of its aggressors. This national integrity has been inherited down to the present so that the people of this nation, divided at the will of world superpowers, have never thought of their nation as two separate ones.

Without a thorough understanding of, and research into the national character, the culture of the nation, torn and bruised by other nations but never advancing to the fore to initiate an attack, it is impossible to ascertain the basis of the phenomenal church growth in Korea.

Uniqueness of culture.--It takes somewhat of an effort to distinguish a Korean, a Chinese, or a Japanese by facial structure; but in regard to their cultures, there is an enormous difference. It is said that the culture of Japan is that of the wooden vessel; of China, the clay vessel; while the Korean culture is that of the copper vessel.

True, in the majority of homes in Korea copper utensils served as wash-basins, cutlery, and bed-pans until only about twenty years ago. This tradition has not died out in some of the respectable households even today.

In all the implements of its culture--clothing, footwear, food, and language--Korea has had a proud tradition unfettered by and independent of its hostile neighbours.

A nation of one race.--Of the 220 or so nations in the world there are very few with a population of around 50 million comprised of a single race. This is even more evident in Asia. Most of the countries in the world are multi-ethnic nations. According to the Ethnologue, the bulk of major nations in the world are multi-racial, multi-cultural, and multi-lingual societies. Great Britain has four registered languages;

Japan has five; France five; Italy four; and China has a sum total of 179 tongues. But Korea has remained a nation of one race, language, and culture throughout its history of five milleniums with the exception of the incipient confusion of culture at the very beginnings of its history.

The fact that the nation had been closed off from foreigners until the end of the nineteenth century imparted to the future generations a policy of self-seclusion that was a major agent in warding off the Japanese imperialists at the turn of the century and the communist aggressors about half a century later. The seemingly defeatist spirit kindled self-consciousness and activated a sense of unity.

Centuries of repeated attempts by the Chinese to assimilate our culture into theirs have proven futile. Even after forty years of determined effort to root out our culture and destroy our language by the mandatory imposition of their tongue and renaming of our people, the Japanese were no more successful.

The fact that this race, so conservative and so exclusive throughout its history, has surprisingly adapted to and accepted the Christian religion as no other race has, must deserve the most profound research and careful analysis.

Uniqueness of Korea's relationship with the West.-- The Koreans had almost no contact with Westerners until about the turn of this century. In fact, the nation had been one of the very few nations in Asia outside the reach of Western colonialism. While the majority of Asian nations have had a master-servant relationship with the West for more than a century, Korea has never been subjected to such a status nor has it ever had any hostile relations with countries of the West. This is in part responsible for the relative obscurity of the nation until after World War II. This fate could be construed to mean that Korea is in a favoured situation to succeed the West in missions as is no other nation in Asia since strong feelings of resentment against the West issuing in strong nationalistic policies are being aroused in many Asian nations.

It is not to say that we are in an absolutely favorite spot, for a lack of antipathy toward the West could also mean lack of understanding and concern for their way of life, thought, and culture. Moreover, a crippling communication gap could result from such apathy. But all these shortcomings could add up to our advantage in missions since these preclude the possibility of our people being taken as servile vassals of the West.

Understanding The Korean Church

Uniqueness of its beginning.--The church in Korea was started by the Korean people. They translated their own Bible with the assistance of missionaries. These are significant facts that point to an essential difference from other countries. Manchuria was a place of active diplomacy, commerce, and scholastic exchange between our race and the Chinese. In the early years of the eighteenth century, some of our enlightened youth travelling in this region came upon Chinese Christians and some missionaries from the British and Foreign Bible Society and the Church of Scotland. They were converted and baptized and returned home with a Chinese translation of the Bible and a mind full of dedication that the Word should be spread to their people even if it meant death.

In face of persecution and deaths of their colleagues they set out on the task of translating the Bible into Korean so that the seeds of His Word might be planted in their fatherland. As a result of repeated persecutions, they had to flee their homes in the northern provinces (Eui-joo) to settle in the village of So-Rae near the Yellow Sea. There they converted their homes into churches and continued fervently to preach the gospel to their race. The unique beginning of the church in this land has characterized the nature of the Korean church ever since.

Unique relationship with Western missionaries. --From the very beginning, Western missionaries came not as church planters but as helpers to church planting already started by Koreans. The church buildings were not patterned after the Western model but built in the style of traditional Korean houses. The ardent Christians who had raw labour potential and material exchange in terms of crops as their only resource gave them freely to their churches.

From the outset, Western missionaries were not burdened with economic difficulties but were able to direct their efforts to the teaching of the Bible and the fostering of local leaders. This was true even in the troublesome times right after the Korean War.

Throughout the history of the Korean church the relationship between the missionary and the local church has been neither one of master and servant, nor of father and son, but one of true fraternity.

Uniqueness of its way of growth.--There seems to be a consensus among people that the phenomenal growth of the Korean church is a result of the adaptation of the so-called Nevius Method by the early missionaries. But the results of the writer's research point to the fact that even before Nevius had come to this land the Korean church was already establishing itself on the principles of autonomy, self-support, and self-propagation which were later to be called the Nevius principles. A requisite for the baptism of believers in those days was that he had to have led another person to Christ before his baptism. An illiterate person was not allowed the sacrament. Even the aged had to learn to read the Bible before he could be baptized. In this way all the believers shared the sense of discipleship in Christ. A life of strict tithes was required of all believers who were also active witnesses of the Word. Junior and senior high school students became self-supporting evangelistic teams to plant rural churches throughout the nation.

During the early years of Christianity in Korea about ninety years ago, there were some exceptional churches ministered by missionaries. But the test of time has shown these to be the slowest in their growth as well as lacking in self-support. Even after the local ministers had taken over the leadership, these remained the most retarded of all and could not be rated with the fast-growing indigenous churches.

A genuine Korean policy, a Korean strategy, a Korean method, and a Korean tactic has provided the fertile soil in which the church could grow. To this end the understanding on the part of the Western missionaries of the nature of the the Korean soil has proven an indispenensable catalyst.

Oppression and Resulting Extroversion

Exodus.--From about the close of the Russo-Japanese War in 1905, many of the Korean people were forced on a fated exodus. The elements of a nation brutally deprived of its sovereignty at the hands of the Japanese imperialists were driven abroad in nomadic groups. Between 1905 and 1945, around five million were scattered over the vast expanses of Manchuria to the northeastern part of China and another two million were taken to Japanese islands. Out of a population of twenty million about a third of the whole were either drifting on the plains of Manchuria in search of freedom or being utterly exploited in the mines and mills of Japan. There was also a considerable number of enlightened youths studying in Japan that fled the woe and agony of the homeland.

The unprecedented exodus of the Korean people at the outset of this century was later to prove a pre-meditated event in the providence of God to prepare this nation and its race as the tool for the evangelization of Asia in the future. The Presbyterian church in Korea set its hands to the task of reaching the nomadic communities in Manchuria and the countless labourers being exploited in Japan together with their more fortunate younger friends pursuing their studies there.

Had there not been the forty years of gruesome exodus much like the suffering of Israel under the Pharaoh and the Babylonian captivity, the Korean church would have become as a snail shut in its own shell.

The exodus from oppression brought extraversive tendencies to the Korean church. The elements scattered over the expanses of Manchuria could breathe in the world and learn of new ways that enabled them to live cross-culturally. Our youths in Japan dug into every new field of study open to them and some brought home with them the theology imported mainly from Europe. As the theology picked up in Japan had largely been German theology, its introduction in Korea brought it face to face with the prevailing American theology.

The exodus and the resultant extroversive tendencies that the Korean church experienced were the parabola of hardship and blessing and a plan in God's providence for the future utilization of this church as a tool for world evangelization.

Expansion.-- The Korean exodus had enabled the Korean church to cross its borders and set foot in foreign lands and constitute a model of what came to be known as the Ethnocentric Evangelization Movement. Successively churches were set up across the border for the people that were scattered abroad. The churches sprang up in Manchuria in 1907, and in 1908 they spread to Siberia, followed in 1909 and 1912 by new ones in Japan and the Shan-tung peninsula of China.

It is significant to note that these churches that sprang

up naturally in communities of a minority race in a foreign land were independent of the Western missionaries and that it was only twenty years or so after the first gospel had been planted in the land.

The subsequent history of Korean churches witness a special blessing in the manner of its expansion. In 1947 a General Assembly was organized among the Korean churches in Japan. In Manchurchia, there were four presbyteries with a total of 200 churches and two theological seminaries up until 1945. The 150 or more Korean churches in the United States by 1970 were all established spontaneously by resident Koreans. The estimates for 1979 show more than 690 Korean churches in the U. S. A. During the nine year period fifty churches were established each year or one church every week.

This phenomenal expansion was not limited to the Koreans but spread to other minorities in different lands. It is significant that all the Chinese churches in Korea were started by Koreans. The people that have founded the Thai church in Los Angeles and the Laotian church in Dallas were not Thais or Laotians, but Koreans.

Contemporary Growth of Korean Missions

The Early Struggles.--It was way back in 1912 that the Korean church started its first cross-cultural mission. The Korean church that had received Christianity through China had decided to send its missionaries to the Shan-tung peninsula in China. Kim Young-Hoon, Park Tae-Ro, and Soh Byung-Hoon were selected. The bold initiatives by Koreans were foolish but dauntless attempts in the eyes of Western missionaries. The Chinese church too considered the proposal presumptuously daring. Although the two seemed to be highly praising the missionary zeal of the Koreans, in reality they were not willing to cooperate. When the three Korean missionaries arrived in Shan-tung they were greatly bewildered, for neither the Chinese church nor the American missionaries there proved to be their partners. They were sent to far places. Eventually they starved, there being no means of communication or transportation. Kim Young-Hoon later fled to the United States and Soh Byung-Hoon died of illness while in China. Park Tae-Ro came to Korea via Manchuria. Thus, the burning aspiration of the Korean church in setting its foot for the first time in missionary work to foreign countries was frustrated. But the Korean church despaired not. The General Assembly commissioned the Department of Missions to visit the places, find the facts, and bring back a report. The secretary of the department, Rev. Pang Hyo-Won, set out to conduct the field studies and brought in a lengthy report on the situation. The report pointed out that:1) The Mission Department had been grossly mistaken in choosing a place where it had not had an on-the-scene survey and with which it was not familiar. 2) Having sent the misionaries without prior agreement with the Chinese church and the missionaries already there was a second mistake. 3) Having sent people not trained for missionary work nor acquainted with the field was still another mistake.

The secretary to the Mission Department who had filed this report, Rev. Pang Hyo-Won, volunteered to go to the same place as a missionary himself. With this determination, he went over to Shan-tung peninsula with a few colleagues. While there, he also summoned his son, Rev. Pang Ji-Il, to join him in his purpose. They remained in mainland China as the last foreign missionaries until August 1957 (right before the Cultural Revolution) although most of the Western missionaries had been expelled from China before 1953.

Unceasing Endeavour.--After the close of World War II in 1945, the peninsula of Korea was divided at the will of the two superpowers. Then in 1950 its fate was worsened by the Communist war. But even from its ashes, the Korean church sent its missionaries, Kim Soon-Il and Choi Chan-Young, to Thailand in 1956 and Geh Wha-Sam and Kim Young-Jin to Taiwan in 1958. Though the war had cost the lives of 300,000 believers and the arrest and abduction of more than 1,000 church leaders together with the destruction of more than 2,000 church buildings, the missionary zeal continued on in the hearts of thousands left homeless.

With the armistice and the perpeutal threat of war, heavy restrictions were placed upon foreign travel because the economy was staggering. But in the midst of thousands being left without parents and spouses, the church nobly upheld the far-reaching vision of world evangelization.

Getting Into Shape in the 60's.--The missionary zeal of the Korean church up to the 50's was contained within the respective denominations. But beginning in the 60's, interdenominational evangelical missions began to spring up. These movements were spearheaded by the the student evangelization movement pioneered by the president of Ewha Womans University, Dr. Helen Kim. The university had sent three missionaries to Pakistan in the beginning years of the 60's. The dissolution of the I. M. C. prompted the vice-president, Dr. Kim, to initiate the student movement. With the death of its founder, the movement slowly withered as it entered the 70's and the last remaining missionary in Pakistan, Chun Jae-Ok, returned to Korea in 1974.

Korea International Mission could be said to be the most sure-footed and research-grounded of all the missions in Korea. Begun in preparatory stages in 1965, its first missionary was sent to Hong Kong in 1968. It also sponsored the missionary conference in local churches which was the first conference of its kind in the nation. So far, it has sent a total of twenty- six missionaries. They are well trained personnel and are reaping substantially.

With the birth of nondenenominational faith missions,

a new wave of awakening arose so that each church began its own program and new movements came into being.

The Front Runner in Third World Missions.—The missions of the Korean church inevitably came to see the need for cooperation among themselves. With the Korea International Mission in the lead, the Korea Foreign Missions Association (KFMA) was founded in 1972. Korea International Mission initiated the conference of all the missions in Asia without the influence of the West for the first time in the history of Christianity. In August 1973, the First All-Asia Missions Consultation was held, followed in August 1975 by the Inaugural Convention of the Asia Missions Association.

The missions consultation in which representatives from Korea, Japan, Taiwan, Hong Kong, Thailand, Vietnam, Cambodia, Malaysia, Singapore, Indonesia, India, Pakistan, Bangladesh, the Philippines and other nations participated, agreed to found the East-West Center for Missions Research and Development in Seoul, Korea, for the development and research of missions in Asia. The Center has set to work on missions leadership, the research of mission strategies, and the training of missionaries since 1973.

The Center has produced about 400 missionary candidates and other leadership personnel up to 1969 and aims to train 10,000 Asian missionaries by the year 2000.

The Asia Missions Association held the second triennial conference in November 1978, and is planning to host a conference for mission leaders from Asia, Africa, and Latin America in the 80's.

Potential Resources of Korean Churches

A Surprising Church Growth Rate.—In the early years of the 70's, the church growth rate for the Korean churches was 12. 5 percent annually. All the churches have set up ten-year development plans since 1975 to mark the first centennial anniversary of the Korean Church in 1985. The Presbyterian General Assembly (Hap Tong) has proclaimed that it will set its goal at planting 10,000 churches to that date and the Presbyterian Assembly (Tong Hap) is advocating the planting of 300 churches a year. With this rate of growth, the annual rate has gone past 12. 5 percent since 1975.

The 10,000 churches that in 1972 were preparing the Billy Graham Crusade '73 had more than doubled to 22,000 by 1978.

The Annual Church Growth Rate (1972—1978)

Year	Growth Rate	Number of Churches
1972		10,000
1973	11.0 %	11,100
1974	11.0 %	12,500
1975	11.0 %	13,700
1976	11.5 %	16,000
1977	12.0 %	19,000
1978	12.5 %	22,000

Even more encouraging is the fact that the rate of growth of the Christian population exceeds that of the growth of churches. In 1972 the average size of the congregation of one church was around 300 persons, but in 1978 the number increased to 330 per church.

Evidence from a different statistical survey indicates that the rate of church growth in Korea is indicative of the potential for evangelization. While in other Third World nations Christianity is gaining ground among the illiterate, the poorly educated, and the economically poor; in Korea Christianity is fast spreading among the younger generation, the students, the military, the engineers, the businessmen, the teachers, and the cultured people of the population.

Among the 30 or so nations comprising the Asia-Pacific region, Korea has the largest number of educated Christians.

About 30 percent of the high class officials of the government, 25 percent of the military, and 25 percent of the students could become a strong potential that would prove of tremendous might when properly utilzed for world evangelization.

There are also to be evinced in Korea, churches set up to meet the special needs of functional communities. Pioneered by the Entertainers' Church started in 1979, churches for athletes, artists, public officials, merchants, and others have sprung up enabling the gospel to be preached far beyond the borders of the conventional church. The use of T. V., radio, newspaper, sports, games, art, music, literature, and a variety of other media are becoming battlegrounds for His Cause.

Leadership Potential.—It has been estimated that as of 1979, there are around 260 theological seminaries in Korea. The smallest among the institutions has a minimum of 100 students. The largest boasts a student body of 2,000. In reality the 60,000 or more students in these seminaries are potential fireseeds for the evangelization of Asia and of the world. The bulk of 10,000 graduates produced annually from these schools are either planting new churches or are being sent to churches without a leader. Also, they have to be sent to the 2,000 new churches being born each year and to the 1,000 or so churches that might see alteration in leadership not to mention service in the military, the schools, police stations, prisons, and in industries.

The cost for education in a theological seminary is by no means low. The students are burdened annually with tuitions ranging from $ 500.00 to $ 1,000.00. Fewer than 10 percent of the students get scholarships or aids. The cost of room and board also falls upon the student. But more than double the number eligible to enter the institutions are crowding into them each year.

The minimal academic requirement for entrance into

these schools is graduation from high school. In a number of institutions in mainline denominations, students earning the Master of Divinity or Master of Theology degree are graduating each year. There are around ten institutions that require three year's training for university graduates.

There are over 400 scholars with Ph. D. or Th. D. degrees in addition to the 5,000 or more ministers holding a Master of Theology degree from institutions in Europe and the United States.

What could be the meaning of this seedbed of leadership potential? Could it not mean the divine hand of Providence is using the land of Korea to train these couriers of the Word for eventual use in evangelizing the countless millions in all Asia?

More than 70 percent of these outreach movements are supported outside the budget of the local church by individual Christians who have been and are willing to give to these para-church organizations solely for the purpose of outreach outside the conventional churches. This fact points to the lack of understanding on the part of the institutional churches of the missionary zeal and the devoted ardent Christians. If so, then this tremendous financial potential of the Korean church will prove an abundant resource when properly utilized for mission and evangelism.

Potentiality of Contribution to World Evangelization

How Korea Turned from a Receiving Status to One in Which the Western Missiologist Could Foresee the Hope of Third World Leadership in Missions.-- In the beginning of the 70's when attention was directed to the problem of Third World missions, scarcely a person paid any serious attention to Korea. When all that could be hoped for in Asia was the role of India or Japan, I strongly argued for the possibility of this country's leadership in Asian missions. But it was only after the All-Asia Missions Consultation was convened in Seoul in 1973 that missiologists began to assess the role of Korea's potential leadership in Third World missions.

1. Missionary Status.

When the Fuller Theological Seminary appointed a Korean as the director of its Asian program which started as a means to reinforce its ministry potential, it was out of recognition of the contribution the nation had made to heighten the Christian leadership resource in Asia.

In the last ten years the Korean churches in the United States have seen a phenominal growth of 90 percent to its present number of 600. The number thus more than doubles the sum of all the other Asian churches in the United States. Most of these churches sprang up spontaneously without aid or prior planning by their fellow American churches. This fact has gradually opened the eyes of church leaders, missiologists and mission leaders in the United States.

In the 70's, the number of church leaders and laymen visiting from countries as varied as India, Indonesia, the Philippines, Thailand, Taiwan, Japan, Australia, New Zealand, West Germany, the Netherlands, the countries of the Scandinavian peninsula, and from overseas Chinese schools totaled more than 10,000. These people came and stayed for weeks and months learning and witnessing the growth of the Korean church as well as giving valuable comments and suggestions.

Christian leaders, aware of the situation in the churches of the world today, slowly came to a realization of the contribution that the Korean churches could make for the development of leadership in the Third World.

2. Geographic and Cultural Environments.

Although attention is being given more and more to Korea's role in developing leadership, the following prejudices often hinder the missiologist's perspective:

a) The fact that Korea is situated toward the north-eastern end of Asia and hence is not suitable as a place of central leadership for the Asian church. Because of Korea's geographical location travel costs are double what they would be were it more favourably located. There is also the problem of the cultural gap in that the nation has not been open to Western culture as some other Asian nations have been. The difficulty of communication in English among the local leaders might prove a handicap not to be found in South-east Asian countries where English is substantially in use. Another potential problem which surfaces is that Korea has extremes of temperature that make it difficult for people from the south to accomodate themselves.

However, if we follow the late great missionary states-man John R. Mott's ideas who said that "Korea is the cap-ital of Christianity of the Orient" and drew Korea as the center of the globe, we would find that the distance and the country is ideally situated where the West and the East meet.

b) Geographically speaking, Korea has the advantage of reaching the United States or Europe more easily than some other lands in Asia. If England is situated to the northern end of the globe when viewed from Asia, then the American continent, not known to Europeans until the 15th century, now assumes greater prestige.

c) There really could not be a more adequate testing ground in terms of climate than this land. For, with the ex-tremes of heat and cold, we also have the temperate spring and autumn which ensure a thorough training in all kinds of temperature. Out in the heat of the Equatorial regions, one could experience only half the world.

What Could be Learned from the Korean Churches?-- The Korean church could be seen as being in a test tube for the experimenters of world missions to see and learn. To be observed are:

The distinctive origin of the Korean church;

The characteristic traits of the Korean church;

The structure and organization of the Korean church;

The distinctive growth pattern of the Korean church;

The leadership structure of the Korean church;

The financial structure of the Korean church; and

The outreach movement of the Korean church.

These are the points that the experimenter will see as different from churches in other Third World nations. The churches in Asia that had hitherto looked to the West for the model of the church can now come and see the experiment being done in the Korean church and learn of new ways. The exchange programs of Asian churches which have been sponsored since 1973 by the East-West Center and the Asian Church Growth Institute and a few others have seen substantial results. The people that were invited--ministers, and students--have studied this model of church growth, its leadership structure, its stewardship training and financial structure, and its outreach program. They have returned to their own lands with the thought of assimilating and adopting the Korean pattern. This does not foster an attitude of rejection of the Western church model but rather brings about an attitude of encouragement concerning what they can do.

Developing Asian Leadership.--The Korean church is fast becoming a model for the Asian church in the way in which it has trained its own leaders. It is giving the churches of Asia the confidence that they can do the same. The problem that all of Asia is facing today is the lack of front runners to fulfill the needs of all and of leaders trained in special fields. To meet this need, we can no longer rely as in the past days on what the Western missions did to foster leadership potential. The Christian leaders in Korea, Japan, China, India, and some other major nations have to cooper- ate to meet this need.

The Korean church is a very likely one to take charge of the burden. The East-West Center for Mission Research and Development started the program for Asian missions lead- ership training in 1973. The Asian Center for Theological Studies and Mission (ACTS) has been in active work since 1974 for the development of theological leadership.

When the nation's top-class theological leaders, the well-experienced church-planters, and the devoted sacrificial missionary candidates come together with other Asian leaders in cross-cultural contacts, reciprocal training, communal life, common research, and common work; then the Asian churches will experience the jubilant sense of self-recognition and the Korean church will rejoice for the opportunity that it will be giving to other growing churches.

With the birth of nondenominational faith missions, a new wave of awakening arose so that each church began its own program and new movements came into being.

The following statistics and the list of the Mission agencies will be accountable information:

1. Analytical Statistics

Catagories	Missions	Missionaries *
Denominational	7	30
Nondenominational	70	250
a. General Faith Missions	27	90
b. Students Missions	4	8
c. Women's Missions	8	20
d. Local Church Missions	31	78
Independent Missionaries	77	280

* Some of the missionaries are affiliated with two missions.

2. Korean Missionary Sending and Supporting Agencies

a. Denominational Mission Agencies:

(1) Korean Presbyterian Church Mission (Hap-Tong)
(2) Korean Presbyterian Church Mission (Tong-Hap)
(3) Korean Presbyterian Church Mission (Koryu)
(4) Presbyterian Church Mission (R. O. K.)
(5) Korean Methodist Mission
(6) Korean Evangelical Church Mission
(7) Korea Salvation Army Mission

b. Nondenominational Mission Agencies:

(1) Korea International Mission
(2) Korea Translation Mission
(3) Korea International Mission for Christ
(4) Missions to North Korea
(5) World Omega's Revival Mission Society
(6) Asia Evangelical Mission
(7) Asian Gospel Mission
(8) Agape Mission
(9) Evangelization of North Korea
(10) Presbyterian Inter-Mission Committee
(11) Korean Christian Medical Mission
(12) Korean Christian Entertainers Mission
(13) World Progress Mission
(14) Korean Christian Mission Center
(15) Korean Indonesia Mission Fellowship
(16) Korea Mass-Media Christian Mission
(17) The Christian Service
(18) Council for Mission in North-East Asian Churches
(19) Korea Mission to Bangladesh
(20) Gospel for Asia Foundation
(21) Asian Evangelical Mission
(22) Han-Kook International Evangelistic Mission

(23) Korea Christian Mission Society
(24) Korea Gospel Mission
(25) Korea Harbor Mission
(26) World Revival Mission
(27) Christian Reach Out to the World

c. Student Mission Agencies:

(1) Korean Inter-Varsity Mission
(2) University Bible Fellowship Mission
(3) Students Fellowship of World Mission
(4) Ewha Womans University Students Mission

d. Women's Mission Agencies:

(1) Korean Presbyterian Women's Mission (Hap-Tong)
(2) Korean Presbyterian Women's Mission (Tong-Hap)
(3) Womens Mission of Presbyterian (R. O. K.)
(4) Korean Methodist Women's Mission
(5) Korea Women's Evangelical Service
(6) The Wheat Seed Women's Mission
(7) The Signal Fire Women's Mission
(8) The Prayer Partnership Women's Mission

e. Local Mission Societies:

(1) Dae-gu Dongshin Presbyterian Church Mission
(2) Seoul Dongshin Presbyterian Church Mission
(3) Choong-Hyun Presbyterian Church Mission
(4) Hoo-Am Presbyterian Church Mission
(5) Nam-Seoul Presbyterian Church Mission
(6) Seoul-Nambu Presbyterian Church Mission
(7) Kwan-Ak First Presbyterian Church Mission
(8) Chang-Sung Presbyterian Church Mission
(9) Yong-Hyun Presbyterian Church Mission
(10) Hyo-Sung Presbyterian Church Mission

(11) Sung-Jin Presbyterian Church Mission
(12) New Jerusalem Christian Church Mission
(13) Don-Am Christian Church Mission
(14) Sung-Dong Church Mission
(15) Mok-Po First Presbyterian Church Mission
(16) Su-Kwang Presbyterian Church Mission
(17) Kwang-Lim Methodist Church Mission
(18) Jong-Kyo Methodist Church Mission
(19) Chang Hoon Dae Presbyterian Church Mission
(20) Dae-Dong Presbyterian Church Mission
(21) Dae-Gu Central Presbyterian Church Mission
(22) Su-Hyun Presbyterian Church Mission
(23) Su-Moon Presbyterian Church Mission
(24) Cho-Ryang Presbyterian Church Mission
(25) Shin Yong San Presbyterian Church Mission
(26) Bu-Kae Presbyterian Church Mission
(27) Soong-Ei Methodist Church Mission
(28) Full Gospel Central Church Mission
(29) Kum-Ran Methodist Church Mission
(30) Dae-Jon Central Presbyterian Church Mission
(31) In-Chon Second Presbyterian Church Mission

Financial Potential and Spirit of Giving

1. The average annual budget of local churches in Korea as of 1979 could be classified as follows:

Class of Churches	Annual Budget	Number
A. Extra-large Churches	Above $ 1,000,000.00	50
B. Large Churches	Above $ 500,000.00	500
C. Average Churches	Above $ 200,000.00	6,000
D. Growing Churches	Above $ 100,000.00	10,000
E. Small Churches	Below $ 50,000.00	6,000
Total		22,550

2. The average living allowances paid to the pastor according to the size of the church are as follows:

Position	A. Extra-large	B. Large	C. Average
Senior Pastor	$ 20,000.—	$ 18,000.—	$ 15,000.—
Assistant Pastor	$ 10,000.—	$ 8,000.—	$ 6,000.—
Director of C. E.	$ 8,000.—	$ 6,000.—	$ 5,000.—
Director of Music	$ 5,000.—	$ 4,000.	$ 3,000.—

3. The budget for outreach is as follows:

Outreach Budget

	Classification of Churches		
	Extra-large	Large	Average
Domestic	$ 50,000.—	$ 30,000.—	$ 15,000.—
Overseas	$ 30,000.—	$ 20,000.—	$ 5,000.—

4. The writer's findings point out that these statistics do not correctly reflect the zeal of the average Christian's giving to the work of evangelism and missions. Since the closing years of the 60's decade there has sprung up spontaneously in the Christian community numerous para-church organizations which could be classified as follows:

a. *Domestic Ministries*
 (1) Ministries to Clinical Patients
 (2) Ministries to Workers
 (3) Ministries to Retailers
 (4) Campus Ministries
 (5) Ministries to Chauffeurs
 (6) Ministries to Merchandise Shoppers
 (7) Military Ministries
 (8) Ministries to Prisoners

(9) Ministries to Garbage Workers
(10) Factory Ministries
(11) Artists Ministries
(12) Entertainers Ministries
(13) Athletes Ministries
(14) Barbers Ministries
(15) Conductresses Ministries
(16) Ministries to North Korea
(17) Media Ministries

b. *Overseas Outreach*
(1) To reach overseas Koreans
(2) Korean workers in the Middle East
(3) Itinerant crusades for the overseas Korean
(4) Lay missionary movement:
doctors, nurses, engineers, overseas representatives
of individual companies, students, professors.
(5) Outreach program for overseas sailors
(6) Cross-cultural ministry

(a) Mainland China	(f) Indonesia	(k) Argentina
(b) Taiwan	(g) Bangladesh	(l) West Germany
(c) Thailand	(h) Pakistan	(m) Sweden
(d) Hong Kong	(i) Brazil	(n) Norway
(e) The Philippines	(j) Mexico	(o) Egypt

Strategic Support for the Development of Leadership.--
The developmental strategy for the Asian churches must be
one that is well analyzed, well-selected, and well-planned.
The participation by Asians in their ministry to the Asians
must not be planned nor interfered with by those
outside Asia. The development of church leadership in Asia
has often lost its sense of direction and been decelerated by
the over-zealous interference and the rush of Western brothers over the past ten years. Asians are preparing for the
development of leadership that is appropriate to Asians and

that which is to be achieved through their effort and planning in Asia's own way.

The tactical problem that Asians have to pinpoint and consider is that of the reconciliation of Asian plans with those of Western missions and moreover that of the effective cooperation of the two in bringing about world evangelization.

God willing, the Korean church might eventually prove to be a bridge connecting the churches of Asia with those of the West. Moreover the church may have more to contribute to the true indigenization of Christianity after the countries have thrown off the yolk of Western civilization that has hung upon them like a blanket for more than 150 years.

Dr. Kim Myung-Hyuk is Associate Professor of Historical Theology and Mission at the Hapdong Presbyterian Theological Seminary in Seoul and Pastor of the Riverside Presbyterian Church. He is a graduate of Seoul National University (B. A.), Faith Theological Seminary (B. A.), Westminster Theological Seminary (Th. M.), Yale University Divinity School (S. T. M.) and Aquinas Institute of Theology (Ph.D.).

Sometimes we naively think that non-Western mission societies and missionaries are the answer for the evangelization of the world. While rejoicing in God's provision of these new resources, Dr. Kim dares to take a critical look at Korean mission structures and missionary motives. There is an urgent need for better selection and training of cross-cultural workers and also need for more extensive research and guidance.

7 KOREAN MISSION IN THE WORLD TODAY AND ITS PROBLEMS

by Kim Myung-Hyuk

The Korean church is well known for her rapid growth and for her enthusiasm for Bible studies, prayers, and evangelism. The great revival in 1907 came out of the Bible study-prayer conferences and resulted in enthusiastic evangelism. In 1907 the Korean Presbyterian Independent Synod organized a mission committee and sent the Rev. Lee Ki-Poong as its first missionary to the Cheju Island which is seventy-five miles from the southern part of the Korean peninsula. In 1912 the Korean Presbyterian General Assembly sent three missionary couples to Santung province in China. Mission activities there continued until China was occupied by the Communists.

The Korean church underwent severe presecution and suffering during the thirty-six years of Japanese occupation. This persecution included the church being barred from active evangelistic mission. After the liberation of Korea from Japan in 1945, the church has slowly become aware of her mission responsibilities. She sent two missionaries to Taiwan in 1949. The tragic Korean War in 1950 stirred the Korean church to be more keenly aware of her mission responsibilities. In 1954 Rev. and Mrs. Choi Chang-Young were sent to Thailand, and in 1956 Rev. and, Mrs. Kim Soon-Il were also sent to Thailand. In the 1960's more than a dozen missionary couples were sent to such countries as Brazil, Bolivia, Vietnam, Pakistan, Ethiopia, Japan, and the United States of America.

The last decade of the 1970's was the "great" decade for the Korean church. The church's growth was unprecedented and the awakening to missions was phenomenal. The growth rate continues to accelerate in the 1980's and the mission awakening continues to deepen. According to Dr. Marlin L. Nelson's report, the number of missionaries and mission societies has increased remarkably during the past three years.

More new societies have been organized and more new missionaries have been sent out during these past two years. More missionaries now have a cross-cultural ministry to people of several different languages and cultures. A brief summary of data included in these two directories is as follows:

	1979	1982
Mission organizations	21	47
Missionaries	93	323
Countries	26	37

....

Marlin L. Nelson, ed., *Directory of Korean Missionaries and Mission Societies.* 1982, p. 7).

The Korean church is gradually becoming conscious of her mission responsibilities. Almost every local church talks about mission. A great number of churches have sent or plan to send their own missionaries for which we should be grateful. There are, however, fundamental and serious problems pertinent to the mission of the Korean church. These problems might be dismissed as growing pains, but they should not be justified or excused. In the remainder of this paper, I would like to point out a number of fundamental problems. On the one hand, I do not want to present merely the positive aspects of the rapidly growing Korean church. On the other hand, I do not want to paint an entirely negative picture full of criticism of the Korean church and her mission. I will try to present the problems honestly and objectively, hoping that this will challenge and help the Korean church to carry out her mission correctly and effectively in the coming days.

Competitive Individualism

Competitive individualism has been the most crucial factor in the Korean church's involvement in mission. A few outstanding mission advocates in the early seventies made a significant contribution in awakening the Korean church to mission. Yet, sorry to say, these pioneers were not immune from the spirit of competitive heroism.

Now almost every church in Korea talks about mission and tries to do something about mission. I dare to say that they are also motivated mainly by this same spirit of competitive heroic individualism. Each church attempts to send out its own missionary. Each church is enthusiastic for its own mission project but not for others. The reputation of the individual pastor or church is a significant motivation for doing mission.

The same is true with each denomination. Denominations do not cooperate in mission; rather, they compete with each other. Some interpret this competitive, even separatist individualism, favorably, saying it makes a positive contribution to the rapid growth of the Korean church. It must also be admitted that church growth theory has encouraged competitive individualism. I would like to stress, however, that even though competitive individualism has been a positive factor in church growth, it has created serious problems in the Korean church and in her mission. Every church is almost entirely absorbed with constructing or reconstructing a larger church building and with expansion. Mission becomes an accessory to satisfy competitive individualism. As a result, the churches have no consistent and comprehensive mission policy for the field. Some are even confused. The doctrine of church and denomination is at stake, posing a serious threat to mission.

Lack of Leadership

The Korean church has enormous potential resources for mission. These spiritual and material resources need to be developed and utilized. They should not be exploited to satisfy individual ambition or to promote an individual's reputation. To avoid these dangers, the Korean church needs unambitious mission leaders who are spiritually as well as morally respected. There is no doubt that the Korean church also needs mission theorists, administrators, and politicians. But what the Korean church needs most of all are unambitious mission leaders who can guide and mobilize the potential mission resources for the glory of God.

Lack of Missionaries

The Korean church has sent a few outstanding missionaries to the field. But the majority of those who were sent lack missionary qualities. More than three fourths of them are not even missionaries in a strict sense. They are

FM-1 diaspora ministers (people who have emigrated to other countries) who have had various motives. The church also has a considerable number of missionary candidates throughout Korea, yet it is very difficult to find truly qualified ones.

Many of these candidates are not rightly motivated. Some even have an imperialistic viewpoint which looks down on underdeveloped and poor people. These "missionaries" are not concerned with serving people with humility; rather, they want to praise the spiritual and material prosperity of the Korean church. For these reasons, the Korean church should be more concerned with training and developing truly qualified missionaries.

Lack of Training

Every so often, I am surprised to learn about some seminary graduate who is sent out as a missionary by a denomination when he had no training at all as a missionary. In such cases, the individual takes the initiative as well as the final decision in becoming a missionary, and the denomination recognizes him as its "missionary" in order to improve its reputation. The denomination does not determine where he goes or what he does. Nor does it require him to obtain missionary training.

Furthermore, even though Korea has a few missionary training institutes, they are not yet adequate. The Korean church must develop denominational as well as interdenom-inational missionary research and training institutes where men and women can learn how to become qualified missionaries.

Lack of Mission Policy

The Korean church is becoming enthusiastic about mission. She is, however, carrying out mission without any consistent planned policies. She has not yet determined the qualifications for a missionary. She has neither studied the situations on the field nor does she maintain a substantial relationship with the church on the field. Instead, a missionary simply goes to a field and then by chance discovers the situation and the needs of that field. I do not deny that a particular mission society may be doing a fine job of deploying missionaries to the right places and for the right purposes. Yet this is not so with most missionaries. A young Korean missionary sent to South East Asia recently confided in me that he was having difficulties with the churches on the field and that he was even thinking of starting a new denomination there. I did not approve of his proposal. But this is one of the unhappy results of the absence of mission policy.

Recently an association of twenty-eight mission societies was organized for fellowship and research. The association arranged a seminar which dealt with such topics as the necessity of establishing a theology of mission, a new direction and image for Korean missions, the mission field and missionaries, missionary support and strategy, and layman mission in different cultures. The organization of such a para-church mission association and the serious discussions which followed are encouraging developments. I personally hope it will not become a political machine or merely a superficial organization. The Korean church needs to develop mission policies on such matters as training qualified missionaries, maintaining and strengthening an organic relationship with the church on the field, developing a long-term educational plan for the missionaries and for their children, and financial support for mission.

Lack of Mission Theology

It has often been pointed out that establishing a biblical theology of mission is an essential task for the church in Korea today. In the liberal camp mission is often presented in the style of minjung (people's) theology. This theology understands that the essence of the Missio Dei (mission of God) in Korea today is to carry out a people's rights movement. In a certain neo-evangelical camp, mission has been recently defined as cultural-nationalism. This camp stresses that without an effort to de-Westernize mission the future of Christian mission is hopeless.

In the traditional conservative camp, mission is mainly understood dualistically as a soul-winning conquest with little interest in social, cultural, economic, and other dimensions of society. Some even maintain an imperialistic and paternalistic viewpoint which looks down on underdeveloped people.

Asia has many complex societies. It is urgent that the Korean church develop a Biblical and realistic theology of mission today which deals with social, political, and cultural complexity.

As pointed out above, the Korean church has serious problems pertinent to its mission. These problems should not be dismissed lightly. These problems do not, however, discourage the Korean church from engaging in mission. The Korean church is determined to pay back the gospel debt which she received 100 years ago. She is preparing to celebrate her centennial in 1984, and, she is keenly conscious of her mission responsibilities.

Korea went through sufferings in the past. Korean missionaries, therefore, should be able to share the burdens of the suffering peoples in Asia. Korea was once totally depraved spiritually as well as materially. Korean missionaries, therefore, might gratefully share their spiritual and material prosperity, which has been graciously granted by God, with the poor in Asia. The enthusiasm of the Korean church for Bible studies, prayers, and evangelism could rekindle the sleeping church around the world.

Seminary graduates are pouring out of more then 100 schools in Korea. If they are rightly motivated and properly trained, they could become an abundant mission resource.

The Korean church has witnessed the heroic sacrifices as well as the imperialistic shortcomings of Western missionaries in the past. Korean missionaries, therefore, might be more able to develop a realistic and appropriate mission strategy for Asia.

The Korean church is struggling to reform and liberate herself from the evils of power struggles, sectarianism, and materialism within her ranks. As long as the Korean church remains dominated by such evils her mission in the world will be at stake. If she is not really willing to reform and liberate herself from these evils and carry out the church's historic task of mission, God may use different means to fulfill the Great Commission. God may even use force or persceution to scatter believers to other lands just as He did with the church at Jerusalem in the book of Acts.

Rev. Jay Kwon Kim, D. D. is Managing Director of the Word of Life Press in Seoul, Korea. A graduate of the Kwon Dong College and the General Assembly Presbyterian Theological Seminary, he served as lecturer and acting chairman of the Bible Department of the Kwon Dong College. In 1982 he received an honorary doctors degree from the Canada Christian College in recognition of his work in translation and publication of Christian literature.

Missions and churches investing money and manpower in the spread of the gospel by mass media will find this article informative and inspiring. Aided by the development of Hangul (Korean phonetic language), a high literacy rate and distribution and sale of Scriptures by colporteurs, Christian literature continues to be an effective way for church growth. The use of radio and TV also have great potential for bringing the gospel into homes and countries closed to the traditional missionary approach.

8 THE IMPACT OF MASS COMMUNICATIONS

by Jay Kwon Kim

Since the beginning of Protestant missions in Korea in 1884, mass communications have played a very important role in presenting the saving knowledge of the gospel to the Korean people. When we consider the history of Christian world missions, it becomes obvious that mass communications have contributed to the unprecedented church growth in Korea, a growth which is faster than the population growth. The chief medium of mass communication in the first half century of Korean church history was literature.

Other mass media, such as radio, film and television, were introduced in the 1950's. In 1955 Korea had only about one million Christians but by 1981, government statistics reported eight million Christians. Of course, other factors stimulated church growth such as the Korean War, industrialization, etc. But we can see from the above indications that when the use of mass media is increased, church growth may also increase.

The twentieth century is characterized by rapid communication, mass production, and population explosion. If any business wants to be successful in this day and age, it must utilize mass media well. And the same is true of successful church growth. For example, the Korean church has utilized mass media efficiently for its growth. Many factors have greatly contributed to the use of mass communications. Ethnically and racially, the Korean people are one integral group. A message is better communicated within an ethic and racial group than between groups. Linguistically, Koreans speak one language and understand each other without difficulty. More about this will be said later.

Religiously, the Korean people are more influenced by animism or Shamanism (folk religion) than Buddhism (organized religion). Missiologists tell us it is much more difficult to communicate the gospel message and to obtain a fruitful response among the followers of an organized religion like Buddhism and Islam than among the followers of a non-organized religion like animism and Shamanism. Since Korea is basically animistic, it is no surprise that so many have responded to the gospel. All of these factors have contributed to the impact of mass communications in Korea.

One Language Makes Communication Easier

The Korean language belongs to the Altaic family which has traditionally included the Manchu-Tungus, Mongol, and Turkic groups of languages. Korean is quite distinct from both Chinese and Japanese. The Korean language has borrowed many Chinese words over the centuries, but grammatical structures of Korean and Chinese are quite different. Korean and Japanese grammatical structures are similar in many ways, but their phonologies differ greatly. A unique language, Korean has been used in the Korean peninsula over the centuries. This language is now spoken by nearly sixty million people including 3,000,000 Korean settlers in Manchuria, about 600,000 in Japan, and some 600,000 in North America.

Historically, geographically, and ethnically Korea is compact enough to be one linguistic whole. No other language is spoken as a native tongue within the Korean peninsula. Korea has only one language. Of course, some minor regional differences can be found in accent and in local colloquialisms, but these do not create difficulties in people's ability to understand one another. It is possible to identify the region from which a native comes by his accent, but this does not affect the understandability of his speech. In recent years even regional accents are fading away due to the Korean War, industrialization, and modern transportation. During the Korean War refugees from the North came to the South and many young people from all parts of the country joined the armed forces and served together. Also many people from the rural areas came to the cities for better jobs as industrialization increased. As a result, local accents became less noticeable.

The construction of modern freeways to most of the main regions of the country reduced travel time by more than one day to six hours or less. Ease in transportation also contributed to the development of one standard language.

As for the written script, Korean can be written in two ways. One is in Chinese characters and the other is in the Korean alphabet which is called "Hangul." The Chinese characters are so hard to learn that their use made it impossible to overcome the illiteracy problem among the common people. Even if a scholar had learned all the Chinese characters, he was still limited in expressing himself because of the different structures in the Chinese and Korean languages.

Hangul was invented in 1446 by King Sejong and his royal scholars. It is the most ingenious and perfect phonetic script in the world. It is so simple that a person can learn how to read and write in a few days. Concerning the superiority of this alphabet and the unfortunate attitudes toward it, Dr. Allen D. Clark writes, "The Korean alphabet (Hangul) is an ingenious and simple system which should long since have made Korea the most literate nation in the world. Unfortunately, its very simplicity worked against it, for the old scholars, who had spent years in mastering the intricacies of the Chinese classics had only a vast contempt for a system of writing that 'even a woman could learn.' The result was that Hangul was largely neglected, used only for low-grade novels..." [1] Certainly Dr. Clark's comment is not at all exaggerted. Dr. Harry A. Rhodes also writes, "This was a great blessing to the missionaries also as they could learn the 'eunmun' (Hangul) in a few days and be reading the Korean Bible and studying the Korean language both written and oral." [2]

The Korean language has twenty-four letters (ten vowels and fourteen consonants). A person can easily learn to read and write the language in a short time. If it were not for this script, the modern educational revival of the nation would been impossible. This simple script pushed the literacy rate up to 90 percent.

The coming of Christianity into the country and the use of Hangul have an inseparable connection. It is with this script that the first Bible was translated into the vernacular. The Bible is the largest single volume ever written in

....

1. Allen D. Clark, *A History of the Church in Korea* (Seoul: Christian Literature Society, 1971), p. 14.
2. Harry A. Rhodes, *History of the Korea Mission* (Seoul: Y. M. C. A. Press, 1934), p. 90.

Hangul. As a matter of fact, Hangul really came into the foreground through the translation of the Bible. It is no wonder that the Korean church has had unprecedented growth. Language, transportation, and political unification of the Mediterranean coastal nations prepared the Roman World for Christ's first advent. It seems that the Lord, in a similar manner, prepared Hangul some 500 years ago to be used for the clear preaching of the gospel to the masses and for the the development of the Korean church.

Early Use Of Literature

The predominant medium of mass communications in the first half of the Korean church was literature. Christian literature work had a rather unusual beginning in Korea. The ordinary way of starting literature work in a mission field is for a missionary to first learn the language of the people and to translate Christian literature into the vernacular, but this was not the case in Korea.

The first translation of the Gospel portions into Korean had taken place in Manchuria and in Japan. The literature prepared in Manchuria had been secretly brought into Korea even before any missionary had placed his feet on Korean soil. The Gospel portion that was printed in Japan was brought into Korea by the very first missionaries who made a stopover in Japan. This means the literature ministry in Korea had an advantageous beginning.

When the first missionaries came to Korea, they laid strong emphasis on the importance of literature and many got involved in this work. During the first eight years of the Presbyterian Mission in Korea, thirty missionaries came to the field. Among the thirty, ten of them produced a great deal of literature. Fortunately, they were gifted with literary and linguistic abilities. This laid a firm foundation for the literature ministries of the Korean church.

Ross Translation of the Bible

Rev. John Ross was a missionary of the Presbyterian Church of Scotland to China. He began his work in Yingkow, Manchurchuria, in 1873. He made an exploratry trip to the eastern region of Manchuria. He found Korea settlements in the course of his trip. Knowing of Rev. Robert Thomas' unsuccessful attempt to witness in Korea, he became interested in this hermit country. Korean settlers told him something about Korea, but they were extremely reluctant to associate with him. This was due to the fact that just a few years earlier thousands of Roman Catholic Christians had been martyred, and the Korean government's hostility toward westerners placed his life in danger.

In spite of this tense atmosphere missionary Ross continued to seek ways to evangelize Korea. Early in the spring of 1874, Mr. Ross visited Koryo Gate, a buffer town where the largest community of Korean settlers resided. The main purpose of his trip was to find a Korean scholar who would teach him the Korean language and history. Fortunately, he found a young man named Lee Eung-Chan who was brave enough to serve as a tutor. Soon Mr. Lee's three friends joined him, and they worked together with Mr. Ross. These four young men confessed Jesus as their Savior and were baptized in 1876. They were the first Korean Protestant believers.

Mr. Ross and his four converts started the Bible translation work, but had difficulty using new believers to translate the Scriptures. In the meantime, a man named Su Sang-Yoon joined in the work. Later this man became the first Korean pioneer evangelist. Mr. Ross describes their method of translation as follows, "First, the Korean translators and I read the Chinese Bible, and when they had translated this into Korean, I then compared it with the Greek original to try to get it as close to the Greek meaning as possible." [3]

....

3. Ibid., Allen D. Clark, p. 84.

After some years of strenuous work, the Gospels of Luke and John were translated. Another difficult task was to print the Gospels for no Korean script in type letters was available in Manchuria. A printing press was secured but how to get Korean in type letters was still unknown. At that time a man named Kim Chung-Song went bankrupt in his medicine business, and he came to Mr. Ross for help. He was so bankrupt that he could not even pay for lodging. He was hired to work in the print shop. This man joined in the work with the other men and they carved the Korean script in type by hand. While setting the type, Kim Chung-Song was deeply impressed and professed faith in the Lord and was baptized. The translation of Luke by Ross was published in 1882. This first printing totaled 3,000 copies.

In the fall of that year Mr. Ross sent Mr. Paik Hong-Joon to sell these Gospels to the Korean settlers in East Manchuria. He made two trips and sold many copies of the Gospel of Luke. As a result, many received Jesus as their Savior. Their lives were full of joy, and they were asking to be baptized. Mr. Ross was unable to go since he was so busy in printing. In 1883, 3,000 copies of the Gospel of John were printed.

Finally, in the fall of 1884 Mr. Ross visited East Manchuria and found many who wanted baptism. He baptized seventy-five people in four villages. This group of baptized people became the first Korean church in history. The work of Scripture distribution continued and 15,690 copies were sold by 1886.

The Bible translation work also continued and 3,000 copies of the entire New Testament of the Ross translation were published in 1887.

Many attempts were made to bring the Scriptures into Korea. However, any religious writing having a connection with Westerners was strictly forbidden in Korea. To bring the Scriptures into Korea was to risk one's life. With a sincere zeal to evangelize his mother country, Mr. Su Sang-

Yoon, a colporteur, got some Gospels and pamphlets from Mr. Ross and set out for Korea in the spring of 1883. When he reached the border, he was carefully inspected, the forbidden Scriptures were discovered, and he was put into prison. Fortunately, two young officials in charge of the prison were Mr. Su's distant relatives, and they arranged to get him a horse so he could escape by night. The next day he was able to reach his home without any trouble. Then he evangelized his family and relatives. Within six months, about twenty people gathered together every Sunday to read the Scriptures and worship. This was the first church in Korea.

In 1884, Paik Hong-Joon and Lee Sung-Ha made another attempt to bring the Scriptures into Korea. But the border was so carefully guarded that this was very difficult. So Lee Sung-Ha left quantities of Scriptures in an inn on the Manchurian side. When the inn-keeper found the forbidden Scriptures, he threw some into the river and some into the fire. When Mr. Ross heard of it, he said: "The water into which the Bibles were thrown will become the 'water of life' to Koreans, and the ashes will be fertilizer to bring about a great growth in the Korean church."[4] Sure enough, this region, later became a strong Christian community and many church leaders came from this area.

Paik Hong-Joon made many trips across the river with quantities of Scripture hidden in loads of old paper and distributed them in the Uijoo area. Eventually, Paik Hong-Joon was arrested and imprisoned for two years. After his release, he died from the effects of his imprisonment.

Meanwhile, a student named Lee Soo-Jung from a noble Korean family went to study in Japan. While he was studying he had contact with some Japanese pastors and was baptized in April 1883. Then he became acquainted with

----

4. Ibid., Harry A Rhodes, p. 74.

some Japanese pastors and was asked to translate the Scriptures into Korean. He used the Chinese Bible and the Japanese Bible as texts and translated a portion of the Scriptures into Korean. In 1884 the Gospel of Mark was published.

When the first missionaries, Rev. Horace Underwood and Rev. Henry Appenzeller, came to Korea, they first stopped in Japan and brought Lee Soo-Jung's translation of Mark with them to Korea. The Korean Protestant church, unlike the Roman Catholic mission, was deeply rooted in the Scriptures from the beginning.

The Bible Society and Translation

Even though the Ross translation of the entire New Testament was available, it could not be accepted as the standard Bible because of its strong Northern dialect and poor rendering. The need for a better translation was so urgent that a translation committee was formed in February 1887. Due to the devotion of the committee members, the translation work progressed very rapidly. It is said that some members of the committee met over 500 times to complete the translation.

The translation was as follows. First, a draft was made by an individual translator; second, a revision of this draft was made on the basis of committee members' suggestions; and lastly, a joint revision was made by the committee which became a tentative version. The committee found this method took too much time and decided to meet as a whole until the entire New Testament was completed. Thus, the New Testament was published in 1900, and 98,498 copies of the New Testament had been sold by 1905.

Finally, in 1910 the committee published the Old Testament and within a year 8,000 copies of the entire Bible were sold. Now with the whole Bible available, the church laid great emphasis on the importance of each believer owning a personal copy and reading it. This had a tremendous impact on Bible distribution and 2,379,751 copies of the

Scriptures were sold by 1918. One of the remarkable methods of Bible promotion was the implementation of the colportage system. In 1928, 177 colporteurs sold Gospels and Bibles. They also witnessed as they went from place to place, and as a result, they started many churches. By 1936, 18,079,466 copies of the Scripture had been sold.

After the Second World War, the work of the Bible Society became even more active due to the freedom of religion. In recent years the Bible Society has had a program to provide the Scriptures for the armed forces. The publishing of an English-Korean bilingual New Testament was another ministry to reach students and other young people.

Now Korea is the second largest Bible publishing country in the world. In the year 1980 alone, 697,548 copies of the whole Bible, 2,675,393 copies of the New Testament, 968,170 copies of the Gospels, and 880 copies of the Braille Bible were published. Since the founding of the Bible Society, 80,242,678 copies of the Bible have been published. Another significant work initiated in 1973 was the publishing of Bibles in other languages such as Spanish, French, Arabic, Polish, Persian, English, Thai, etc. By the end of 1981, 600,000 copies of the Bible and 600,000 copies of The New Testament in forty languages had been published and exported to forty-nine different countries. The Bible Society subsidizes $ 50,000.00 annually for publication of the Bible in other countries.

The Christian Literature Society

In October 1889, plans were made to form a society for publishing Christian literature. The following year, The Korea Religious Tract Society was established. The first publications were a booklet on the "Doctrine of Christianity" and ten different Gospel tracts.

There was an unsuccessful revolution in Korea in 1894 and many noble patriots were imprisoned. A missionary visited the patriots and gave them literature published by the Christian Literature Society, as it is now called, and as a result twelve of them became Christians. This was a great encouragement to the literature work.

In 1919 the Society's name was changed to The Christian Literature Society of Korea (CLS). In order to produce better literature a new editorial committee was formed. Different subjects were given to each writer including devotionals, Bible study, theology, sermons and sermon material, church history, exposition, biography, catechisms, worship and forms, tracts, etc. In the 1927 catalog of the society, 525 titles were listed. By 1939 the Society had published forty-six million copies of various books.

The Society's main income was sales, but it also received contributions from its membership, grants from missions and donations from individuals, organizations, and churches.

The Society's work was crippled during the Second World War when the Japanese interfered in its operations and finally confiscated the property. In March 1948, the first board meeting was held after the war and the work was revitalized. The board decided to improve publication quantitively and qualitatively to meet the needs of the church. Since then many large volumes have been published, among which *The Dictionary of the Christian Church* is monumental. Now the Society has over 1,000 titles and forty new titles are added yearly. Among these, the uniform Sunday School lessons and two hymnals have had the widest circulation.

The Society also publishes several periodicals.: *The Children's Friend, Theological Thought, The Upper Room, New Light* and the *Braille Magazine.* Of these, *The Upper Room has the widest circulation reaching student* armed forces personnel, and the rank and file of people. *The Children's Friend* magazine has the longest publication history of twenty years.

In order to secure regular readers, the Society established The Book Club plan in the 1960's. Under this plan its 2,000 registered members receive new copies of books as they come out.

Until the early years of 1950's the Bible Society and CLS were the only agents producing Christian literature. They have published millions of volumes of various Christian books. Their contribution to the unprecedented church growth in Korea should in no way be underestimated.

Word of Life Press

The Evangelical Alliance Mission (TEAM) began its ministry in 1953 when the Korean War was still going on. One of its main ministries was literature work. Shortly after TEAM arrival in Korea it established the Word of Life Press for publishing tracts and pamphlets for this devastated country. Thousands upon thousands of tracts and pamphlets were printed and distributed by the missionaries in cities and towns and in farm and fishing villages. Many national pastors and Christian workers obtained literature from the press to distribute in their localities. Among the pamphlets, "What Must I Do to Be Saved?" by John R. Rice was printed in exceptional numbers and was effectively used in mass evangelism. As is generally the case with missionary publishers worldwide, Word of Life Press went on to publish larger volumes to meet the needs of the Korean church. The main themes of books were devotional thoughts about God, apologetics, and evangelism. Of these books, *Power Through Prayer* by E. M. Bounds was the most outstanding volume and is still one the best sellers, having sixteen reprints.

The publication of the *New Hymnal* in 1965 was a new milestone for the publishing house. The largest Presbyterian denomination (Hap Tong) and another Presbyterian Church (Koshin) adopted this hymnal in commemoration of their merger. Some other churches also began to use the *New Hymnal*. Now 300,000 copies of this hymnal are distributed yearly and a total number of 3,000,000 copies had been published up to the end of 1981.

The Book Club plan has been in operation since 1972 and now over 2,000 members are enrolled. Each member of the club receives two or three new books monthly by mail. This plan was set up to supply books to those who have difficulty in getting to a bookstore due to their work or distant place of residence.

The Church Library Plan was set up in 1975 to especially help churches with Christian literature. The finances of most rural church believers are not sufficient to buy the books that they want to read. To encourage reading, the church buys Word of Life Press books at a low cost and lends them out to the church members. Up to the present, 769 church libra- ies have been established.

The publishing of the *Living New Testament* is another outstanding Word of Life ministry for the Korean people. The English *Living Bible* is one of the most understandable Scriptures for modern people. This makes it especially useful in evangelism because it uses the language of the average man. This is also true of the Korean *Living New Testament*. In December 1977, 50,000 copies of the *Living New Testament*. were published and distributed through bookstores, Christian organizations, and churches. In 1978 and 1969, 500,000 copies of the *Living New Testament* were printed with decision slips inside. These *New Testaments* were distributed by mail to homes in six major cities in Korea. These addresses were selected at random from telephone directories. Many phone calls and return post cards were received saying that the recip- ients had received Christ and asking what church they should go to and how they should join. This program was sponsored by *Bibles for the World* in Wheaton, Illinois, U. S. A.

Word of Life Press has seventy franchised Christian bookstores throughout the country. They all carry Word of Life Press books for the local people. The number of book- stores continues to increase as new churches are started and believers are added to them. Word of Life Press sold over 1,000,000 books in 1981. The increase of sales from 1971 to 1981 was 2,900 percent.

It is to be regretted that no more publishers can be mentioned because of limited space. Korea has other good sized publishers like Kyo Moon Sa, Voice, Agape and many others. At this time 115 Christian publishers operate throughout the country.

1970's seems to have been a revival for Christian literature work in Korea. Many large volumes of Christian writings were translated and published. Among these were *The Pulpit Commentary, Calvin's Commentary, Lange's Commentary, Lenski's New Testament Commentary,* and *Barclay's Commentary.*

Newspapers and Magazines

The first Christian newspaper, *The Christian News* appeared in April 1897. Christians and some non-Christians read this paper. The Korean government subscribed to 450 copies for its officials all over the country. Two copies went to the palace and brought a note of appreciation from the King.

The first Christian magazine, *The Church,* was published in 1889 and continued for ten years, Since then many different Christian newspapers and magazines have appeared and some have been discontinued. However, the following chart gives the listing of the ones being published today. This will give the reader an overall view of the Christian periodicals in Korea.

NEWSPAPERS (weekly)

NAME	FOUNDED	CIRCULATION	PUBLISHER
The Catholic Times	1927	85,000	Roman Catholic
The Christian Public Press	1946	25,000	Presbyterian (Tong Hap)
The Christian Press	1960	30,000	Inter-denominational
The Gospel Times	1960	20,000	A Branch of the Methodists
The Christian Times	1964	20,000	Presbyterian (Hap Dong)
The Church Union Times	1966	20,000	Non-denominational

Magazines (most are monthly)

NAME	FOUNDED	CIRCULATION	PUBLISHER	READERS
War Cry	1907	15,000	Salvation Army	Christian Workers & Laymen
Church Compass	1916	10,000	7th Day Advent.	Laymen
Presbyterian Theol. Quarterly	1916	5,000	Hap Dong Sem.	Theologians Christian Workers
Christian World	1930	30,000	Methodist	
The Christian Home	1953	6,000	Women's Missions	Mostly women (discontinued)
Word of Blessing	1954			
Theological Thought	1957	6,000	CLS	Pastors
New Light	1960		CLS	The blind

Christian Education	1961	5,000	Inter-Denom.	S. S. Teachers
New Life	1961	5,000	Lutheran	Laymen
Anglican Monthly	1962	2,500	Anglican	Christian Workers & Laymen
The Upper Room	1962	60,000	CLS	Students & Laymen
World of Faith	1962	5,000	Non-Denom.	Laymen
New Friends	1963	10,000	Non-Denom.	S.S. Children
Church Administration	1964	1,000	Baptist	Pastors, Christian Workers
The Christian Life	1965	8,000	Non-Denom.	Christian Workers & Laymen
True Light	1966	2,000	Church of Christ	Christian Workers & Laymen (discontinued)
Victorious Life	1967	15,000	Victorious Life	Pastors & Laymen
World of Faith	1967	85,000	Assemblies of God	Christian Workers & Laymen
Separation News	1971	10,000	Presbyterian (ICCC)	Christian Workers & Laymen
The Prayer	1973	12,000	Every Home Crusade	Laymen
The Sunday School Teacher	1974	8,000	Christian Ed Research	S. S. Teachers & Christian Workers
The Living Stream	1975	5,000	Presbyterian (Daeshin)	Christian Workers & Laymen
Pastoral Monthly	1976	5,000	Pastoral Monthly	Pastors
Modern Pastoral Monthly	1982	30,000	Assemblies of God	Christian Workers

Christian Use of Radio

Christian Broadcasting System

The first Christian programs to be broadcast over government radio stations were limited to Christian music. Music programs continued for only a few years and stopped. After the Second World War, the church was unable to buy time for a greater variety of Christian programs from the government radio stations. So the church decided to start a Christian radio station. After many difficulties the government granted a permit for a private Christian radio station. A building was secured and transmission antennae were set up. Finally on December 15, 1954, the Christian Broadcassting System (CBS) went on the air with 5,000 watts of power and the call letters of HLKY. The establishment of CBS was very timely and appropriate because it helped meet the spiritual needs of people who were unmercifully attacked by the Communist invasion. Later, four branch stations were set up so that HLKY reached a potential listening audience of fifteen to twenty million people (over 50 percent of the total population). Surveys showed that HLKY had a wide listening audience.

A general breakdown of the daily program schedule, prior to 1980, was as follows: news and commentary (19 percent), culture-education (22 percent), entertainment (12 percent), religious (13 percent), and music (13 percent). Not only the evangelistic programs but the other programs also had a tremendous influence upon non-Christians. The religious programs included sermons sponsored by churches; documentary drama based on personal experiences and Korean church history; testimonies of Christians as to how they had overcome hardship in their daily lives. One of the best-rated and longest-lasting evangelistic programs has been "The Lutheran Hour," which used a drama format of Christian stories from daily life. These first went on the air in 1959 and were called "This Is the Life." This program is also broadcast over six commercial stations. Those who became interested in the gospel because of these broadcasts were followed up by a correspondence course.

In 1960, a simple pamphlet which explained what a Christian is and how to study the correspondence course was mailed out and 100 of the inquirers registered to study the course. After a while those studying the course told their friends about it and a total of 2,500 registrations a month were received. Up to now, 589,123 have registered and 143,556 have received a diploma of completion.

In 1980, CBS had to change their programs drastically because the govenment initiated new mass media policies. The government cancelled their commercial license, which allowed 30 percent of the programs to raise 90 percent of its income from sponsors. Now CBS is turning from secular society to the churches for revenue. The churches expressed great sympathy and began to support CBS so it could continue to broadcast.

Far East Broadcasting System

A second radio station, Far East Broadcasting System (FBS), with the call letters of HLKX and a 50,000 watt transmitter, was established by The Evangelical Alliance Mission (TEAM). They aired their first message in December 1956. FBS broadcasts fourteen hours daily in the Korean, English, Chinese, Mongolian, and Russian languages. The purpose of this studio is to broadcast the gospel message, not only to the Korean people, but also to the people living behind the bamboo and iron curtains. The antennae are so directed as to make it possible for people living in Communist countries to clearly hear the Word of God. For some time TEAM had no way of knowing whether these people were listening to the broadcasts or not. Finally, in the early 1960's a letter was received from a listener in interior China. Shortly after that a letter was received from Siberia. This greatly encouraged the radio staff and the Korean church. Since then until the end of 1981, 1,414 letters were received from these areas. The largest number of letters were sent by the Korean settlers in Manchuria. Some of the letters are heart rending.

A sixteen-year-old Korean boy in Manchuria actually copied the whole New Testament while it was read over the radio. A lady said in one of her letters that she had saved some money for the radio station but had no way to send it. Another person wrote and said he had received Jesus as his personal Savior just from listening to the radio, without any other help.

FBS programs emphasize evangelistic and gospel preaching. Many sermons by local pastors are aired daily. To strengthen the believers and to help win new believers, various levels of Bible studies conducted by Bible teachers and theologians are broadcast. The follow-up department is making every effort to help the new believers grow in the Lord by correspondence and telephone conversations. Many conferences have been conducted over the years for the listeners. These conferences led some listeners to Christ and others to a deeper fellowship with the Lord. The programs where believers share their testimonies as to how they found the Lord and how He enabled them to overcome hardships and live a victorious life have been very encouraging.

The English Bible study program is instrumental in leading many students and professional people to Christ. At first they are attacted by the opportunity to study English, but eventually some of them are won to the Lord by the ministry of the Word and by the Holy Spirit.

Far East Broadcasting Company

A third radio station, Far East Broadcasting Company (FEBC) with call letters HLZA and 250,000 watts of power was established in June 1963. Like FBS, the main purpose of FEBC is to broadcast the gospel message further into the interior of China and Russia. Its signal is stronger and covers a wider area than FBS. It broadcasts ten hours daily in the Korean, Chinese, Russian, English, and Japanese languages. Its program is very similar to that of FBS but it has much better response because of its stronger signal.

In 1980 and 1981, 15,890 letters were received from listeners in China. Radio waves are the only means of carrying the gospel message to the interior of Communistic regions where a missionary cannot go. Often we forget the importance of this ministry. It is said that a great revival is going on in China today. Some China research groups in Hong Kong estimate that China has thirty to fifty million Christians. Of course, we have no way of knowing the exact figure but it would seem that China has at least twenty million Christians. This large number may be partly due to radio ministries. A radio ministry serves two purposes: on the one hand it encourages the listeners and on the other hand it strengthens those who participate in the ministry.

In conclusion, it must be said that the mass media have been excellent tools to evangelize Korea and have yielded outstanding results during the past 100 years. Mass media found very fertile soil in Korea with its closely knit, basically animistic society which had one standard language which was easy to learn to read.

Furthermore, Korea's political struggles helped break up the soil, preparing for an even greater response to the gospel. Coupled with this receptivity, the Holy Spirit led dedicated and skilled missionaries to translate the Scriptures very early. These missionaries widely distributed the Scriptures as well as preached the gospel and led Bible studies. All of this, in turn, brought thousands to Christ and helped build them up in the faith.

This response laid a broader base for wide acceptance of Christianity even in the government. The government, then, allowed mass evangelistic rallies and wide literature distribution and granted permission for Christian radio stations to broadcast the gospel even beyond the shores of

Korea.

One more thing that must be noted is the utilization of television for church growth. From 1956 to 1968, the government television station and two commercial stations gave some free time for Christian programs. During those years, a total of 238 Christian programs utilizing films, dramas, choirs, puppet stories, and panel discussions were broadcast over these stations. Since 1968 free time has no longer been available. Television broadcasting in Korea has become extremely expensive, so the church cannot afford to buy time. The only programs aired since then have been some announcements for rallies. Should we forget about using Christian television programs for evangelism and church growth? No because the most popular and effective mass medium in Korea today is television. The saving gospel of Christ must be conveyed to the masses through television.

Today in Korea the church continues to be challenged to make effective use of the mass media for the reaching of the sixty million Koreans in the North and South and for reaching others around the world.

Note: On November 10, 1983, the Korea Times reported the election of Rev. Han Kyung-Chik as director of the newly organized Korea Video Evangelical Society. The purpose of this Society is to do evangelism in hotels, hospitals and military installations by use of video tapes of sermons by noted pastors. The first project is to donate tapes to 300 express buses. We rejoice in this innovative use of VTR for evangelism.

PART TWO

HISTORICAL, CULTURAL AND
RELIGIOUS ASPECTS

Dr. Ro Bong-Rin is executive secretary of Asia Theological Association, editor of Asia Theological News and Asian Perspective, church historian and professor of Missions and Asian Studies and teaches part-time at the Tung Hai University in Taiwan. Educated in the Seoul National University, Columbia Bible College (B. A. in Biblical Ed.), Wheaton College (B. A. in History), Covenant Seminary (B. D.), and Concordia Seminary (S. T. M. and Th. D.), he is presently serving with the Overseas Missionary Fellowship (formerly C. I. M.) in Taiwan, Republic of China.

Most of the contributing authors in other chapters have emphasized various and significant spiritual factors that have contributed to the explosive growth of the Korean church. In this chapter Dr. Ro Bong-Rin gives insight concerning cultural, historical, educational, social and political aspects. Though many of these are unique to the Korean situation, he emphasizes principles that can apply to countries where Christianity is still a minority.

⑨ NON-SPIRITUAL FACTORS IN CHURCH GROWTH

by Ro Bong-Rin

The rapid church growth in Korea is not entirely due to spiritual factors in Korean Christianity. Non-spiritual or situational factors deeply rooted in the history of the nation have contributed to this growth. Many Korean intellectuals welcomed Western influence including Christianity as a means of liberating Korea from the Japanese colonial power. Christianity introduced new ideas of political democracy into Korea through mission schools. The missionaries popularized the use of the Korean phonetic script, started education for the masses, and ministered to the people's physical needs through Western medicine. Christianity has filled the spiritual vacuum created by the traditional religions of Buddhism and Confucianism, which have made little impact in their lives. The sufferings experienced by Korean Christians during the Japanese occupation in Korea (1910—1945) and during the Korean War (1950—53) and the constant threat of Communism from North Korea have encouraged the people to find their security in God rather than man.

"How many legs does a Korean have?" asked an entrance examination of freshmen in a certain American college to test the students' knowledge of world events. This was before the Korean War. The answers varied from "one" to "fourteen." Not many knew much about this nation until the Korean War in 1950 when Korea became more prominent in world news. Virtually a hermit nation, Korea's doors to the West gradually opened in 1882 with the Open Door Treaty.

The recent phenomenal church growth in Korea cannot be understood apart from the historical and cultural background of the Korean people. The author will attempt to depict here situational or non-spiritual factors such as historical, cultural, and environmental reasons which provided a fertile soil for the spiritual fermentation of the Korean people.

I. The Historical Background

According to the Korean calendar, 1984 is the 4317th year of history. The country was divided into several kingdoms for several centuries. The following brief outline indicates the political development of Korea up to the present time.

Pre-historic legendary period:
Tangun Mythology (2333 B.C.-   ): pre- historic legendary
                                      period

Divided Three Kingdoms:
   Kokuryu Dynasty (37. A.D.—668 A.D.) in northern half
   Silla Dynasty (57 A.D.-935 A.D.) in southeastern part

Paik Che Dynasty (18 B.C.-935 A.D.) in southwestern
Koryu Dynasty (935-1392): Golden Age of Buddhism
Yi Dynasty (1392-1910): Age of Confucianism
Japanese Annexation (1910-1945)
Divided Korea (1945-   ) by Yalta Conference
    North Korea: Communist control by Kim Il-Sung and
                his son Kim Chung-Il
    South Korea: Republic--Syngman Rhee, Park Chung-
                Hee, Chun Du-Hwan
    Korean War (June 25, 1950 - July 27, 1953)

The first modernization efforts in Korea can be traced back to the 17th and 18th centuries. Far Eastern political history, in which the church has been intimately involved, throws some light on the problem. Korea is surrounded by the larger and more powerful nations of China, Japan, and Russia. Thus, Korea has been described as a "shrimp crushed in the fight of the whales." The Chinese Han dynasty invaded Korea in the second century, B.C., the Sui and Tang Dynasties in the seventh century, A. D., the Khitan in the tenth and eleventh centuries, the Mongols in the thirteenth and fourteenth centuries, the Japanese in the late sixteenth century and the Manchus is the seventeenth century. With this background, it was understandable that Korea practiced political isolation from 1864 to 1876.

From 1876 to the time of the Japanese protectorate of Korea in 1905, the conservative bureaucracy which favored China struggled with the progressive group which was pro-Japan. This conflict resulted in a bloody and abortive coup in December, 1884. The coup consequently led to the Sino-Japanese War (1894-1895) for the domination of Korea. The pro-Chinese conservative bureaucracy which paid tribute to China from 1627 was defeated by Japan. Furthermore, Russia's interest in Manchuria and the Korean peninsula led to a conflict with Japan which caused the Russo-Japanese War (1904-1905). Japan then became the dominant ruler of Korea for the next forty years.

Western powers also put pressure on Korea. The United States signed an Open Door Treaty with Korea in 1882, and other European colonial powers followed the Americans making their way into Korea through treaties in the following four years.

In addition to external pressure from neighboring invaders and internal political disintegration through factionalism, Korea had no strong philosophical rationale that provided a basis for any political or intellectual ideologies. The country was in deep trouble in every way. Dr Lee Won-Sul, Vice-chancellor of the Kyung Hee University, succinctly describes the condition of Korea at the end of the 19th century:

> Politically inept, economically stagnant, socially disequilibrated, and morally corrupt, the old system could not cope with the tidal challenge of the West, and people were in the state of total despair (Gospel Light, February-March 1983, p.9).

During this time of national crises, Christianity played a very significant role. Belief in Christianity gave a sense of patriotic national identity as an alternative force to Japanese colonial assimilation. Korea welcomed Western powers which were "Christian" as a means to restore political independence and to introduce political democracy. Christianity introduced the new concept of modern education, uplifted the status of women in society through education, and injected a new Christian etical standard.

Among the many contributions of Christianity to the nation, four areas listed below are particularly related to the growth of the church in Korea.

1. The Independence Movement Against Japanese Colonialism

Unlike China where the colonial powers were Western nations, Korea faced colonialism from Japan. Therefore, the Korean people welcomed Western influence including Christianity in order to liberate themselves from the hands of the Japanese. While the gentry class in China rejected Christianity, many Korean intellectuals eagerly grasped Christianity.

Western missionaries fostered the concept of national independence and trained the younger generation in modern ideas so as to be free from the old-fashioned and conservative bureaucratic Korean culture. For example, the Korean Independence Association at the beginning of this century had several key leaders such as former president Syngman Rhee who were Christians. Christians played a leading role in the independence movement.

When a nation-wide revolt against Japanese rule occured on March 1, 1919, the national independence declaration was proclaimed by thirty-three patriots, of whom fifteen were Christians. Christian schools promoted patriotism in their classes; and many intellectuals accepted Christianity not only for spiritual reasons but also because of its political persuasion.

2. Christian Contribution to Modern Education

The elite minority had educational opportunities to learn from Chinese classics, but the vast majority was illiterate. Pioneer missionaries translated the Scriptures into the Korean language and taught Koreans, through Sunday schools, vacation Bible schools, and Bible institutes, how to read the easy Korean phonetic script rather than the difficult Chinese characters.

Two of the best known pioneer missionaries, Rev. Horace G. Underwood of the Presbyterian Mission and Rev Henry G. Appenzeller of the Methodist Mission, further popularized the Korean script by starting their own respective newspapers in the Korean script. These were the weekly *Christian News* and the *Korean Christian Advocate* in April 1885. It is not an overstatement to say that Christian Koreans were the only Koreans able to read the Korean script.

A number of Christian schools were opened by missionaries. A boys' Christian school, Baejae School, was started in 1886 and a girls' Christian school, Ehwa School, was started in 1887. Korea's former president, Syngman Rhee, had part of his education at the Baejae School when he was young. Several Christian colleges were opened at the beginning of the 20th century: Sung Shil College (1906), Ehwa College (1910), and Yunhee College (1915). Ehwa University today is the largest women's university in the world with 15,340 students. And Yonsei University, with 17,947 students, which developed from Yunhee College is one of the best universities in South Korea today. These two Christian universities along with others have produced a large number of Christian lay leaders in all segments of Korean society.

3. Medical Missions

In 1884 a pro-Japanese political party incited a coup against the ruling pro-Chinese party and seriously injured the prince. Dr. Horace N. Allen, a medical missionary from America, was requested by Mr. Min to treat him. Within three months, Mr. Min recovered through the use of Western medicine. As a result of this incident, Dr. Allen was allowed to start a mission hospital. This was the beginning of the well-known Severance Hospital in Seoul. The introduction of Western medicine into Korea as an alternative to the traditional Oriental medicine was certainly one of the main contributions of missionaries to the Korean people.

4. YMCA and Social Service Agencies

The contributions of YMCA, which was established in 1903, cannot be ignored. The YMCA introduced both vocal and instrumental Western music and modern sports such as baseball, soccer, volleyball, basketball, ping pong, and track.

Hundreds of Christian social service organizations have sprung up throughout the country to assist needy people. During the Korean War (1950-1953) the churches received enormous amounts of assistance from the West and played the major role of distributing food and clothes to hungry people.

II. Religious Factors

Like other people Koreans were religious even before adopting the imported religions from China and the West. A half dozen religions are prominent today in Korea: Shamanism, Buddhism, Confucianism, Taoism, Chondokyo, and Christianity.

Buddhism entered Korea from China during the Koguryo dynasty in 372 A.D. and became a dominant force in every area of Korean life during the Three Kingdoms Period. It reached its peak during the "Golden Age of Buddhism" (935-1392) during the Koryo dynasty (935-1932). Buddhism became not only a religious force but also a political power in the dynasty. Consequently, the political opponents to the controlling Buddhists in the Yi dynasty cooperated with Confucianism to drive out the Buddhist rulers. In 1456 the Yi dynasty even decreed to forbid monks from entering into the capital city of Seoul.

The decline of Buddhism in the early years of the Yi dynasty encouraged an increase in the influence of Confucianism among the intellectual classes. The decline also left ignorant peasants and women without a viable religion so they turned to superstitious Shamanism. For many centuries

Buddhism lost contact with the people; however, some signs of a resurgence of Buddhism in recent years in Korea is evident.

Confucianism emphasized ethical conduct in individuals and government, and maintained a high standard of education. The Yi dynasty adopted Confucianism as "the national religion." Neo-Confucianism prevailed during the Yi dynasty. It adopted the philosophical, metaphysical. and religious terms concerning human existence and nature of reality. Confucianists erected many Confucian schools throughout Korea, such as Songyunkwan in Seoul. Even though Confucianism met the intellectual needs of the elite (the Yangban), it ignored the vast majority of the Korean people.

Chon dokyo or "The Sect of the Heavenly Way" is another important religion which was founded by Choe Che-Wu (1824-1864). He created a syncretistic religion which was known then as *Tonghak* or the "Eastern Learning" in opposition to *Sohak* or "Western Learning" which meant Roman Catholicism. Choe believed that all religions, from primitive Shamanism to Western Christianity, were valid and embodied truth. But each person had to seek truth according to his own ways. For Koreans *Tonghak* was the best way. The leaders of this religion played important roles in the independence movement, as also did Christians, during the Japanese domination of Korea. Yet *Chon dokyo's* spiritual impact on the people is negligible.

During the spiritual vacuum in the Yi dynasty, Shamanism, which is said to be the original religion of Korea, grew among the common people. The religion teaches that a shaman can communicate with the spirit world in an attempt to better the fortunes of man. Taking over some of the supernatural characteristics of Buddhism and Confucianism, Shamanism to this day appeals to the common masses who are ignored by rational Confucianism.

Therefore, the majority of the people do not practice Buddhism and Confucianism in the form of cultic exercises.

Many experience a spiritual vacuum, and for a significant number, Christianity has filled the void.

Since the traditional religions have lost their grip on the people, most Koreans have become skeptical of their fore-fathers' religions. This is explicitly expressed in the survey statistics which show that the majority of people do not practice any religion at all. When the former President Park Chung-Hee of South Korea was asked whether he was a Christian, his reply reflected a typical feeling, "My father and mother were Buddhists, but I am nothing."

III. Political and Economic Factors

In order to understand the characteristics of the Korean church, one has to remember how she *suffered* for many decades from external invasions and internal revolutions. The Japanese government tried to enforce Shinto shrine worship upon the Korean people; some Christians believed it was idolatry to bow down to the Emperor of Japan. Others believed that it was merely a political matter; they participated in the Shinto shrine worship under the pressure of the Japanese. Those who refused to compromise were imprisoned and beaten. Many Christians were killed or later died in prison. On the day Korea was liberated in 1945, more than three thousand Korean Christians were released from prison.

Instead of gaining its hoped-for freedom in 1945, Korea once again became a victim of a larger power struggle between the United States and the Union of Soviet Socialist Republics. The ideological struggles between Communists and the free people mushroomed and ultimately divided the country. By the thousands, Koreans under the Communists in the North began to escape to find freedom in South Korea. The tragic *Korean War* impoverished the people and brought added sufferings to the nation.

After 1945 the Communist Party of North Korea under

Kim Il-Song began to impose a tight control on the people. The Party set the national election day on Sunday, November 3, 1946, to hamper Sunday worship services, and demanded loyalty from the Christian churches. The Christian church in North Korea requested the government to observe five principles. The fifth principle was to guarantee religious freedom.

Christians in North Korea ultimately lost their freedom of worship and became an underground movement as a result of Communist persecution. North Korea, where the Northern Presbyterian Mission was particularly successful, had the largest Christian population in the nation. In fact, three-fourths of all the members of the Korean Presbyterian Church were in North Korea. Before 1945 approximately ten percent of Pyongyang, the capital of North Korea, claimed to be Christians, and more than fifty percent of Sunchun city was Christian. But during the Korean War, when the United Nations forces arrived, more than 100,000 of these Christians, many of them pastors, fled south. Almost three hundred Presbyterian pastors were martyred.

The Korean War also produced many Christian martyrs in South Korea. At the end of 1950 some 500 Christian leaders in Seoul alone were either killed or kidnapped by the Communists. During the war, 727 pastors and evangelists were arrested, 360 captured and in Seoul 39 prominent Christian pastors were martyred. Psychological tension during the war and the ensuing economic poverty indelibly marked the minds of the people. The Japanese persecution and the Korean War were the two decisive events which influenced every phase of life in the country.

In the midst of intense suffering and toil, the Korean church was able to give hope to the hopeless, food to the hungry, and shelter to the homeless. Christians looked forward to their heavenly home as a relief from the painful earthly conditions that surrounded them. They learned to trust God in time of troubles. Churches were filled with people who needed help and peace of mind.

The political and economic suffering and religious fervor

of the Christians reminded the Christians of the New Testament church. Dr. Stephen Moon, a professor at Hanguk
Seminary, cites the similarities between the Jews in the first
century and the Koreans in the twentieth. Pointing to the
physical sufferings of both peoples under foreign domination,
he compared the ancient zealots to the legalistic Christians
in Korea.

One of the most salient features of the Korean Church
was its strong apocalyptic hope. Christians longed to get away
from this painful, sinful, suffering world to their heavenly
paradise. This emphasis on a future hope as a release from
mundane daily struggles was explicitly expressed in many
hymns, sermons, and prayers in Korea. Hymns such as "Bright,
Heavenly Way," "I'm Pressing on the Upward Way," "Traveling to a Better Land," "Out of My Bondage, Sorrow, and
Night," and "I Must Tell Jesus" became very popular. The Pil-
grim's Progress story was well accepted.

The presence of the Demilitarized Zone(DMZ), North Korean tunnels into the South, the constant threat of Communist attack and possible persecution of Christians by the
Communists are still providing a very important motivating
factor to many Christians to renew their faith. People look
for spiritual security rather than earthly uncertainties. The
land is ripe for spiritual harvest. Therefore, the present uncertainty has been a real blessing to the Korean church. Tertul-
lian of Carthage in the third century once said, "The blood
of the martyr is the seed of the church." The church, like iron
which is tested by fire, becomes stronger. I believe that the
Korean church will continue to grow and to make enormous
spiritual contributions to the world.

Conclusion

Korea has a long national and religious history, but the
religions have lost their influence upon the majority of the population. Political, sociological, cultural, and religious circum-

stances in the country were favorable to the spread of the Christian faith in Korea. Protestant missions, with one hundred years of history in Korea, have been most successful in gathering converts into the church. The Holy Spirit has used these situational factors, combined with the tireless efforts of missionaries and the spiritual fervency of many national Christians. Working through all these factors, the Spirit has brought "wildfire" church growth for His glory.But rather than being puffed up with pride over the church's past accomplishment, every Korean Christian should rededicate himself to Christ for the "Christianization of Korea" and for the evangelization of the world.

Dr. Harold S. Hong (Hong Hyun-Sul), director of the Korea Research Institute for Mission and Education and president of the Methodist Theological Seminary for twenty-five years, graduated from the Methodist Theological Seminary in Seoul, Kwansei Gakuin University in Japan, Drew University in New Jersey, the Union Theological Seminary in New York (S. T. M.) and received the Doctor of Divinity degree from the Evansville University in Indiana. He has served as chairman of the National Council of Churches in Korea, the Christian Literature Society, the Christian Academy of Korea, the National Committee of the YMCA, and the Central Committee of the Nationwide Evangelistic Movement in 1965.

Theologians frequently think only of doctrinal reasons for growth or non-growth of the church. Dr. Hong makes a significant contribution to this compendium by carefully analysing and illustrating ways people think, act and feel about religions. Though Koreans are a very religious people, the traditional religions failed to change their lives, the society and the nation as Christianity later did. What does this say to nations where Christians are still a struggling minority?

I ⦾ SOCIAL, POLITICAL, AND PSYCHOLOGICAL ASPECTS OF CHURCH GROWTH

by Harold S. Hong

It is rather difficult to single out just one or two factors when there are multiple reasons for the rapid growth of the Protestant church in Korea. But in this chapter, I will limit myself to the social, political, and psychological factors.

Some scholars insist that we need to consider the pre-understanding or the preparation of the people for the gospel before Christianity was introduced to them. To do this we must understand the native religions ideas--namely, Confucianism, Buddhism, Shamanism, and so forth. Korea was not a religious void when Christianity came to the country; rather, a rich religious culture had shaped the Korean world view for thousands of years. In a certain sense, dominate religions such as Confucianism and Buddhism had been indigenized to the Korean context. But if we speak about the theological formulation, there was no such evidence of it at all.

The Buddhist doctrine of *nirvana* is somewhat similar to the Christian doctrine of salvation. But Buddhism has a high level of intellectualism as well as fatalism. Salvation in Buddhism comes from mental awakening. Because Buddhists believe that all evil comes from ignorance, they have little sense of guilt or need for penitence.

In contrast, Confucianism is a practical way of life based upon a utilitarian type of human relationships. Confucianism always defends the social order and the hierarchy of authority at the cost of individual rights and freedom. We seldom find any sense of repentance or unconditional forgiveness in Confucianism. These factors made the Korean people psychologically unprepared to understand the meaning of the gospel of Christ.

Nevertheless, in some ways the Korean people were prepared for the gospel. Dr. Yun Sung-Bum, the late president of the Methodist Seminary in Seoul, Korea stated six major reasons for the rapid church growth in Korea as follows:

A. Christianity was understood as a religion of plain men, the common people of society. It was contrasted with neighboring Japan where Christianity was received mostly by the military knight class.

B. Under the dominant Chinese culture, Christianity stressed the use of the original Korean language which was invented by King Sejong and his royal scholars during the Lee Dynasty. The Bibles and hymnals were printed in the Korean language so that people of little education could read them. This vernacular language became the most effective media in the spreading of the gospel.

C. The idea of heaven and hell of Christianity was a kin idea to the Buddhist idea of Paradise or Nirvana.

D. The social situation was also favorable to the propagation of the gospel. There were several attempts of independent movements, but all of them failed tragically. Therefore, people shifted their thought to a long-range national movement, and people thronged to the church. Among the people there were outstanding national leaders who were later converted to Christianity.

E. Personal evangelism: Mass evangelism was more often used and popular, but personal evangelism was the most characteristic Christian witness.

F. Finally, Korean Protestantism contributed to the modernization of Korea. The modernization impact was in many fields, such as in education, in medicine, in social work, and so forth.[1]

---

1. Sung-Bum Yun, *Christianity and Korean Thought* (Seoul: The Christian Literature Society, 1964), pp. 248-250.

Some other factors could be mentioned, but the above are some of the main reasons given by our theologians for the rapid church growth in Korea.

Social and Political Aspects

Rev. Roy E. Shearer, a former Presbyterian missionary to Korea, stated that the common error in the study of missions is to simplify the reasons for successs to a few categories-namely, the missionary method and the environment.[2]

Rev. Shearer claimed that the same mission methodology could produce different results, depending on the geography or the folk psychology of the people. Therefore, no generalization can be made about methods. But environmental factors are not so determinative in Korea. The same Nevius method was successful in certain areas, but a failure in other areas. The real cause of church growth is revealed when we study the local church in depth.

Korean society in general was feudalistic and aristocratic. The structure of such society was influenced by the Confucian ethic. Chinese culture respected the learned elite. The elite were an intellectual aristocracy which always despised the common people, the rank and file. Korean society was dominated by such ideas.

But Christianity revolutionized this classical status system by making vital contact with the common people. Rev. Shearer pointed out that the secret of success for the Korean church was in rooting her foundation in the independent farmers, or free farmers who owned their land.[3] They had the freedom to make their own decisions. And they also had the economic power to support the church financially. The democratic way of life was more prevalent in the western

2. Roy E. Shearer, *Wildfire: Church Growth in Korea* (Seoul: The Christian Literature Society, 1966), pp. 273-274.

3. Ibid, pp. 277-278.

part of Korea, which as a result, was more responsive to the gospel.

Equal status of women with men was unthinkable when Christianity first came to Korea. Usually, a woman was called "the indoor person." A woman was supposed to stay inside the house and do the housework. Whenever a woman was converted to Christ she was ostracized from society. This social rejection was a severe trial for a female in a paternalistic society. She suffered a sort of martyrdom, indeed.

Fortunately, Korea had no caste system. The whole society was sharply divided into camps: The *Yang-ban* and *Sang-nom*, meaning the class of nobility and the class of low birth respectively. The *Yang-ban* had plenty of opportunities to be promoted to government officialdom, but the *Sang-nom* had none. The butchers, craftsmen, and tenant farmers constituted the *Sang-nom* class. The *Yang-bans'* status and property were inherited by their descendents.

In the olden days the order of occupational preference in Korea was first the scholar, then the farmer, next the technician, and finally the tradesman. A national slogan says that farming is the most fundamental human activity in the world. This is why the Christian church in her early stages in Korea found a more fertile ground in the rural areas than in the cities.

Christianity attacked the so-called *Yang-ban* system and promoted the idea of the equality of every person before God. Consequently, the church's door was wide open for people long alienated from social status. Churches were packed with mostly women and children. For some time the sanctuary was partitioned or screened in order to separate the male and the female worshipers. This sort of sex segregation was the only segregation found in the major public gatherings in Korea in those days.

Only one democatic movement was attempted outside the Christian church. This movement was actually a revolt of the people against the tyranny of the totalitarian government; tendoism (*Chun-Do Kyo* in Korean language) was the name. It was founded by Choi Soon-Woon in 1860. Political confusion had reached the crisis stage. On the one hand foreign invasion threatened and on the other hand inner corruption in the government invited protest. Mr. Choi claimed to be the Messiah who would deliver the people out of chaos. His movement was a reaction to Christianity which was called at that time *Seo-Hak* (the Western religion); while Mr. Choi called his new religion *Tong-Hak* (the Oriental religion).

Tendoism promoted national identity and indigenous culture in opposition to a foreign Christianity and its accompaning Western culture. Tendoism also strongly propagated human rights based upon the idea that man is no other than the heaven, that is, the god. Every man carries in himself the divinity of heaven. This divinity makes man as the absolute value and invests in him an inalienable right.

Choi Soon-Woon was executed as a revolutionary before his movement firmly took root. In 1905 Son Pyung-Hee, the third successor of Tendoism, made great progress in expanding this movement. Mr. Son was one of the planners of the famous 1919 Independence Movement against Japanese imperialism. He cooperated closely with Buddhist, Confucian, and church leaders in planning for independence. But of the thirty-three patriotic national leaders, Christian ministers and laymen were in the majority.

Throughout their history, the Korean people have been strongly family centered. It is common to find three generations living in the same house. Walter Rauschenbush claims that the family was tyrannical in its primitive stages and that it was also paternalistic and male dominated. But it gave weak protection against enslavement and death. The uneducated were made to work and the idle people to sweat in order to make human labor more productive. People were forced to cooperate with each other. We observe this pattern in the early stages of the church. The church was gradually democratized after becoming an ecclesiastical tyranny in the Dark Ages. Eventually, it became a free fellowship of God's people.

Christianity has been family centered from its beginning. "To make the whole household Christian" has been the motto of every true Christian. Though we now see some signs of family disintegration in Korean society, it will be a long time before we witness total collapse.

The average Korean seldom had any social experience other than his home life. Korea has been a closed society for a long time. The old Chinese saying reflects this viewpoint: "Cultivate yourself, control your family, and then govern the state...these are the proper order of achieving peace."

Politically speaking, Korea is tragically located among surrounding major powers such as China, Japan and Russia. Korea has been constantly invaded, especially from China who subjugated Korea several times in our history. Eventually Japan annexed Korea in 1910.

The Japanese ruled Korea thirty-six years and caused much physical and mental damage. Japan was determined to control Korea not only by military power, but also by thought control. Christianity was the first target of Japanese imperialism. The Japanese thought the Christian churches in Korea were strongly supported by America through her missionaries. Actually, the American missionaries, although politically neutral, shared the sufferings of the Korean people.

Korean political refugees used to find temporary shelters in the missionaries' residences. Most of the Korean patriots were products of mission-related schools. These mission schools were the seedbeds of democracy. Christian leaders were the most respected and trusted above any other people because of their fidelity, honesty, and trustworthiness. Though the Korean church has been very nationalistic, she never endorsed a narrow, exclusive nationalism.

The Korean church has been a folk church because

of her comprehensive function and purposes. It was inevitable that the church would become the spiritual center for a nation which had lost her sovereignty and had no other spiritual center for renewing the hope of national restoration.

The 1919 Independence Movement is widely known as resembling the non-violent resistance movement of India under Mahatma Gandhi. The Independence Declaration document is considered to be one of the best such documents ever proclaimed. The spirit of tolerance and forgiveness prevails throughout the document.

During the movement, earnest prayers were offered by the Christians in the churches. The churches were like Jewish synagogues during the period of the Babylonian Captivity. The immediate task of the churches was to achieve national emancipation. National deliverance was then regarded as the prerequisite of spiritual salvation. While Christians were fighting secretly for independence, they had a vague hope of arousing international public opinion against Japanese oppression. Secret envoys were sent to the League of Nations with Korea's urgent appeal for help.

In 1918 the President of the United States of America, Mr. Woodrow Wilson, advocated the well-known Self-Determination of the Nations document at the Paris Peace Treaty Conference. The Korean government in exile was greatly impressed by it. Overcoming despair, Koreans renewed their hope of national restoration.

In a word, the Christian churches became the spiritual centers of hope for the oppressed nation. Protestant church history is filled with imprisonment and persecution. However, these adversities turned out to be God's blessings in many ways. Christian pastors and laymen who were in prison had excellent opportunities to share the gospel message with their fellow prisoners. The prisoners gladly accepted Christ as their Savior. When these Christians were spread around in several prisons the opportunity was wider than ever. It has been true that God turns the darkness into daylight.

The Korean church suffered a great deal not only during the Japanese occupation but also during the Communist invasion in 1950. The Communists also considered the Christian church as their main target for suppression. During the Communist occupation of South Korea, many stories of heroic Christian witness were brought to light, but many still remain unknown. Conservative Christians used to say, "We have no business with politics." Actually they have been deeply involved, though unconsciously, in political struggles.

The present-day Christian witness should include politics, and Christian obedience should involve obedience to the state, by all means. This is why the theology of Dietrich Bonhoeffer has great appeal to Korean Christians today.

The Psychological Aspect

Now I come to the psychological aspect of Korea's church growth. Missionaries opposed Korea's traditional religious service for deceased ancestors. The missionaries did not oppose the idea of ancestral veneration, but they opposed the pagan style of the ceremonies. Consequently, Koreans regarded Christians as having abandoned one of the most fundamental ethical duties in Korean society. This was because ancestral worship was considered to be the extension of filial duty to one's parents.

The missionaries encouraged Christians to transform the pagan ritual ceremonies into Christian memorial services. Traditional religious services for deceased ancestors have been a national custom for several thousand years. Confucian scholars were especially indignant over this condemnation of an ancient national custom by a foreign people. Consequently, it took many years to convert the stubborn Confucian scholars to Christianity. Even the first believers developed some psychological resistance.

Many brave Christians thought that breaking a traditional custom was an expression of heroic faith. They were willing to endure any resulting sacrifice. It is true that the heavier the persecution, the stronger the faith. During the years of the Pacific War some fifty Korean pastors died in prison because they refused to participate in the Japanese Shinto shrine worship.

Professor Chee Myung-Kwan, former Seoul National University professor, pointed out the following in his book, *The Religions of Asia and the Logic of the Gospel:*

> The true meaning of the suffering of the Korean Christians during the years of Japanese persecution was, though quite different from that of The German underground churches, not to keep the eternal church of God, but to achieve their personal salvation through their pietistic type of faith. They thought they could keep their faith pure by not bending their knees to Baal so that they could enter the Paradise and enjoy their eternal life with the everlasting God. It was not actually to share the tribulations with their fellowmen. Martyrdom was not for the sake of the eternal church but it did matter only for the personal conscience to be cleared. But it was unreasonable to ask the Christians in these young churches to embrace any higher quality of faith. [4]

Out of total despair of clean self government, Christians turned their eyes to the eternal world which has no oppression, cruelty, or violence. The wholehearted dedication of Korean Christians to their Savior was due to their complete despair of earthly hope. They anchored their faith in

4. Chee Myung-Kwan, *The Religions of Asia and The Logic of the Gospel* (in Japanese) (Tokyo, Japan: Shinkyo Publishing Gompany, 1970), p. 163.

God's power which would eventually triumph over evil powers.

The popular psychology of the Korean people was to ascribe both fortune and misfortune to the gods and to divine beings rather than to themselves. In this sense, Koreans may be called more religious than any other people. The prevailing animism was due to this kind of psychology. It will take many more years to wipe out the Shamanistic element from the Christian faith because Shamanism is so deepy rooted in Korean soil.

Buddhism is an example of syncretism in religion in Korea. Pure Buddhism is practically nonexistent in Korea today.

It would be unfair to say that the Korean people were more receptive and responsive to the Christian gospel than any other nation in Asia. But we strongly believe that we are now the chosen people of God and that we are under the special providence of God. This strong faith has actually made the Korean church the most rapidly growing church in the world.

Marlin L. Nelson came to Korea in 1956 with World Vision International. He is presently seconded to ACTS (Asian Center for Theological Studies and Mission) as associate professor of missiology. A graduate of the University of Minnesota (B. A.) and Fuller Theological Seminary (M. Div. and D. Miss.), he has written several articles and books on church growth and Third World Missions.

We remember how three blind men described the elephant as a wall, a pillar and a rope as they felt the side, leg and tail. Some foreigners visiting Korea give a glowing report of the church while others become almost cynical. Dr. Nelson presents a "long-view" of the church which will help the reader to gain a proper perspective of God's work through redeemed sinners.

II A FOREIGNER'S VIEW OF THE KOREAN CHURCH

by Marlin L. Nelson

As a foreigner, I will try to serve as a catylyst and write about the various views of foreigners concerning the Korean church. This will include work and attitudes of the past as well as contemporary views.

Because of space limitations, I must take a general view of the Korean church. There will be exceptions to most of my observations. When writing and speaking about the Korean church, some may exaggerate the many achievements and idealize the church. But others may become extremely critical of the weaknesses of the church and thus fail to recognize the miraculous working of God in this nation. Paul wrote of the glory and power of the gospel put into earthen vessels (2 Cor. 4:6-7). The visible church has all the weaknesses of a clay pot. But all who are redeemed are appointed "ambassadors for Christ" (2 Cor. 5:20). Hopefully these two truths can be kept in proper perspective.

From the beginning, how did foreigners view the Korean people? Members of the Korean Embassy regularly visited the embassy in Peking. In 1631 Chung Du-Won contacted Matthieu Ricci, a Jesuit missionary, and brought to Korea a copy of Ricci's book on the *True Doctrine of the Lord of Heaven.*

In 1783, Yi Seung-Hoon went to Peking with the annual embassy; he was converted, baptized, and given the name Peter. It was hoped that he would be the first foundation stone of the Korean Church. But instead suspicion and persecution broke out and the Christians were ordered to give up their faith or die. In 1866 the greatest persecution of all began. In September over 2,000 Koreans were martyred including many priests and bishops. A monument was erected in Pyong Yang to testify to the fact that at last the Catholic faith had been completely destroyed in Korea. But the seed had been planted and was well watered with the blood of martyrs. In 1982 the Roman Catholic church reported a membership of 1,439,778.

In 1832 the first French Catholic missionary priest, Bartheleme Brugiere, was appointed to Korea. The first Protestant missionary, Carl A. F. Gutzlaff, a German, also briefly visited Korea in the same year. Gutzlaff distributed Chinese Scriptures along the coast and the Lord's Prayer was translated into Korean. He even sent two copies of the Chinese Bible to King Hun Choung.

In 1865 Robert J. Thomas, a native of Wales, attempted to enter the forbidden land of Korea but was turned back. He returned aboard an American ship, the "General

Sherman," in 1866 as an interpreter. The effort to open trade with Korea met with failure. The ship was burned and Thomas was martyred. It is reported by Allen Clark that Lee Young-Tai, the nephew of the man who assassinated Thomas, became a Christian. Lee Young-Tai graduated from Soongsil College in Pyong Yang and later helped Dr. W. D. Reynolds to revise the Bible (Clark, 1971:63).

The first Presbyterian missionary actually to arrive in Korea was Horace N. Allen, M. D., an American who was transferred from China. He arrived in Korea on September 20, 1884. He served as physician to the American Embassy. On December 4, 1884, a significant event helped to open the way for missionary work. A political revolution was attempted and the young prince, Min Young-Ik, was wounded. The American Embassy secretary called Dr. Allen to treat the wounded prince who was at the point of death. It required three months of constant medical care before the prince was out of danger. This care won the confidence of the King and Queen, who granted Dr. Allen's request to start a Royal Hospital which was opened in Seoul on April 10, 1885. This pivotal event encouraged the missionaries in their witnessing. Few could have anticipated the quick response to the gospel, with many soon seeking baptism. Others, mindful of the previous persecution of Roman Catholic Christians, feared lest they lose favor with the Korean government.

On Easter morning, April 5, 1885, Rev. Horace G. Underwood and Rev. Henry G. Appenzeller, the first ordained missionaries, arrived in Inchon, Korea. The story is that they held each other's hands and jumped ashore together so that no one might later say that either the Methodists or the Presbyterians had arrived first (Clark, 1971 : 91). Though this is an interesting story, Mrs. Appenzeller was probably the first to step ashore. However, the attitude reflected in this story is typical of the friendly spirit which has characterized the relationship between missionary groups. The missionaries desired to establish one Korean church, with one Bible and one hymnal, and so on, thus exemplifying the unity of the body of Christ. Unfortunately, various events later destroyed this ideal, and the early comity agreements were broken.

In the providence of God, the Rev. and Mrs. John Nevius, Presbyterian missionaries in Cheefoo, China, came to Korea in June 1890 at the invitation of the infant Presbyterian Mission. For two weeks these seven young missionaries discussed the principles involved in starting a mission work in a new country. They had been influenced by Dr. Nevius' book entitled *Methods of Mission Work* (Shearer, 1966 : 45). Dr. Underwood reports that "after long and prayerful consideration we were led, in the main, to adopt these Nevius methods" (Clark, 1971 : 114). These were principles, not for the organized church, but for the beginning stages of work in a new area. Later on, conditions might call for a modification. Dr. Underwood gave the main points as follows:

1. Let each man "abide in the calling wherein he was found," teaching that each was to be an individual worker for Christ, and to live Christ in his own neighborhood, supporting himself by his trade.

2. To develop church methods and machinery only so far as the native church was able to take care of and manage them.

3. As far as the church itself was able to provide the men and the means, to set aside the better qualified to do evangelistic work among their neighbors.

4. To let the natives provide their own church buildings, which were to be native architecture,

and of such style as the local church could afford to put up (Clark, 1971:114).

To this may be added the following from C. A. Clark's *Korean Church and the Nevius Methods.*

1. *Missionary personal evangelism* through wide itineration.

2. *Self-propagation.* Every believer a teacher of someone and a learner from someone else better fitted. Every individual and group seeking to extend the work.

3. *Self-government.* Every group under its chosen unpaid leaders; circuits under their own paid helpers, who will later yield to pastors.

4. *Self-support,* with all chapels provided by the believers; each group, as soon as founded, beginning to pay toward the circuit helper's salary.

5. *Systematic Bible study* for every believer under his group leader and circuit helper.

6. *Strict discipline* enforced with Bible penalties.

7. *Cooperation* and union with other bodies, or at least territorial division.

8. *Non-interference in law suits* or any such matters.

9. *General helpfulness,* where possible, in the economic life of the people. (Clark, 1971:114-115).

From this, it will be evident that the Nevius methods are not merely a system of self-support and refusal to pay subsidies. Its real core was in the Bible study system, which encouraged every Christian to study his Bible and to be able to pass on to others what he found there. The new little groups were encouraged to grow in the faith under the best local leadership available. These local leaders took turns in leading worship and in teaching what they found in their Bibles. Obviously, in order to have something to teach others, they had to study their own Bibles first!

To avoid being a mere matter of the blind leading the blind, district leader's conferences were carried on annually or more frequently. The local leaders came to these conferences for ten days of Bible study. On their return home, these men passed on in their preaching what they had learned. Later, to help the average member in his Bible study, district Bible conferences were held for the average member. Later, similar Bible study conferences were conducted in local churches under a visiting Bible teacher with evangelistic services in the evenings. And still later, this practice led to the founding of Bible institutes. These institutes were carried on in central places for a month or more during January and February when those from farming communities were not too busy to come for study. These Bible institutes were intended for teaching the Bible to all church members who wished to come. They were not intended to train professional church workers. These winter Bible institutes are still carried on today and are a great blessing to the church.

The first converts naturally led and taught persons in their neighborhood who later came into the church. These leaders needed instruction themselves and were formed into Leaders' Classes. They in turn held local classes in their districts. The missionary, on his periodic itinerating trips, chose centrally located places for holding special classes for ten days to two weeks. Annual classes were held in still larger centers to which each church or group was urged to send as many representatives as possible. Those who attended these central classes went home and often held other local classes.

Classes for men and women were held wherever possible. Instruction in sanitation and hygiene was given in addition to the Bible study. Women were also instructed in the care of children. The day's program for a village class might be something like this: assembly with prayer and singing, division into two or three classes for the study of some book of the Bible, assembly for a singing lesson, then another period of Bible study. After the noon meal, another period was given to instruction in hygiene. Then part of the afternoon given to house-to-house visitation where advice on the care of children might also be given. The evening was for further study or for evangelistic services (Clark, 1971 : 116-117).

Humanly speaking, the Nevius principles were a significant factor in the growth and strength of the Korean church. These ideas were not new, but timely. Henry Venn, an Anglican and general secretary of the Church Missionary Society for thirty-one years from 1841 to 1872, was keenly aware of problems missionaries experienced (Neill, 1964:259-260). Likewise Rufus Anderson, a Congregationalist, was secretary of the American Board of Commissioners for Foreign Missions (A. B. C. F. M) for forty years from 1826 to 1866. His ideas were similar to Venn concerning missions. But the time and place for implementation apparently had not appeared as clearly as in the Korean situation. Here was a people ready to receive the gospel which was presented in a manner that would help to build a nation. This nation would soon face added persecutions and have an increasing influence throughout Asia.

The early missionaries traveled extensively by foot and by horseback. Some planned 100 days per year for itineration and some covered over a thousand miles. In this way the missionaries came to understand well the minds of the people and their real-life situations and to learn the Korean language fluently! Unlike itineration in most countries, their primary purpose was not for distributing literature or "wide seed-sowing." Rather, they went first to teach and examine those who had decided to become Christians and wanted to become catechumens or to be baptized, and second, they went to conduct baptism and the Lord's Supper (Shearer, 1966: 124). We see church growth as both God's blessing and the result of hard work by the Christians.

There is a high rate of literacy (92 percent) in Korea. The Korean alphabet was invented in 1446 by King Sejong and a group of Korean scholars. It is one of the most perfect alphabets in the world. It is so simple that the Koreans should have become the most literate people in all the world; but its simplicity hindered its acceptance. Scholars who spent years mastering the Chinese classics had great contempt for a system of writing that even women could learn. So the Hangul was neglected until the Protestant missionaries came in 1885.

We need to remember that the Korean people are one race, with one language and culture. Though the dialects are different in some provinces, yet all can freely communicate with each other; Koreans read the same newspaper, listen to the same radio, and watch the same TV. We must contrast Korea with such nations as India with its population of 620 million consisting of 20,000 castes and sub-castes speaking over 225 languages. Indonesia has a population of 145 million with 54 different tribes speaking over 200 languages and dialects. The Philippines has 46 million living on 7,107 islands with 50 tribal groups speaking 80 different languages and dialects. The problems in communication as well as those of transportation help us to understand the difficulties other peoples have to evangelize their own nation. However, Korea does not have these obstacles. This is an important factor in the evangelization of the Korean people.

Missionaries also helped to establish Christian institutions such as hospitals, schools, colleges, universities, and seminaries. They also began orphanages, widows' homes, old peoples' homes, leprosariums, and other service facilities. From the beginning, evangelism and social work were both emphasized. Many of the leaders in society today attended Christian schools. The Methodist mission gave special emphasis to education as a method of evangelism. Unfortunately, this strategy was hindered by the Shinto shrine issue during the Japanese occupation when many schools were closed.

The revival of 1907 is well documented and is an inspiration to Christians around the world (Clark, 1971:159-165). But few are aware of the emphasis upon Bible study that preceded this movement of the Spirit of God. The origin of the revival may be traced to a meeting in 1903 when a group of Methodist missionaries met together for a week of prayer and Bible study in Wonsan. Miss M. C. White, a missionary with the Southern Methodist Mission in China, was the guest speaker.

Among this group was Dr. R. A. Hardie, a medical missionary from Canada. His work in the northern part of Kangwon Province had progressed slowly. As Dr. Hardie examined his heart and motives, he experienced a great filling of the Spirit of God. The Wonsan conference was repeated in 1904 with even a greater outpouring of blessing. These outpourings were repeated in many places under the leadership of Dr. Hardie. There was a longing for such a revival as Christians were experiencing in Wales and parts of India.

Bible training classes were being held in both rural and urban areas and contributed toward the growth of the church. The education of the whole church, young and old, literate and illiterate was undertaken systematically; the textbook was the Bible. In 1904 it was reported that 60 percent of the church members and catachumens attended one or more of these classes. The 1907 revival is described by other writers in this book so I will include only a comment by Dr. L. George Paik.

The most convincing argument for the genuineness of the revival is the result that followed. The great awakening marks the spiritual rebirth of the Korean Church. The religious experience of the people gave to the Christian Church in Korea a character of its own. Following the revival, the religious experience was severely tested but it has survived as a moral and spiritual force. Korean Christians look back on the movement as the source of their spiritual life. One of the most important sequels was the proof that the Christian religion had a hold on Korea and was not unadapted to the country. Another interesting result was a better understanding between the Korean Christians and the missionaries. Still another was a change in the moral tone of the Christian community, and fourth was the establishment of important religious habits of Bible study and prayer (Clark 1971: 166).

Another important factor influencing church growth is the structure of the Korean society. In Korea we are dealing with a society based on the family, not a tribe. This family unit is strong even today and is the basic social unit in the country. The soundest way for a man to come to Christ is in the setting of his own family. Its members make the move as individuals, but still belong to the family. Chun Sung-Chun declares, "The family was the basic unit in society so it was not unusual for all members of a family group to adopt Christianity at the same time" (Chun, 1979: 16). He affirms that the great numbers who rushed into the church came because whole family units moved together.

We read of Korean Christians engaged in intensive evangelism. Often they traveled away from home on evangelistic trips, but more often they led people to Christ in their own villages. Even today, most of the people in villages will be related to each other by marriage if not by blood. The Christians did not go out and "beat the bushes," talking to strangers about their faith, but they talked to people they knew and to people with whom they had strong family ties. These ties were the means by which the Korean church multiplied ahead of the missionaries. Because of the close-knit web of family relationships and the inter-family relationships through the clan, no one wished to take the great step alone of accepting a new religion which would break down these family ties. A person who heard the gospel of Christ or read it from a Bible sold to him would go back to his own village and talk it over with the members of his family and clan. If they made a positive decision, the entire group would often quite naturally become Christian while holding fast to their family relationships. If all were not immediately won, each family member in his own time would often become Christian until soon the whole family and sometimes the entire clan turned to Christ (Shearer, 1966:147-149).

Another major contribution to the growth of the Korean church is the Wesley class meetings. This Methodist system is used by nearly every denomination in Korea and has recently received much publicity by those reporting on the Full Gospel Central Church in Seoul. This church with 325,421 members as of September 1983 is undoubtedly the largest in the world. But those who attend are not merely "statistics" but are members of 19,380 cell groups or "house churches". Such meetings are conducted weekly by trained leaders in the homes of laymen. This plan of pastoral care for members according to their geographical location is carefully described in chapter 17, "Ministry Through Home Cell Units" by Drs. Cho and Hurston. Critics of the emphasis on numerical growth of the church need to carefully study this internal structure which provides nurture, care, and assistance to members experiencing spiritual, social, or economic difficulties.

I have tried to present some of the views, attitudes, and activities of foreign missionaries active in the planting and early growth of the Korean church. As we approach the centennial celebration of the Protestant church, what is the present attitude of missionaries? Some see the church as God's people destined to take the gospel not only to Asians, but also to those in Latin America and the Western world. But others are critical of the indifference of many church leaders to social, political, and economic injustices. Others spurn "quantity" growth and long for more "quality" within the church.

At a church growth seminar conducted for missionaries working in Korea held October 16, 1980, I gave a lecture suggesting several secrets of the marvelous growth of the Korean church. During the discussion period that evening, the leader of a well-known interdenominational mission submitted a list of twenty-eight weaknesses in the growth of Korean churches. His reasons are as follows:

> Pride of bigness; preoccupation with money; love of power and place seeking; mishandling of money by leadership; hedonism; pretense of long prayers; authoritarianism of pastors; manipulation of people by appointment to offices; high rating of finances for qualifications of elders; neglect of family life; widespread lack of personal and family Bible reading; salvation by church attendance; excessive stress on tithing that produces burdens; lack of social impact, especially of doctors; lack of social concern; poverty of biblical teaching, discipling of men to men rather than to God; rarity of real fellowship; mixed motivation for missions; denominationalism; regionalism; pressures on young ministers to conform; appeal to the miraculous; Confucian structures; Buddhistic view of the church; Shamanistic view of ministry; materialistic view of the kingdom; and humanism.

Perhaps his observations come as the voice of a prophet to warn of future dangers.

Are Western missionaries still needed in Korea, a nation where 15-20 percent are considered Christians? Should missionaries live and work in Seoul with a population of nine million where perhaps 25 percent are considered Christians, or should they move to rural areas where less than 5 percent are Christians? This decision will reflect the goals, policies, and strategy of each mission.

Chua Wee Hian says that we still desperately need dramatic changes in missionary policies and practices. In his article "Missionaries Must Change" (Chua, 1958:20), Chua states that nationalism is booming in Asia and old religions are being reformed and revived. Why is Christianity still weak after 100 years? Why are most churches still not self-supporting and sadly lack missionary vision? To answer these questions, Chua observes that before World War II, theological liberalism emphasized social reform rather than conversion. Institutions had priority over the indigenous church. Another reason is that missionaries ran everything, and the Asian Christians were mere spectators. The strange thing is that the church members did not rebel against such a passive role! Rather, they rejoiced to have "professional men" to care for their souls as doctors care for their health. Their missionaries were like the priests and monks of other religions. Chua then states:

By failing to train local believers to positions of spiritual leadership and to pass on our Lord's missionary mandate to them, they made the Asian Church feel that it must regard itself as the receiving church and not the sending church. Where there is no evangelistic thrust and missionary commitments, there is no growth. No wonder the Asian Church is not virile and strong (Chua, 1968:20).

After World War II, there was a new restlessness among people in Third World countries. They wanted political independence. Many missionaries promised "nationalization" but realized the serious lack of capable leadership. Recognizing the impossibility of a "go it-alone" policy, "partnership" became the watchword. The missionary role must change from that of a performer to a trainer, from a patron to a servant, and from a director to a catalyst.

What then should be our attitude concerning a moratorium on Western missionaries and / or Western money? I agree with C. Peter Wagner who considers the moratorium as a very pragmatic issue.

> To the degree that a moratorium on missionaries facilitates the fulfillment of the Great Commission of our Lord, it should be supported by Bible-believing Christians. It hardly needs to be mentioned that the reverse equally holds, if a moratorium on missionaries hinders the progress of world evangelization, it should be opposed (Wagner, 1975: 165-176).

Wagner continues by suggesting the necessity of a moratorium in four areas: (1) missionaries who extend Western cultural chauvinism, including economics, politics, technology, or methods of communication; (2) missionaries who indulge in theological and ethical imperialism; (3) missionaries who are dedicated to paternalistic interchurch aid, the syndrome of church development; and (4) missionaries who are involved in counter-productive activities as described in the first three points.

The above mentioned attitudes in the fields of culture, theology, ecclesiology, and missiology cry out for a moratorium. However, simultaneously with that cry we need a new movement in the same fields by which the Spirit of God can work out His purpose through us. A major shift in this movement will be an explosion of Third World missions.

We must remember that the Great Commission also applies to Christians in Western countries. As Paul was called by God to become an apostle to the Gentiles, some Western Christians will be called to go as missionaries to preach the gospel to people of another language and culture. Some will be involved in evangelism and church planting, others in Christian nurture, and others in social service. These Western people must become obedient to the call of God and seek the right place for an effective ministry.

A foreign missionary from the East or the West adds a vital and significant element to the church in any land. Seeing the worldwide aspect of the church reduces nationalistic pride. Becoming aware of the needs of other people reduces selfishness and complacency. Experiencing the grace of Jesus Christ reduces the natural human barriers between nationalities.

There is one world, one gospel, one church, and one Lord. Though the gospel is a pearl of great price, the visible church consists of men and women characterized by clay. We are not yet perfect, but await the return of the Lord Jesus Christ who will establish the kingdom of God. To this end, may God use the church in Korea to fulfill His will and to also become an example and challenge to Christians in other Asian, African, Latin American, and Western nations.

Bibliography

Chua, Wee Hian. "Missionaries Must Change." *Eternity,* Vol. 19, No. 5, May 1968.

Chun, Sung-Chun. *Schism and Unity in the Protestant Churches of Korea.* Seoul, Korea: The Christian Literature Society of Korea. 1979.

Clark, Allen D. *A History of the Church in Korea.* Seoul, Korea: The Christian Literature Society of Korea, 1971.

Clark, Charles Allen. *The Korean Church and the Nevius Methods.* New York: Revell, 1928. (reprinted in 1937).

Neill, Stephen. *A History of Christian Missions,* Harmondsworth, Middlesex, England: Penguin Books Ltd., 1964.

Nelson, Marlin L. *The How and Why of Third World Missions: An Asian Case Study.* South Pasadena, William Carey Library, 1976.

Paik, L. George. *The History of Protestant Missions in Korea 1832-1910.* Pyengyang, Korea: Union Christian College Press, 1929.

Shearer, Roy E. *Wildfire: Church Growth in Korea.* Grand Rapids, Michigan: Wm. Eerdmans Publishing Co., 1966.

Wagner, C. Peter. "Colour the Moratorium Grey." *International Review of Mission,* Vol. 64, April 1975, pp. 165-176.

PART THREE

RENEWAL OF THE LOCAL CHURCH

Dr. Park Cho-Choon, Pastor of the Young Nak Presbyterian Church since 1966, is a graduate of Seoul National University (B. A.) and Princeton Theological Seminary (M. Div. and Th. M.). In 1971 he was conferred an LL. D. by the Azusa Pacific University. Dr. Park is also chairman of the Presbyerian Theological Seminary Board of Directors and has served as Moderator of the Seoul Presbytery.

The Young Nak Presbyterian Church in Seoul, established by Dr. Han Kyung-Chik, is the largest Presbyterian church in the world. During a recent International Pastors' Seminar, Dr. Park lectured on "Secrets of Church Growth." This article was prepared from lectures presented at that time. Training of laity is emphasized plus a balanced concern for evangelism and mission, education, and social services.

I2 THE DYNAMICS OF YOUNG NAK PRESBYTERIAN CHURCH GROWTH

by Park Cho-Choon

Historical Background

The Young Nak Presbyterian Church was established in 1945 by Rev. Han Kyung-Chik, with 27 Christian refugees from North Korea. There had been much suffering under the domination of the Japanese for 36 years, and we had hoped for peace following liberation on August 15, 1945. But the Russian Communists immediately began moving their military armaments into North Korea and persecution of Christians began again. Rev. Han was among the early groups of refugees that fled south.

Rev. Han secured land in the center of Seoul that had been previously used as Korean headquarters for the Shinto religion. This was rennovated into a place for Christian worship while the church was being built. By 1947 it was necessary to hold two morning worship services because of the increasing attendance of North Korean refugees.

The new sanctuary was completed in June 1950, but on Sunday June 25th the North Korean Communists attacked. The members again fled further south to Taegu, Pusan and Cheju Island, once again becoming refugees. During the Communist War (1950-53) Young Nak Churches were established in several cities and the members were later urged to replace themselves with new Christians before they returned to Seoul.

The Communists had used the Young Nak Church in Seoul as a place to store ammunition. During their final retreat, they ignited the ammunition, but miraculously, the fire went out. Thus God protected our church from destruction. The sanctuary was cleaned out and dedicated in 1954. Since then there have been several new buildings constructed to meet the growing needs of our members and our surrounding community. From the beginning Dr. Han emphasized evangelism, education and social works. I will describe these activities more later.

In 1973 when Dr. Han was installed as Pastor Emeritus, it became my honor and responsibility to become pastor of this church. Though I felt most unworthy, God has been faithful to me, and Dr. Han continues to counsel and help in many ways, even preaching once a month in my place.

Secrets of Korean Church Growth

Visitors from abroad often ask me the reasons for the growth of our church. I think there are many reasons why not only our church, but many churches in Korea are growing. Let me explain a few of these briefly.

1. The Korean church is built on the blood of martyrs. Years ago someone said, "The blood of the martyrs is the seed of the church," and this is certainly true in Korea. The Catholic church began 100 years before the Protestant church in Korea, and scores, even thousands of Catholic Christians were persecuted and killed. A large percentage of these were women who had begun to experience human dignity and hope through the gospel. Then for 36 years our people suffered much under the Japanese rule. After a brief period of peace, persecution broke out again as the North Korean Communists invaded our country, and killed and captured many pastors, Christian teachers and leaders in society.

2. The Korean church is a praying church. You will remember the 1907 revival when the Holy Spirit brought conviction of sin and cleansing and then empowered Christians to win their family and friends to Christ. There was much rapid growth following this period of prayer and purification.

But during the years of Japanese occupation, many Christians compromised their faith and bowed to the Shinto Shrine. If the leaders remained steadfast, often their schools and churches were closed and sometimes burned. As the Japanese sensed impending defeat, the persecution increased.

The World War II finally ended August 15, 1945, and we all gave much thanks to God. Also, many Christians repented of compromising their faith. At that time several churches began the dawn prayer meetings which have become well known around the world. Then during the Communist War, people prayed even more, realizing the uncertainty of even life itself.

With increasing urbanization and industrialization, it is no longer convenient for many church members to attend the dawn prayer meeting as they did earlier in the rural areas. Even so, most churches continue to have an early morning prayer service often attended by 20 to 300 people.

Recently many churches have begun all night prayer meetings on Fridays from 10:00 p. m. to 5:00 a. m. During this time there is singing, preaching, testimonies, group and individual praying. And some sleep too! We have a social time about 2:00 a. m. and many enjoy a cup of coffee.

We also have a Wednesday night prayer meeting in our church. In fact, we have two services, 6:30 and 8:00 p. m. as our auditorium seating 3,500 is filled to capacity, mostly with young people. This is one of the most encourging aspects of my ministry as these are the future leaders of our church.

Many churches have a prayer mountain or retreat center where groups and individuals can go for prayer, Bible study and meditation. Our church also has a prayer center on the northern side of Seoul which is used by many of our members. I truly believe that our church is growing because people are sincerely praying.

3. The Korean church is growing because Christian are enthusiastic about evangelism. Since 1974 we have had personal evangelism classes in our church. Classes consist of 50-70 members and they must attend for three hours, twice a week for four weeks. And our training is strict. They must be present 10 minutes before class begins and if they are absent more then two times or if they fail to complete their assignments, they cannot graduate. The teaching materials have been prepared by our church, using ideas from CCC, the Navigators, Evangelism Explosion and others.

Thus far we have trained over 3,000 lay persons and our church has grown much because of their zeal to witness. We find this not only an effective way to get new members, but also to develop the vitality of our present members. Many churches are becoming institutionalized and the members think evangelism is the duty of the church staff, and "not our job." Such churches usually don't grow.

Though people often resent hard training, they actually appreciate it when they experience more fruit in their lives. I emphasize again and again that this is important and that I cannot do everything alone. Actually we have many kinds of training. We train our choir members, church school teachers, lady officers, elders, deacons and others. It was most difficult to train elders as they thought they were already mature Christians. So I began having four day seminars in September. We go to a nice place where we can relax and be comfortable as we *plan* for the new year and *evaluate* the activities of the past year. This is most important as they then become more committed.

Let me suggest another way in which our lay people become actively involved. Our congregation of 60,000 members is divided into 19 parishes with each having an ordained pastor. Each parish has 1000 families and we have annual visitation. How is that possible? The parishes are sub-divided into districts or cells with 12 families and each cell has three or four church officers who help with visitation and report special needs to the pastor. These cell leaders (1362) meet every Monday morning at the church to receive Bible teaching which they in turn pass on to others. How thankful we are for this practice which was begun by John Wesley and brought to Korea by the Methodist missionaries and has been adopted by nearly every denomination.

4. The Korean church is growing because the heart of the Korean people is as a vacuum. Historically Korea was influenced by Buddhism and Confucianism, but practically speaking, they have no strong influence now. The government gives statistics for these religious groups, but they are not very active. Some may visit a temple once a year or when there is a marriage, illness, or death in the family. Actually the Buddhists are beginning to immitate the Chris-

tian forms of worship, organizing a Sunday school, singing hymns and wearing modern clothing. Yet without Christ in their heart, they are still empty and cannot offer a message of hope and eternal life to those suffering spiritually and physically.

We know that Pentecost happened in Jerusalem and the church spread to Europe, to America, and now into Asia. For various reasons the church had become "dead" in these other countries, yet the ministry of the Holy Spirit is still very active in Korea. I believe God is giving the Korean Christians a great opportunity. If we are faithful, God may use the Koreans to evangelize the world. But if we are unfaithful, the Holy Spirit may move elsewhere.

Special Characteristics of the Young Nak Church

While I was describing reasons for church growth in Korea, I mentioned some of our church activities. But let me continue with some other aspects which I consider essential for a healthy growing church.

1. Positive leadership. A growing church needs positive leadership. I believe it was John Calvin who said that the church can grow according to the pastor. Not above this. The pastor has a great responsibility. He must be a man of faith. Moses sent 12 spies into the promised land and all said it was a great land. But 10 men said the land was filled with giants and that they could not conquer such a place. Naturally this disappointed the Israelites. But the other two men said that God was greater than the giants. God had promised the land to them. The difference in these two reports was faith in God's promise. If God is with us, we can do all things. Some pastors have faith and others do not. God will bless us and our congregation according to our faith.

2. Unity in Christ. The Bible teaches, that we all have spiritual gifts and talents, but they are different. God in his wisdom gave variety to our society and likewise to our churches. I often consider my role as that of a symphony director rather than as a spiritual dictator. Some members are like the violin and others like the tuba or the drum. Sometimes they make too much noise and I wish they would keep quiet or move to another church. But each person has a special gift or talent. If the drummer plays at the right time, he makes a great contribution. But if he plays according to his own will, he makes a horrible noise. Part of my ministry is to maintain this unity in diversity.

3. Inspiring services. Our members come to church emotionally and spiritually weary from their activities in society during the previous week. Many of them face various temptations in business and difficulties at home or at school. Therefore they need to have their spiritual batteries recharged. This is done as we bring them into fresh communion with the living God. The entire worship service must be carefully planned—selection of hymns, Scripture reading, prayer, choir anthem, and especially the sermon.

In the Protestant church proclamation of the Word of God is of primary importance. Sometimes while visiting in the States, I see two or three churches in the same neighborhood. One is filled and may even be planning to enlarge their sanctuary, while the others appear to be dying churches. What makes the difference? I believe an important reason is the preaching. A sermon needs to have three ingredients:

1) Be biblical--we may occasionally refer to political issues, but not continually. I like expository preaching, but· this needs variety otherwise the people lose interest. A pastor is like a cook who must learn how to prepare spiritual food in a tasty manner.

2) Be theological--each sermon must have a definite aim and I believe the supreme and highest aim is the salva-

tion of the listeners. This encourages people to bring unbelievers to church. I then use words that are easily understood
rather than scholarly theological terms. My concern is not
to impress my congregation but to bless them.

3) Be existential--by this I mean that a minister must
understand the problems and situations of people listening.
Jesus exhorted His disciples saying, "Feed my sheep; Tend
my sheep." This requires a close relationship between the
pastor and the people. Because my congregation is so large,
this is difficult. Yet as I mentioned before, our staff is well
organized so that every family is visited once or twice a
year. Special cases are reported to me so I too can visit and
pray with them as time permits.

4. Special groups. In addition to our home cell units
that usually meet on Friday, we encourage people to form
groups according to their particular interest or hobby. Our
church has groups for lawyers, medical doctors, businessmen,
as well as for people concerned for evangelism among the
military, college students, policemen, prisoners, etc. Each
member needs to become involved personally. This increases
their interest in church activities and also allows them to
become better acquainted with each other.

5. Culturally relevant. The Korean church is not the
same as the Western church. Of course we must teach and
preach the same biblical truths, but application of these teachings needs to be adjusted to our Korean society. Christianity
must be meaningful to our people. We are to be the
light and salt in this present world. The church is still in
this world, not yet in heaven. So we need a Christian faith
not only for Sunday, but a Christian way of living during
the week too. We urge our members to become involved in
community activities.

6. Clear planning: As mentioned earlier, I work

with the elders in setting new goals for the coming year as well as evaluating our ministry for the past year. We are in a changing world, so we must work hard to maintain effective strategies of mission. Our church is growing about 10% a year. Therefore by 1990 our expectation is to have 100,000 members. This is why we have purchased land on the southern part of Seoul and plan to build a sanctuary that will seat 10,000.

But our primary concern is not to just get bigger, but to enlarge the influence of our ministry. Therefore we have established many new churches and already over 200 have become self-supporting. And many of these have likewise started other new churches so we see a multiplying effect. If we think of these new churches as daughter churches, Young Nak Church is not only the mother church but has become a grandmother church and she is still producing more daughter churches!

Our church also has a vision for foreign missions. On the front of our weekly church bulletin, we list not only the names of our church staff, but also the names of those serving overseas. We have seven ordained missionaries in Guam, Philippines, Indonesia, Taiwan, West Germany, Chile and Singapore, and eight laymen working and witnessing in Pakistan, India, Nepal, Somalia and Malaysia. We believe that a church concerned about foreign missions will also be a church burdened for the evangelization of those nearby.

You see that our church is interested not only in evangelism and missions, but also in education and social service. In 1957 we dedicated our Christian Education Building located beside our sanctuary. We have established The Young Nak Junior High School, The Young Nak Girls High School and also the Young Nak Womens Seminary.

As Korea is a rapidly developing country, there are still many poor people. Others suffer because of some unexpected catastrophe as fire, flood or drought. On the last Sunday of each month we emphasize social services, and collect rice, clothing and other things for the needy. We continue to maintain an orphanage, kindergarten, widows home, and an old folks home. We even have our own cemetery.

With our staff of 22 ministers and 24 evangelists (unordained pastors), seven choirs plus scores of dedicated laymen and women, our concern is to preach Jesus Christ as savior from sin and hope for our future. We presently have five worship services on Sunday and use closed circuit TV for those in nearby buildings.

Though all growing churches may not be healthy churches, I firmly believe that a healthy church must be a growing church. When we cease growing, we begin dying. With these convictions, our prayer is that the Young Nak Church (meaning eternal joy) may continue growing and may be a place where God is worshiped, obeyed and served by our members.

Dr. Oh Pyeng-Seh is dean of the Graduate School, Kosin College and Korea Theological Seminary and President of the Korea Society for Reformed Faith and Action. A graduate of the Korea Theological Seminary, his conservative faith was further developed at the Covenant Seminary (B. D.) and Concordia Seminary where he received S. T. M. and Th. D. degrees. As pastor, scholar, teacher and administrator, he is well qualified to write about the doctrinal struggles of the Korean church.

Presbyterian missionaries from the United States, Canada and Australia cooperated to establish the Jesus Presbyterian Church in Korea. But between 1940 and 1960 a division caused the formation of the Christ Presbyterian Church and later the Jesus Presbyterian Church was divided into the Hap Tong and Tong Hap groups. Dr. Oh explains how the church has suffered to keep the doctrine pure, referring to the Shinto shrine issue with the Japanese and the influences of the World Council of Churches (WCC) and the National Association of Evangelicals (NAE) upon the historic biblical teachings.

13   KEEPING THE FAITH PURE

by Oh Pyeng-Seh

The Korean people share many things in common with the Israelites. Like Israel, Korea frequently became a battleground when neighboring countries had wars. She is among the fewest of all people, and she has many mountains with no fertile resources (Deuteronomy 7:7-8; 11:10-11). Korea is also a land the Lord God cares for. The eyes of the Lord God are continually on her from the beginning of the year to its end (Deuteronomy 11:12). As the Israelites were not supposed to live depending upon the resources of the earth, so I feel that the Korean people are to live looking up to heaven. In this respect the Korean church is blessed in a special way. Although she has had many difficulties here on the earth, I thank God for them as the church's faith has been purified through those difficulties.

Early Missionaries Were Evangelical and Conservative

Dr. Harvie M. Conn speaks about early missionaries who introduced the gospel to the Korean church as follows:

> The history of the Korean church in its early years is the history of conservative, evangelical Christianity. That history must be credited to the missionaries of the Presbyterian faith who brought it. As with any church, younger or older, convictions are molded by those who plant the seed. The missionaries who led the Presbyterian church in its early, formative years were men of sound convictions, and they did not hesitate to ground the church in those convictions. [1]

Like many churches in countries where Christianity was introduced, the Korean church was under the influence of foreign missionaries for a period of time. Early Korean Christians were not prepared to govern their churches independently or to conduct theological education. Therefore, the influence of missionaries was evident from the beginning. This influence was felt especially from September 1, 1912 when the first Korean Presbyterian General Assembly was

....

1. Harvie M. Conn. "Studies in the Theology of the Korean Presbyterian Church (Part I)," *The Westminster Theological Journal*. Vol. XXIX, No. 1 (Nov. 1966) p. 26.

established until 1930 when foreign missionaries left Korea because of oppression under the Japanese rule.

From the founding of the Pyung Yang Theological Seminary until 1927, faculty members were all foreign missionaries. The first Korean professor was employed in 1927 fifteen years after the Korean Presbyterian General Assembly was established. Until that time the missionaries had the theological leadership. Mr. A. J. Brown, who was general secretary of the Board of Foreign Mission of the Presbyterian Church U. S. A., commented on the theological opinion of foreign missionaries in Korea before 1911 as follows:

> The typical missionary of the first quarter century after the opening of the country was a man of the Presbyterian type. He kept the Sabbath as our New England forefathers did a century ago. He looked upon dancing, smoking, and card-playing as sins in which no true follower of Christ should indulge. In theology and biblical criticism he was strongly conservative, and he held as a vital truth the premillenarian view of the second coming of Christ. The higher criticism and liberal theology were deemed dangerous heresies. [2]

Thus, Korean churches were characterized by conservative and Calvinistic theology from the beginning. They have grown more rapidly than churches in other countries. The theological thinking of our early missionaries can be grasped by examining the founding spirit of the seminary in Pyung Yang and the theological background of those missionaries who taught there. Missionary Herbert Blair reported as follows about the theology taught at Pyung Yang Theological

....

2. A. J. Brown, *The Mastery of the Far East* (New York: Scribners, 1919), p. 540, quoted in Harvie M. Conn, op. cit., p. 26.

Seminary:

> The Bible is the one textbook emphasized and
> studied. The seminary, which sets its theological
> impress upon all pastors alike, has been large-
> ly also in the hands of missionary teachers,
> but is now beginning to be transferred to the
> control of the General Assembly step by step.
> Presbyterians, with their historic Calvinistic
> background, accepting the Westminster standards
> and Presbyterian form of government have, as
> of old, unquestioningly accepted the Scriptures
> as the very Word of God. On this basis the
> gospel story centering in the cross of Christ,
> with its frank Pauline supernaturalistic interpre-
> tation has been taught by the missionaries and
> accepted by the Korean church without reserve. [3]

The theology of Pyung Yang Seminary can be discussed in the context of its relationship with Princeton Theological Seminary. Founded in 1812, Princeton Theological
Seminary was the cradle of reformed theology for the whole
Presbyterian denomination in the United States until the
school became liberal in 1929. The fact that the majority
of the missionaries to Korea were Princeton graduates
holds great significance for Korea. The professors at the
Pyung Yang Theological Seminary published *The Standard
Bible Commentary*. Dr. Samuel A. Moffett, who was principal of Pyung Yang Theological Seminary at that time, wrote
in the preface of the standard commentary as follows:

> The authors of this commentary, moreover,
> not only believe that the whole Bible is the

----

3. *Report of the 50th Anniversary Celebration of the Korean Mission* (1934),
   p. 121.

Book of books, and the very Word of God; they also believe that the system of truth taught in the Bible is well summarized in the Westminster Confession of Faith and the Catechisms of the Presbyterian Churches. These standards constitute the creed of the Presbyterian Church in Korea, and the authors of this commentary believed in this creed because they believe it is taught in the Word of God. [4]

The leading figures in the Presbyterian Seminary in Pyung Yang were Samuel A. Moffett, Charles A. Clark, and William D. Reynolds.

Samuel A. Moffett came to Korea in 1890. He was the founding president of the Presbyterian seminary in Pyung Yang. He was a good organizer. He did not write many books, but his influence was great and his theology was conservative and Calvinistic. Recalling the first time he came to Korea, he said, "I have done what I prayed and decided before God when I first came to Korea. That is, I decided not to preach anything except the cross of Christ. If I preach any other gospel, I should be cursed." [5] We can see his theological thought in this saying.

Dr. Charles Clark was a missionary whose influence was also felt greatly in the formation of Korean church theology. He belonged to the Northern Presbyterian Mission and started to teach in 1908. His influence was great as he wrote many books. His thoroughly conservative theology was set forth in *Shin hak ji nam* (*A Theological Guide*) which was published in 1918.

....

4. H. N. Park, ed., *The Standard Bible Commentary* (Seoul, 1937), *Proverbs, Ecclesiastes, Song of Solomon* (Seoul, 1937), Forward, p. 2.

5. Kim Yang-Son, *The Ten Year History of the Korean Church After Liberation* (Seoul: Korean Presbyterian General Assembly Educational Department, 1956), p. 173.

Mr. W. D. Reynolds came to Korea in 1892 as a Southern Presbyterian missionary. He worked in Korea for forty-five years as a missionary lecturer, Bible translator, and professor at the seminary. He contributed to the establishment of a conservative theology based on the Bible by introducing C. Hodge and A. A. Hodge's theology.

As shown above, the early missionaries received conservative Presbyterian theological training before they came to Korea and this theology formed the early theological foundation of the Korean church.

Early Bible Translation-Christians
Taught To Read

Early efforts to evangelize Korea had been made for a long period of time indirectly. Evidence of this effort can be seen in Rev. Gutzlaff's coming to Korea and the martyrdom of Rev. Thomas. They both tried to distribute Bibles wherever they went. The Bible was preeminent in their ministries; this emphasis is a unique aspect of the Protestant church in Korea. This is in sharp contrast with the Roman Catholic church. However, Protestant missionary effort was obstructed because Korea remained closed to any contact with foreign countries. Missionaries in neighboring countries such as Manchurchria tried to evangelize Korea by translating and distributing Bibles. Rev. John Ross in Manchuria translated the Scriptures into Korean with the help of Korean Christians such as Suh Sang-Ryoon.

He published the Gospels of Luke and John in 1882, and 3,000 copies of John and Acts in 1883. Matthew and Mark were completed in 1884 and the New Testament in 1887. [6]

Mr. Lee Soo-Jung, who was in Japan, also translated

---

6. Min Kyung-Bae, *History of Korean Christianity* (Seoul: Christian Literature Society, 1977), p. 144.

the Bible into Korean by comparing Chinese and Japanese Bibles He published the four Gospels and Acts in 1884 and 1,000 copies of the Gospel of Mark in 1885. Rev. Horace G. Underwood entered Korea with these Scriptures. [7]

The fact that the work of Bible translation into Korean was started in Manchuria and Japan before any missionaries came to Korea was a big help in the future evangelization of Korea to Christianity. The hope of the evangelization of Korea was realized when missionaries came to Korea after the Bible was translated and distributed to Koreans. At first the missionaries either translated or corrected the existing translations independently as long as time permitted. The Bible Translation Association was later organized in February 1887 and published the Gospels of Luke and John. The Gospel of Mark was revised by Mr. Underwood and Mr. Henry G. Appenzeller in 1890. This Bible association also appointed Mr. Underwood and Mr. Scranton to publish the New Testament within two years. However, this work was delayed because they returned to the United States before the task was compeleted. [8] Afterwards Mr. S. J. Gale and Mr. Reynolds took part in this work and the New Testament in Korean was published in 1900. The Board of Bible Translators then translated the Old Testament which was published in 1910.

In the meantime, many capable missionaries participated in this work, but among them Messrs. Underwood, Gale, and Reynolds were the most prominent. Mr. Underwood was president of the Board of Bible Translators during all that time except when he was in the United States. Mr. G Gale was a careful and faithful scholar; and Mr. Reynolds was a learned writer.

....

7. *Ibid.*, *p.* 142. p.
8. Paik Nak-Joon, *History of the Protestant Church in Korea* (Yonsei University Press, 1973), pp. 159-160.

The distribution of the Bible grew rapidly. According to the American Bible Society's report, 151,230 Bibles were distributed before 1910, but in 1910 there were 666,178 Bibles distributed. What is remarkable is that 1,000,000 Bible were published during the campaign of "A Million People to Christ." The Bible is the foundation of our faith and church. Therefore, the quickest way to tell others about Jesus Christ is to deliver the message of the Bible in which the life of Jesus and His instructions are written. It was surely a wise thing for the early missionaries to Korea to translate the Bible into our language, The translation and distribution of the Bible made the fast growth of the Korean church possible.

Winter Bible Institute-Laymen
Taught the Bible

The importance of the Bible was stressed in the Korean church which had adopted the Nevius plan for evangelism. In fact, the foundation of the Korean churches was the Bible which became the basis for church activities. In the Korean church the Bible was accepted as God's word bearing powerful authority and spoken directly towards man.

The Nevius plan was devised by John Livingstone Nevius, a Southern Presbyterian missionary who went to China in 1856. The group of seven young Presbyterian missionaries which had arrived in Korea requested him to lead a special two-week meeting for them in 1890. When he spoke, he added to the so-called "Three-Self Formulas" that Henry Venn, general secretary of the Church Missionary Society and Rufus Anderson, general secretary of the American Board of Commissioners for Foreign Missions had used. (The "Three-Self Formulas" include the self-support, self-govern-

....

Ibid., p. 432. *Ibid.*,
10. *Ibid.*, p. 433.

ment, and self-propagation of indigenous churches.) It was called the "Nevius Plan." Later, the Nevius Plan was chosen as an evangelistic strategy for the new Presbyterian church in Korea.

A. D. Clark describes the essence of this plan as follows: "The Nevius methods are not merely a system of self-support and refusal to pay subsidies. Its real core was in the Bible study system which encouraged every Christian to study his Bible and to be able to pass on to others what he found here." [11]

Dr. Moffett also commented "I do not hesitate to state the conviction that the unique and pre-eminent place given to instruction in the Scriptures as the very Word of God has been the outstanding factor through these fifty years in the evangelization of Korea." [12]

As we have seen above, Bible study played an essential role in the early Korean church and has become a main force in the church's growth. Many reports and statements indicate that the early Korean church enthusiastically studied the Bible. Those who gathered for Bible study shared lodging and board together and enjoyed the Bible's teachings in a festive spirit.

The purpose of Bible study was to strengthen the faith of each Christian and to find and train promising laymen to be pastors. These studies took four different forms. First, Bible study was held during the winter season for those who lived in an area belonging to one evangelical district. Farmers were free during the winter to attend. They would all come to a big central church in the area and study the Bible. Second, one single church or a few neighboring churches held Bible study for the local people

....

11. Allen D. Clark, *History of the Korean Church* (Seoul: Christian Literature Society, 1961), pp. 87ff.

12. *Report of the 50th Anniversary Celebration of the Korea Mission,* (1934) p. 40. ,

individually or as a whole. Third, Bible study for the church staff was held for two or three weeks in the summer. Fourth, stemming from the above three forms, theological education was provided for the pastors.

Quite a few gathered for Bible study and their enthusiasm was great. In one Bible study held at Shincheon in 1901, people from all the neighboring villages gathered together bringing sacks of rice on their heads (a common way of transportation for Koreans). In a men's Bible study at Pyung Yang in 1902, 400 people had come from all over the country. According to one statistic, 610 people gathered in Pyung Yang and 434 people in Shincheo in 1904; and in 1905, 733 people gathered at Suncheon. The first Bible study in 1890 was attended by only 17 people. That number increased every year until by 1936 Bible studies were held in 2,344 different places with a total attendence of 178,313. We can clearly see that in the early evangelical movement, Bible study made an important contribution to church growth.

As the Christians increased in number, Bible study for laymen usually began during the lunar New Year holidays and lasted for seven to ten days. During that period, the Christians supplied their own meals. They also studied hygiene and general knowledge, but the main subject was Bible study. Sometimes they visited each house, winning souls to Christ. When early spring came, women's Bible study began. Individual churches had Bible study for three to five days at the most convenient time. In the morning the women studied the Bible, and in the afternoon they visited non-Christians and held evangelistic meetings at night.

Bible studies were also held to train would-be pastors. Dr. Paik Nak-Joon comments:

For the training of would-be pastors, mainly Nevius Method was applied to Bible study. The purpose of Bible study was clear. It was not only for education but to help encourage them to render devoted Christian service. But training the Korean pastors was not so simple. Among the new Christians, outstanding persons were not many who could be trained to be respectable Christian leaders. Sufficient finance to secure qualified teachers was not available. Among the missionaries who had good command of the Korean language and had ample experience in evangelical field, the majority were already serving in other posts. Furthermore, the leading missionaries were engaged in evangelism for the local people so they were not available. Facing such difficulties, missionaries held winter Bible studies lasting from one to six months in Seoul or Pyung Yang in the very early days of training the would-be pastors. In those days, mission boards paid transportation expenses, lodging and board and held Bible studies for trainees in the area where missionary groups resided. The curriculum included theology, history of the Bible, and guidelines necessary for Christian life and pastoral care. Their responsibilities for their fellow citizens were inspired and they were trained in such a way as to get ready for participation in local evangelism. As trainees increased in number, summer and winter Bible studies were held in many areas.[13]

As we have seen above, the essential factor in Korean church growth was faith in God's Word.

Shinto Shrine Issue

During the years just before Japanese colonialism came

---

13. Paik Nak-Joon, *op. cit., p. 314.*

to an end, the imposition of so-called Shinto shrine worship deprived Koreans of their freedom of religion. The Japanese attempted thereby to eradicate the Christian faith from Korea. All of the Korean churches suffered and were severely tried. The Japanese imperialists forced Koreans to worship at idolatrous Shinto shrines. The purpose of this policy was to make Koreans subjects of Japan. Shinto worship was also designed to wipe out the Christian faith. Christians who worshipped Jehovah God as their only God could not bow to the Shinto shrine nor could Korean patriots who yearned to preserve the national spirit. As a result their battle for the Christian faith or patriotism began.

However, those Christians who believed in liberal theology in the 1930's, accepted Shinto shrine worship as a national ritual and cooperated with the Japanese imperialist. While those who believed in Presbyterian doctrine declared, in the light of the Bible, that Shinto shrine worship was the sin of idolatry. Accordingly, they began an anti-Shinto shrine worship drive.

In 1935, the Japanese ordered the Christian students in Pyung Yang to regularly worship the Shinto shrine. In November 1935, Dr. G. F. McCune, headmaster of the Pyung Yang Soongshil Junior College, and Mrs. V. V. Snook, headmistress of Soongeui Girls High School, rejected the Japanese order. Therefore the Japanese launched the nationwide enforcement of Shinto shrine worship.

The Korea Mission of the Presbyterian Church in the U. S. (Southern) decided to close its schools and to retire from secular education rather than comply with Japan's

....

14. Lee Man-Yul, *End of the Lee Dynasty and the Nationalistic Movement,* (Seoul: Pyung Min Publisher, 1976), p. 14.

15. Paik Nak-Joon, *op. cit.,* p. 314. i

16 Kang Keun-Hwan, "Influence of the Early Missionary Policy on the Growth of the Protestant Church in Korea, "*Theological Thought.* Vol VI (Sept. 1974), p. 630

demands concerning shrine attendance. The Korea Mission of the Presbyterian Church in the U. S. A. (Northern) did not take final action. This was because a minority of the missionaries and the mission board in New York which was influenced by liberal theology, did not see any great harm in shrine worship. The Methodist Mission decided to comply on the basis of official assurance that shrine attendance was a patriotic rather than a religious act. In 1938 eighteen Christian schools including the Union Christian College in Pyung Yang, were forced to close because of this issue.[17]

When the Japanese Governor General in Korea and his associates found their requirements satisfied the schools, they began to concentrate on enforcing shrine worship on the churches.

The General Assembly of the Korean Presbyterian Church was called in September 1938. The Japanese police checked the delegates to the General Assembly who were strongly against bowing at the shrine; they were refused permission to travel. Only those who would vote for shrine worship or who would maintain silence on the issue at the meeting were allowed to go. The General Assembly was held in Pyung Yang under police surveillance. An affirmative vote for shrine worship was called for and given scattered assent, but no negative vote was called for. The missionaries tried to protest the unlawful procedure of the moderator, but police interrupted their protests. Thus, the Presbyterian Church was forced to give its approval to shrine worship. Then the vice-moderator with the representative of each presbytery was appointed to go to the shrine at Pyung Yang to represent the General Assembly of the Presbyterian Church.

The Methodist Bishop had already submitted to the

....

17. K. S. Lee, *The Christian Confrontation with Shinto Nationalism* (Philadelphia: Presbyterian and Reformed), p. 168.

shrine worship, as had the representatives of the Holiness Church and the Seventh Day Adventist Church. The Roman Catholic Church had also earlier complied, preserving the position of the priests on the field.

Although the General Assembly of the Presbyterian Church and other ecclesiastical bodies collapsed under Japanese Shintoism, a minority of ministers and Christians stood against the issue. Nearly 200 local congregations closed their doors; about 2,000 persons were arrested; and among them more than fifty died in prison and twenty to fifty were released at the end of the war.

After the General Assemby of the Korean Presbyterian Church in 1938, the police forced the Christians to worship at the Shinto shrines. But the ministers who resisted courageously stood against shrine worship. They began the "Non-Shrine Worship Movement." They used every possible means to strengthen and to link the resisting Christians together to fight for the faith. In order to prevent the spread of resistance among Christians, secret police agents pursused the ministers constantly. Their words and deeds were recorded in detail by the police and later, when they were arrested and imprisoned, they were charged with violating the law for maintaining public order and peace.[17b]

From February to September 1938, most Christians and pastors rejected Shinto shrine worship. In early 1939 the anti-shrine movement expanded systematically throughout the nation. The headquarters of this campaign was the Sanjunghyun Church in Pyung Yang, and its pastor was Rev. Joo Chi-Chul. The Sanjunghyun Church was closed after enduring Japanese threats. In addition, Rev. Joo was imprisoned for seven years until his death in the cell at 9:00 p.m. on April 21, 1944. Rev. Joo's imprisonment and the unswerving resistance of the church against Shinto shrine

....

17b. K. S. Lee, *Ibid.*, pp. 169-171. 17a.

worship became a symbol which fueled the anti-shrine movement. This movement resulted in the imprisonment of more than 2000 people, the martyrdom of some 50 people, and the closing down of more than 200 churches. These were obvious signs of the glorious victory of the Korean church.

The anti-Shinto shrine worshippers held firmly to conservative Presbyterian theology. This belief can be summarized from their testimonies as follows:

1. They believed the Bible to be God's infallible Word that should be applied to their Christian faith and life. They tried to yield total obedience to God's Word and commandments.

2. They believed in the surety of the second coming of Jesus Christ as is prophesied in the Bible. They believed that the last days of this world were near. Submitting to Jesus and relying upon Him, they resisted anti-Christian beliefs at the cost of their own lives.

3.They were convinced that spreading of biblical truth benefited the country and mankind. "If only for the sake of God's glory," they were willing to be loyal to God to their death. In contrast, those who submitted to Shinto shrine worship did so because according to liberal theology they were helping to build Christ's kingdom under the Japanese imperialists. The Shinto shrine issue was, therefore, not only a severe trial for the Korean church, it also drew the line between conservative and liberal theology.

Evangelical and Liberal Conflict

Since 1958, the Presbyterian Church of Korea had two major divisions--namely, the pro-World Council of Churches (W. C. C.) movement and the pro-National Association

----

18. Kim Yang-Son, *op. cit.*, p. 187.
19. *Ibid.* Ibid.

of Evangelicals (N. A. E.) movement. These two groups opposed one another, and their confrontation led to more serious differences that made mutual reconciliation almost impossible. Consequently in 1959, the church divided into the Tong Hap and Hap Tong groups. The reasons behind this split were matters related to the purchase of land for the seminary, the issue of withdrawal from the W. C. C., and the election of the representative for the Kyunggi presby tery. These three problems were closely related to each other because they were expressions of the conflict between the ecumenical position and the evangelical position.

The N. A. E. was organized in St. Louis, Missouri, in 1942. An international meeting of evangelicals was convened in Switzerland in 1948. In 1950 two meetings were held in England and in the United States. In 1951 the N. A. E. movement was enlarged and renamed the World Evangelical Fellowship (W. E. F.). Representatives from twenty-four countries met in Holland and developed a doctrinal statement for this international organization. Their beliefs are as follows:

1. The Bible is truly the Word of God.

2. The Trinity of God.

3. The Diety of Christ, His sinless life, redemptive death, resurrection, and second coming.

4. Salvation is through faith by the Holy Spirit.

5. Christians lead a holy life with the help of the Holy Spirit and witness for Christ.

....

20. Lee Young-Hun, *History of Korean Christianity* (Concordia Publishing Co., 1978, 9. 318. p.

6. The saved enter eternal life after resurrection and the unsaved suffer eternal punishment.

7. Christians are united as one in Christ and they serve the church which is Christ's body.

The N. A. E. movement in Korea began around 1948. Fifty-one Chosun Seminary students and ten other persons who were against liberal theology agreed to organize the Korea branch of the N. A. E. during a summer conference in July 1952. In December, an application for regular membership was submitted to W. E. F. where Dr. Park Hyung-Ryong was advisor.

The Korean church's relation to the W. C. C. began with the dispatch of Rev. Kim Kwan-Shik to its first meeting held at Amsterdam in 1948. Its second meeting was at Evanston, Illinois, U. S. A. in 1954. Rev. Kim Hyun-Jung, Rev. Myung Shin-Hong, and Rev. Yoo Ho-Joon attended. Conflict between the W. C. C. and the N. A. E. brought disintegration inside the Korean Presbyterian Church. And the conservative N. A. E. continued to resist the pro-liberal W. C. C.

Liberalism, Humanism, Neo-Orthodoxy

The infiltration of liberal theology into the Korean church can be traced to the influence of a number of factors: (1) pro-liberal missionaries, Scott and Frazier, from the Canadian Mission Board, (2) the Northern Presbyterian Church's theological leftism, (3) the return to Korea of those who had access to liberal theological study in Japan, and (4) the comity agreement by missionaries which allowed liberal

---

21. *Encyclopedia of Christianity* (Korea Christian Literature Society), p. 401.
22. Kim Yang-Son, *op. cit.*, pp. 179-185. pp.

theology to develop faster in certain provinces without outside interference.

During the twenty-third General Assembly in 1934, liberal theology became a controversial issue as a result of Rev. Kim Yung-Joo's denial of the authorship of Gensis by Moses, and Rev. Kim Choon-Bae's thesis on women's rights. This was the first incident in which the Bible came under criticism and liberal theology appeared to challenge the whole church. Regarding these two issues, the study committee declared that criticism of the Bible's authority was wrong and anyone having such opinion should be disciplined according to regulations. Rev. Kim Yung-Joo and Rev. Kim Choon-Bae accepted the assembly's resolution and announced the annulment of their opinion. Thus the problem was settled for the time being.

At the twenty-fourth meeting in September 1935, another issue arose, that is, the controversy over the authority of the *Abingdon Bible Commentary*. On the occasion of the fiftieth anniversary of the Methodist Church, Abingdon's commentary was translated by Rev. Song Chang-Keun, Chae Phil-Keun, and Han Kyung-Jik and published with Rev. Yoo Hyung-Ghi as editor. The General Assembly resolved that since many points in the commentary contradicted Presbyterian doctrine, Presbyterian churches should not use it and the translators should publish statements of apology in the Christian paper.

Rev. Chae and Rev. Han agreed to accept the resolution and apologized right there in the meeting. Rev. Song, however, flatly refused to apologize, insisting that any apology for the reason of doctrinal contradiction was absurd and that the General Assembly's resolution discouraged freedom of religion. This was the first time liberal theology directly challenged conservative theology in the

Presbyterian church.

The Pyung Yang Seminary which had forty years of tradition as a stronghold of conservative theology, was ordered to close in September 1938. As the Japanese Imperial power increased, evangelical ministries were forced to stop and missionaries returned home. Rev. Park Hyung-Ryong and Rev. Nam Goong-Hyuk fled abroad, and it seemed unlikely that the school would ever reopen. Later, leading conservative pastors including Rev. Joo Chi-Chul were imprisoned, and thus, the conservative line became weakened. As a result, pro-liberalism appeared again. On April 19, 1940, the Chosun Seminary opened in Seungdong Church, Seoul, with Elder Kim Dae-Hyun as principal and Kim Yung-Jo, Hahm Tae-Yung, Lee Jung-Keun, Yoon In-Koo, and Kim Jae-Joon as teachers. Later, it was legalized as the seminary sponsored by the General Assembly of the Presbyterian church.

Kim Jae-Joon's educational ideal was the opposite of Pyung Yang Seminary's ideal. Liberal theology had apparently declared war against conservative theology. Undeniably, Chosun Seminary, as directed by Kim Jae-Joon, was the base for starting, developing, and eventually introducing liberal theology into the church.

In April 1947, fifty-one Chosun seminary students who were against Kim Jae-Joon's view of theology submitted a statement refuting his teaching to the Thirty-third General Assembly held in Taegu. One year later at the Thirty-fourth meeting, the Board of Directors resolved to send Kim Jae-Joon to the United States for studies and to supplement the teaching staff with Rev. Park Hyung-Ryong, Hong Myung-Shin, Kim Jin-Hong, and Shim Moon-Tae. Nevertheless, Kim Jae-Joon disapproved, and kept criticizing orthodox theology. Finally, he was ostracized, and he and his followers organized the R. O. K. Presbyterian Church.

....

24. Ibid., p. 192. *Ibid.,*

On August 15, 1945, when the Japanese surrender ended World War II, Korea became politically and religiously independent. On August 17, anti-Shinto shrine worshippers were set free from imprisonment where they had suffered for five to six years. Among them were Rev. Han Sang-Dong and Rev. Joo Nam-Sun who had been praying in prison for a three-way plan to rehabilitate the Korean church if God would give them an opportunity. Their plan was as follows:

First, build reclusive prayer houses for pastors whose Christian conscience was tainted under the Japanese persecution in order to help them become strong believers.

Second, seminaries which were closed because of refusal to accept Shinto-shrine worship should be reestablished to train pastors who would fight for biblical truth at the expense of their lives.

Third, large numbers of evangelists should be trained to help start revival meetings.

In September 1946, pastors Han and Joo established the Koryo Seminary in Pusan in order to help train pastors who would be orthodox in faith and pure in life. During the past thirty-six years, Koryo has trained many Christians to be faithful servants of God in Korea and in other countries. The churches which have a close relationship to Koryo Seminary are called "Koryoists" or "Koshinists." This denomination is a steadfast stronghold of Korean reformed theology.

In 1959 the Jesus Presbyterian Church was split into two groups, the Tong Hap and Hap Tong. The Hap Tong is oriented to conservative theology, while the Tong Hap is pro-conservative but also follows the ecumenical line in theology. A majority of the Korean churches are for orthodox theology based on the Bible, and their efforts to witness provide a solid basis for Korean church growth.

---

25. Min Kyung-Bae, op. cit., p. 360.

Mrs. Lee Youn-Ok graduated from the Presbyterian Theological Seminary in Seoul, received the Master of Christian Education degree from the Presbyterian School of Christian Education in Richmond, Virginia, and also received the Master of Educational Administration from the University of North Carolina. She has served as principal of the Jung Shin Girls Middle and High School, chairman of the board of directors of the Kyung Min Commercial Middle and High School and is now president of the National Organization of the Korean Presbyterian Women.

The changing role of women in society is not only a concern in Western countries, but affects women throughout the world. Mrs. Lee, an educator, administrator and pastor's wife, documents accomplishments by women in Korea and clearly sets forth the increasing responsibilities of women, especially in the church. Mrs. Lee hopes that the Presbyterian General Assembly will soon allow women to become elders and to be ordained. Her writings will bring encouragement to other women leaders and inspire women to fulfil their God given responsibilities.

14 THE ROLE OF WOMEN IN KOREAN CHURCH GROWTH

by Lee Youn-Ok

Korean women have contributed much to the growth of the Korean church during the 100-year history of Protestantism in Korea. We can find many stories in the history of the Korean church about church women's devoted service, patriotism, and their willingness to sacrifice for the realization of social justice. The National Women's Evangelistic Association, which is the only women's organization in the Korean Presbyterian churches, published an *Outline History* in 1968 in commemoration of the fortieth anniversary of its founding.

The same organization in 1978 published the *History of Presbyterian Women* in commemoration of its fiftieth anniversary; it also published the *Management Guide of the Women's Evangelistic Association* which contained the church activities, mission strategy, and women's role in the churches. The above three books have been used as resource materials in the preparation of this summary of the role of women in the growth of the Korean church. Our brief sketch will embrace the past, present, and future.

Early Role of Women in the Korean Church

Protestantism entered Korea on September 20, 1884, when Dr and Mrs. Horace Allen arrived. Rev. Horace G. Underwood and Rev. and Mrs. H. G. Appenzeller entered Korea on April 5, 1885. In the same year, Dr. Scranton and his mother, founder of Ewha school, came to Korea. Earlier, when the Catholic church had entered Korea, the country was closed to any contact with foreign nations. However, Protestantism entered when the Korean political situation was in turmoil and the majority of Koreans were longing for a solution. Also, the government was willing to accept anything positive. Moreover, Dr. Allen provided medical care for the royal families of the Yi Dynasty and had close contact with them. It was a propitious time for Protestantism to enter this country. The wise evangelistic policy of the missionaries received no negative response from the government.

This policy was to evangelize people and then establish churches and Christian schools as the center of the new Western culture.

There were 501 Presbyterian schools, 158 Methodist schools, 2 Seventh Day Adventist schools, 1 Interdenominational school, 46 Catholic schools, and 84 other schools by February 1910. This meant that there were 796 Christian primary, middle and high schools and colleges. (*Management Guide of the Women's Evangelistic Association, page* 42)

Missionaries established not only men's schools but also women's schools.

An essay in the *Chosun Christian Bulletin* on December 29, 1898, said "Education of housewives is such an urgent task. The thriving of the household, revival of the nation and power of people depend upon the education of Korean women." Truly, the missionaries' founding of women's schools based on the spirit of equality of the sexes was the first torchlight for liberating Korean women and opened the way for Korean women's education. The purpose of this education was to equip church women to awaken fellow Korean women from the deep sleep of social and political ignorance.

Church Women Were Pioneers. God created men and women in His own image. However, in Korea only men were educated while women spent all their time bearing children and doing household chores following the tradition of Confucianism. Church women came to know through the Bible that they should have equal rights with men and that our country could become prosperous only when men and women cooperated together. Women who were oppressed by men began to resist and to introduce changes in the family, society, and nation. For instance, the "Women's Friendship Association" was organized in March 1899. About fifty housewives became very indignant about powerful and rich men who had concubines and yet felt no guilt. These women strongly protested against our social system which allowed this evil behavior. They staged the first sit-down demonstration in front of the Duksoo Palace to express their disapproval. They wanted King Kojong to ban such a corrupt system.

Educated women began to work in the various sectors

of society. For instance, in 1896 Ms. Shin Maria was appointed as the first vice-principal at Jung Shin Girls' School the first Presbyterian girls' high school, having been founded in 1887. She was also the first deaconess at Yun Dong Church. Ms. Kim Pil-Rye was the principal of Jung Shin Girls' High School. She also founded the Young Womens Christian Association (YWCA) in April 1922; she was also the president of the National Presbyterian Women's Evangelistic Committee. Mrs. Choi Eun-Hee became the first woman reporter for *The Chosun Ilbo* (a newspaper) in 1924. She was only twenty-one years old at that time. It was a job which few women of that day would even dream of filling. Since many women have worked as principals of Christian girls' high schools, we can see that the role of women has changed profoundly.

Church Women Were Patriots. Korean church women who learned of new values of life through the gospel could no longer endure the oppression of Japan, the intruder. Their faith filled their hearts with righteousness and warm patriotism toward their country.

The March First Independence Movement was widespread. Over 1,000,000 people from 212 communities in different provinces took part in 1,214 demonstrations over a sixty-day period. The Presbyterian Assembly of October 1919 reported that 2,125 men and 531 women from Presbyterian churches had been imprisoned. Working together in this movement, many organizations sought to free our country from Japanese rule. Among them was a organization called the "Korea Patriotic Women's Association" which received its orders from Korea's temporary government in Shanghai, China.

To aid the March First Independence Movement, women church leaders and representatives of the Patriotic Women's Association throughout the nation gathered together and appointed Kim Maria president of the National Presbyterian Women's Evangelistic Committee. The organization's main purpose was to recover human rights and to free our nation from Japanese rule. They said, "We should love our country as we love our home. Just as our home cannot function well unless we love our home, so our nation is not preserved when our people do not love our country." They proclaimed that all should march forward to accomplish that purpose. However, Japanese police imprisoned all of the staff members of the Women's Patriotic Association.

Church Women Were Witnesses. The evangelistic task of the Church Women's Witnessing Committee was organized at Nul Dah Ri Church in Pyung Yang in 1898. Lee Shin-Haeng was the first president of the committee. She dispatched evangelists to the places where no churches existed and founded many churches. Many Protestant churches were established by women in Korea. Here I quote one of the examples from the *Presbyterian Women's History:*

> Korean women played a remarkable role in establishing new churches. In 1899, about forty housewives gathered and organized a witnessing committee in Chang Yun, Kyung Sang Nam Do. They opened the map of the five neighboring subcounties and marked places where the gospel of Christ should be spread. They visited each place, witnessing for Jesus and established churches. They not only made efforts in establishing churches in our country, but also in evangelizing the whole world. The National Women's Evangelistic Association sent Mr. Kim Soon-Ho to Sang Dong City in China along with five women missionaries in 1931.

Korean church women are expediting the goal of world evangelism in many homes and institutions in Korea where missionaries are being trained.

Church Women Were Educators. The National Women's Evangelistic Association began to establish Bible schools such as Pyung Yang Women's Seminary and Wonsan Martha Seminary and many others in different areas. Many women leaders and laymen were trained and given intensive Bible instruction in these' schools. This great task achieved by women will be highly praised forever.

The Present Role of Women in the Korean Church

Though I will not make an interdenominational survey of today's church and the role of women, I will summarize the contributions Presbyterian women made to the growth of the Korean church from the year of 1970 until today.

National and International Evangelism. The strength of Korean church women is their vision for evangelism. For example, the budget of 1981-1982 for the National Presbyterian Women's Evangelization Association was 12,000,000 won (U. S. $ 17,140.00) for evangelism out of the total amount of 20,000,000 won (U. S. $ 28,570.00). National and international evangelistic work includes special evangelism for underprivileged people in our society. The activities of the association in cooperation with the various branches of the denomination may be tabulated thus:

Purpose of Activity	Location	U.S.Dollar Value
Establishing new churches	359	$ 117,412.00
Special evangelism for prisoners, prostitutes, women laborers, mine workers, policemen,		

crew members, and industrial evangelism	335	83,600.00
Military evangelism	335	170,360.00
	Total	$ 371,372.00

The above figures do not include the work of women's evangelistic committees in each local church.

Ever since the gospel of Christ entered Korea, church women have had a strong spirit of evangelism. They sent missionaries to Indonesia ten years ago and established kindergartens and primary schools and are planning to establish the Hope Middle and High Schools in 1984. More than 500 church members and primary school students witness for Jesus to Indonesians. The women are reaching Korean residents in Japan, China, and Hong Kong and are eager to reach people in Mainland China.

Church Democratization and the Development of Women's Abilities. Generally speaking, in the 1970's women's rights and issues were greatly emphasizad internationally. Presbyterian women pleaded for the ordination of women elders as early as 1933, but ordination was not even made a subject of discussion at the General Assembly. Women have been continually bringing up the subject for discussion in the Presbyterian General Assembly during the past forty years.

They have now come to the conclusion that their objective can be realized only when the churches are democratized. To make their dream come true in the near future, they have conducted seminars since 1974 on the "Development of Women's Abilities" to enlighten church women about the practical utilization of their resources. Their educational policy to democratize churches is to awaken women to their potential so they will be good stewards of their God-given gifts. The women adopted the following resolutions and petitioned the General Assembly meeting for:

a) The establishment of a laywomen's training center.

b) The improvement of the position of women evangelists and their participation.

c) The establishment of an old people's college for the use of their surplus resources and as a lodging place for women evangelists.

d) The democratization of Christian homes (democratization of the church begins at home).

To establish the Scriptural view of Christian homes, church women studied the Bible and conducted various seminars and panel discussions on children's education. They invited leading Bible scholars and researchers on the Christian home to teach them. They also held a special lecture on two themes, "Women's Liberation" and "Women's Law," in 1974. They signed a petition requesting revision of the family laws and submitted it to the Republic of Korea National Assembly.

From the beginning, church women, believing they were doing God's will, took the initiative in seeking social justice and in recovering women's rights. Certainly women play an important role in democratizing their homes. Their position and responsibilities in the home not only contribute to the formation of their children's character but also deeply influence their family's mental and physical growth.

Humanization of Women. I mentioned the role of women in democratizing churches, but now I will discuss women's issues, illustrating with some examples.

Three-fourths of the people in Korean churches are women. Therefore, the issue of women in the church is of great concern for we know that training them correctly and utilizing their power will make a unique contribution to Korean church growth. They cannot make a positive contribution to church growth unless they are rightly trained. Even when the Korean church was growing rapidly in number, many laymen were led into heathenism or mysticism. About 90 percent of those so misled were women. This shows the urgency of training women. Generally speaking, people think "Women's Rights," "The Fourteen Movement," and the "Women's Liberation Movement" are the only women's issues, but Korean Presbyterian women face many other issues.

Laywomen should have an opportunity to study general theology, women's theology, and missiology so they can effectively serve the Lord in the church. Plans to establish an education center for women for this purpose are being made. Laywomen need to understand missiology correctly so that they can understand their proper role in evangelism.

The humanization of women means they should serve in their proper roles according to their ability without discrimination. Women enter and graduate from theological seminaries with the same qualifications as men but women cannot serve as church pastors. Also laywomen who have the ability to administer and the qualifications to be elders cannot become members of the highest decision making committees.

The women of the presbytery made up a questionaire on women's ordination. They asked why women could not be ordained. The answers and the percentages responding are as follows:

Women cannot be ordained because of the
traditional custom of men's superiority
complex.   41%

Women's ordination is not the teaching
of the Bible.   26%

Women's ordination is not a proper time
yet, and many other reasons.   14%

Therefore, democratizatization and humanization of the church should soon be obtained.

The evangelism committee of the Sixty-sixth Presbyterian General Assembly sent questionnaires in 1981 for the study of evangelism policy to its 642 members. One question asked was: How do you think we should handle the task of women's ordination (women pastors and elders) which has been suspended for such a long period of time?" The answers and percentages of responses were as follows:

We should allow it for the conscience of
our faith and the extension of human
rights.   31.66%

We don't oppose it, but it is not yet
the proper time.   35.74%

We cannot permit it according to the
tradition of our General Assembly
meeting.   30.70%

We believe that the ordination of women will eventually be realized. Some expect it to be granted in 1984 when we celebrate the 100th year of Protestantism in Korea.

Cooperation Between Men and Women. In the Bible, women are to be men's helpmates. Men and women should not struggle against each other. The women's rights movement is not taking away men's rights but changing our present system which puts men first. The movement seeks to establish a system of cooperation between men and women. Both men and women should work together to build a bright and harmonious society. Women need to take part in the different areas of our society to develop their abilities. (God created the different characteristics of men and women). The army and other areas of society need men who have physical strength, but women are most needed in bringing up children. Surely, these differences do not mean that men are superior to women; these are only differences of personal ability and adaptability between men and women.

Future Role of Women in the Korean Church

We rejoice that the present membership of Korean churches is rapidly increasing. The large number of laywomen in the church can be a powerful force to stimulate the growth of the church in the future. To accomplish this, the social system must be revolutionized so as to improve the role of women in the homes and the utilization of laywomen in the church, based on equality of the sexes and human dignity. At the same time, the skills of laywomen should be continually developed so that they can rise to the challenges of our time as wise and faithful stewardesses of the Lord.

Church women are witnesses--all of us are evangelists. The fact that our number is so large means that we can expect much of ourselves. What then are the urgent tasks for the Korean church in the 1980's as it celebrates the centennial of Protestantism in Korea?

In planning for the future, we should consider three basic matters.

First, we should train laywomen who are dedicated to evangelism. No group in the church is as strong in the spirit of evangelism and as devoted to service as the church' women. Thus far, we have committed our lives and possessions to God. Therefore, it is our great responsibility to help establish evangelistic policies, to encourage Bible study, and promote practical theology among the laymen. These are the foundations upon which the spirit of evangelism rests. And these foundations are badly needed in our pluralistic, industrialized society. This society challenges our sense of duty, demands a lifetime of service, and expects us to remain faithful unto death and to cope with its highly developed culture.

The *second* reason why laywomen need to be trained as witnessing women is that our society can no longer keep women in the roles of the traditional system. If churches do not make use of their varied talents, women will seek fulfillment in secular activities. The church will suffer from the loss of these talented and capable workers. The church's evangelistic outreach will be greatly reduced by this loss.

Third. The church in Korea not only sends missionaries around the world, but she also feels a keen sense of God's providence as it relates to world evangelism. Without further elaboration, it is obvious that God is working through the Korean church in a special way.

A number of Korean young people are being trained in theological seminaries here and abroad. They study the evangelistic policies of world church leaders, the Korean church, and the trends of the ecumenical movement. We expect Korea to produce world evangelistic leaders who, because of a background of centuries of suffering, will be able to meet the needs of a suffering world.

Looking to the future, Korean church women should recognize the church's potential not only in terms of numerical and financial strength and the size of her churches. Women should also recognize the qualitative aspects as well. We want to see trained laymen and laywomen become effective saints who have the assurance that God has called them. We want to see believers who abide in God's Word and who become true disciples of Jesus. The person who proclaims the cross of Christ must share the sufferings of others.

The church should also seek to extend the service of the church through its laywomen. Korean church women have contributed so much to the church's growth during one hundred years of Protestantism, but very much still needs to be done. If they are to respond to this challenge, church women need to do the following:

1. They will need to study evangelistic policy and cultivate administrative ability.

2. They will need to promote Bible study so as to establish a spirit of evangelism.

3. They will need to promote women's evangelistic work by discovering talent and developing financial resources.

4. They will need to strengthen the church women's sense of responsibility to society.

5. They will need to cultivate the church women's ability to promote church growth.

We must confess that in comparison with church women in other countries we have our weak points. To overcome these weaknesses and to become even more effective in the years to come, our Korean church women must give top priority to the following:

1. They must be encouraged to have intensive Bible study and to publish reference works suitable for the laity.

2. They must concentrate on the study of church educational materials, such as helps for Christian mothers on how to rear their children in the fear of the Lord.

3. They must make use of such media as newspapers, mag-

azines, and other Christian literature plus radio and television broadcasts in their evangelistic outreach.

4. They must experiment in the development of new methods. The experiential knowledge obtained through diagnosis and evaluation should save time and money and contribute toward effective evangelization strategies.

5. They must have a sense of responsibility for world evangelism and cultivate the potential for church growth through interdenominational and ecumenical cooperation.

6. They must maintain contacts with women's organizations in general so as to develop effective strategies and programs for evangelism.

7. They must emphasize the training of female Christian leaders by strengthening their ties with other world organizations of church women.

Finally, I emphasize again the importance of the ordination of women pastors in the near future for the evangelization of the whole world.

Rev. Kim Chang-In, founder and pastor of the Chung Hyeon Presbyterian Church is also president of the Chung Hyeon World Mission Center and the Mission For North Korea. On 1967 Rev. Kim organized the Police Evangelism Association and in 1970 was elected moderator of the Presbyterian Church.

The practical application of church growth principles that have caused the Chung Hyeon Presbyterian Church to increase from 18 believers in 1953 to 10,000 members today are emphasized by Kim Chang-In. This paper was presented at the Wheaton '83 Consultation, Wheaton, Illinois, June 20-July 1, 1983.

15 A CHURCH IN MIDDLE CLASS SUBURBIA: SECRETS OF GROWTH IN THE CHUNG HYEON PRESBYTERIAN CHURCH

by Kim Chang-In

Historical Background

I thank the Lord for giving me this opportunity to report about the growth of the Chung Hyeon Presbyterian Church. Instead of giving only theoretical principles, I want to share experiences from my past 40 years of pastoral life, especially the 30 years that I have ministered at the Chung Hyeon Church. I sincerely hope that some of the principles emphasized in this case study will contribute to the growth and development of the church worldwide.

I was born November 18, 1917. at Euju-kun, Pyungan-buk-do, North Korea. Even though my childhood was spent under Japanese occupation, I embraced the Christian faith of my parents. When I was in middle school, I had been already commissioned as a servant of the Lord so I did not hesitate to preach the gospel in the pulpit from that time on. At the age of twenty-three, I was a leader of Christians who stood against the Japanese government over the Shinto shrine issue.

Furthermore, I attempted a religious renewal movement in North Korea which the Communists tried to suppress. Many Christians who had joined with my spiritual tutor, Rev. Lee Ki-Sun, to stand against the Shinto shrine worship were imprisoned. They also joined with me in this renewal movement. However, we ran up against a stone wall as the Communists began to persecute Christians severely. So I came to South Korea for religious liberty.

When the Korean War was over, many Christians returned to Seoul to rebuild the churches. It was at that time that eighteen believers established Chung Hyeon Church. The church's facilities were built in a place which was surrounded by several markets. For this reason, middle class merchants have been actively involved in the growth of our church from the beginning. I began to minister in this church on September 6, 1953.

Before Korea came under the rule of the Japanese government, Christianity exerted great power in the northern part of Korea, which was then called the Jerusalem of Korea. These Christians kept their faith pure although they all suffered much under the Japanese and Communists alike. They played a vital role in the churches which became prosperous. Many of these North Koreans became members of our church.

Chung Hyeon Church, which was then established by

eighteen persons, now has 10,000 members, We hold five services every Sunday to accommodate 4,500 adults, as well as
many girls and boys who attend our Sunday school.

I have briefly mentioned the historical background of
our church to explain why it has developed as a church of
middle class people. Now I want to introduce some secrets
of the growth of the Chung Hyeon Church.

Some Secrets of Chung Hyeon
Church's Growth

Spiritual Power and Godliness

In 1907, the Korean churches experienced a great
revival much like the working of the Holy Spirit in the days
of the early church. At first, Chung Hyeon Church consisted of those Christians who had experienced this revival,
and they set a good tradition for our church. Chung Hyeon
Church has always emphasized the work of the Holy Spirit.
It was the Holy Spirit's personal presence, seen in the experience of Ananias and Saphira in chapter five of Acts,
that created the spiritual dynamic of Chung Hyeon Church.
One of the characteristics of this church is godliness in the
presence of God the Father. This pious attitude is shown
clearly in our worship. I have tried my best to see that every
service gives all the glory to God. I have taught · our church
people to root out idolatry and to keep the Lord's Day
holy.

During the worship service I emphasize not only tithes
and hearty thank offerings but also a solemn and pious
attitude of devotion before our Father. Our church people
have accepted my advice with joy and outsiders enjoy our
church's atmosphere and teaching. Many have decided to be
our church members. This is due entirely to the Holy Spirit's
presence which is as personal and powerful as it was in the
early church.

The Pastor's Example of Death to Self

The Apostle Peter says in I Peter 5:3: "...but being examples to your flock." Pastors should be exemplary Christians in every respect. I have made this my motto for my pastoral life at Chung Hyeon Church. I have resisted the big temptation to follow the liberal betrayal of the faith and have defended the conservative, biblical faith to the last, which the church of Korea accepted in its early days.

One day while praying I receved a vision from the Lord. I did not hesitate to carry it out although I received no help and much opposition from others. When I sent missionaries overseas, many people criticized me saying it was premature to attempt it. And when I organized the Mission Foundation for North Korea, I was told it was an impossible, empty dream. Also, when I purchased a lot on which to build our new church fifteen years ago, it was a field of little value. At that time nobody else thought we should buy it, but it has now become a valuable piece of land in Seoul, so my vision has not proven to be a vain dream. All these things have contributed greatly to Chung Hyeon Church's growth.

Since my childhood, I have suffered from consumption with tuberculosis. My pastoral duties have often made me ill from overwork and to cough up blood. However, I have never excused myself from preaching the sermons on Sunday because of illness. I made up my mind that "If I perish, I perish." Witnessing my active faith, our church members have been moved deeply to make strenuous efforts for God, which have stimulated our church's development.

I went ahead before others for the glory of God, and I did not spare my life so as to be an example of the Christian faith. This has given me the wonderful experience written of in 2 Corinthians 4:12: "So then death is working in us, but life in you."

Well-trained Laity

The homogeneous characteristics of our nation have had a great influence on Chung Hyeon Church's growth as well as on the growth of other Korean churches. These characteristics are as follows:

A homogeneous people. An important characteristic of Koreans is that they are a homogeneous people. Our people have the same culture which includes a common language, history, and customs. This common culture has contributed to the remarkable growth of Korean churches and to the speedy propagation of the gospel. Likewise, the growth of Chung Hyeon Church is a result of this common culture.

A persecuted people. In its early days, Chung Hyeon Church consisted of Christians who had been severely persecuted for their faith under the Japanese occupation. Moreover, religious persecution of North Korea made Christians come south over the border. A very large number of refugees flocked to our church. The homogeneous characteristic of these refugees made our church grow in quantity.

A similar occupation. Our church is surrounded by market places. Most of our church members who came from North Korea conducted their businesses in these markets. These Christian merchants preached the gospel to their fellow workmen. Their homogeneous occupation brought them into close association with one another and provided an easy way to lead unbelievers to Christ. This characteristic is one of the secrets of Chung Hyeon Church's growth.

A discipled, united people. Chung Hyeon's people have been discipled and disciplined well. Through tribulation and persecution, the faith of the members of Chung Hyeon Church has been purified and become stronger.

I did not neglect to strengthen our unity by discipling our church members. For example, Chung Hyeon Church appointed pastors to every department of our Sunday school. In 1967, we published our own Bible Teaching Text Books for all groups in our Sunday school. At that time even the

General Assembly of our denomination had not begun to publish Sunday school materials. We also founded many Sunday school departments.

I established the Mission Foundation for North Korea and the Special Evangelical Crusade at a time when nobody else dared it. This undertaking was due totally to the amazing grace of our Lord in that I attempted them at that time. Now about 1,000 volunteers of the Special Evangelical Crusade are being trained within and without the church.

Because I am convinced that Bible teaching is vital for the church and its growth, we are operating the "All-the-church-members Bible Class" at the Chung Hyeon Bible Institute. This class is divided into a pastors class, an elders class, a class for ordained deacons, and a church employees class.

The Establishment of Church Goals and Strategy

In 1963 on the tenth anniversary of our church's founding, I found it very necessary to determine principles for my ministry. While I meditated on this, God reminded me of Psalm 18:1, "I love you, Oh Lord, my strength," which I then adopted as the permanent motto for our church. My pastoral goal, however, is not only to make the Lord my strength but also to disciple our church people to love God with all their heart and soul. My goal is also to raise up workers for the Kingdom of Heaven. Accordingly our church established five goals, such as, "to train Christian workers," "to evangelize North Korea," "to evangelize our whole nation," "to evangelize the world," and "to build a new church building." Our church members pray constantly for these definite goals.

These five goals have become one of the secrets of Chung Hyeon Church's growth. These goals challenge us to pray about our responsibilities for the church worldwide as well as for the local church. From the early stages Chung Hyeon Church established goals and objectives like these and developed strategy to carry them out.

A Concerted Effort to Evangelize the Nation

In the early days of Western missions in Korea, Korean churches were diligent to preach the gospel to people. Chung Hyeon Church solidified its footing by developing faithful Christians who dared to risk their lives for the Lord. Our church has done its best to disciple them well. Consequently, our members hearts burned with love to lead their family, friends, and neighbors to Christ through their church. Not only young men, but children, and even the aged devoted themselves to the growth of the church. As a result, Chung Hyeon Church was so crowded with people that it had to enlarge its space every week.

At first the objective of this evangelization was to convert mainly people who lived around our church. Then our goal was extended to the evangelization of our nation, including fishing and farming villages and the military.

Chung Hyeon Church expanded its ministry systematically. In 1954, the Women's Mission was organized. Its members provided the church with necessities such as raising funds for expanding our church facilities and supplying labor if necessary. Moreover, they provided financial support to build churches in the country and to help weak churches until they could support themselves. Through these activities, Chung Hyeon Church was well known to the country churches. And when their members moved to Seoul, they became our church members.

As of 1960, our church began to be more directly involved in evangelizing rural and country churches. For the first time a Young People's Mission was delegated responsibility for the rural churches to enlighten people there. They preached the gospel while they worked together with its farmers and fishermen.

In 1966 the Pastors' Committee for Police Mission was organized to evangelize all the policemen in our nation. I was elected as first chairman of the committee. To this day this mission has contributed to the evangelization of policemen.

The military provides golden opportunities for fishing for souls. We discipled the soldiers at our church, who in turn, have won other soldiers to Christ. On April 25, 1972, several assistant pastors and I had the privilege of baptizing 3,473 soldiers at one time.

Also our church organized Bible Clubs for boys and girls who had to work because they could not go to school. We also organized an Office Workers Mission for office managers and their staff. The Prison Mission was organized for criminals, and some of them became our church members if a good opportunity was given to them after they were released.

To carry out such diversified missionary work, our church organized a Mission Committee. We also enlarged its organization and designated pastors to supervise its ministries.

I suppose someday South and North Korea will be united under one government. At that time we may determine by voting what type of government we want to establish in Korea. In order to prepare for this, I think churches in South Korea should have over twenty million Christians. Therefore, we can not be too diligent in evangelizing our people, and this would also benefit our respective churches. For this reason, I hope all of our churches will take an active role in evangelizing our nation.

Christian Education for Training Workers

A representative example of the growth of our church can be seen in our Sunday school. I realized early in my ministry that God regards this to be very important. As Christian education is very important for us, I adopted the goal for our church on the tenth anniversary of the church's founding: "To raise up workers for the Kingdom of Heaven."

Our Sunday school has sixteen departments, classified

by the age, type of occupation, etc., of our members. For these respective departments thirty-seven ministers are on hand to give the benediction and to disciple useful workers. We organized a Teachers Training Department for our Sunday school in 1971. People who want to be Sunday school teachers must be trained in this department.

We are the first church in our country to organize an Infants Department, a Newly-weds Department, and a Department for the Aged. The special programs of these departments have contributed greatly to the growth of our church.

The Infants Department was born in 1975 when the parents of our church realized the importance of early education. As they realized more and more the importance of early Christian education, our Infants Department was expanded. So by 1977, the Infants Department held two services and by 1978 it had three services on Sunday. Today, its members have increased so greatly that the department holds five services every Sunday. Besides these, we have special departments such as the New Believers Department and Office Missions, etc., which are very productive, also.

In the future, I plan to emphasize the Sunday school and to strengthen its potential more and more, rather than to establish an ordinary day school managed by our church.

We have appointed good leaders in each department of our church who are willing to serve for their entire lifetime. We are sure that fruitful results can be expected from well-trained Christians. Many pastors from our church are studying in the United States of America so as to be capable workers for the Kingdom of Heaven.

Home Visitation and Cell Groups

Chung Hyeon Church had much concern for home visitation in its early days. We divided and expanded our home cell groups continuously. The cell group system is very productive in Korea because the Korean people have good neighborhoods.

The Korean churches, including Chung Hyeon Church, were convinced of the importance of home visitation in its early days, so pastors devoted much effort to it. When Chung Hyeon Church was established, we assigned many evangelists for home visitation and strengthened the cell group system as the number of church members increased continuously.

In 1955 our Church had 16 cell groups and by 1983 it had 631 cell groups. Since 1973 our church has trained the cell group leaders with a regular curriculum. The subjects in this curriculum are as follows: how to study the Bible, worship and godly life, Christian fellowship, the doctrines of our church, stewardship, personal evangelism, follow-up of new Christians, home visitation, the cell group system, and the Christian's social life.

At present one cell group usually consists of five families. Through this cell group system and home visitation, we extend our fellowship. Our church members, especially cell group leaders, are greatly concerned about their witness in matters of personal importance such as weddings, sixty-year-old birthdays, funerals, etc. As a consequence, some unbelievers who attended these ceremonies were deeply moved and became Christians.

Our church especially takes care of people who are over seventy years old. I have personally visited these people in order to comfort and encourage them to hope in heaven.

Mission to North Korea and to the World

Though I am not a specialist on missions, I am convinced that missions is a battle. To engage in missions is to fight with the powers of evil so as to deliver people and to protect them from Satan. Therefore, missions are really difficult as we Christians must fight with the enemy. As soldiers we cannot spare ourselves.

For this reason, as the pastor of Chung Hyeon Church, I sent missionaries for overseas battle even when it seemed to be very premature for our church to engage in such an endeavor. I am convinced that the more we are concerned about missions overseas, the more we will accelerate the growth of our church. Therefore, in spite of many difficulties, we organized the Overseas Evangelical Missions Association November 24, 1968, in our first step towards world evangelization. Three years later on September 9, 1971, Chung Hyeon Church sent Rev. Su Man-Soo to Indonesia as our first missionary.

During fifteen years of mission, we have sent seventeen missionary couples to twelve countries and at present, there are twelve couples ministering in twelve regions. Some of them minister to Korean residents abroad and some of them minister to the natives in these regions.

In January 1983, the Overseas Evangelical Missions Association enlarged its organization and it has been renamed "Chung Hyeon World Mission," whose staff is busy to prepare for moving its office to the Mission Center in our new church complex on August 15, 1983. Until now world missions have functioned and will continue to function as one of the most important elements in the growth of our church worldwide.

As I mentioned earlier, the Mission Foundation for North Korea was organized several years ago and the Special Evangelical Crusade workers have been trained. Their initiative in evangelizing North Korea and other Communist nations has refreshed our church.

I emphasize evangelizing North Korea, believing God will surely give us an opportunity to build a church at Pyung-Yang in North Korea as He allowed us to do before the Korean War. For this purpose we are attempting indirect evangelization through Gospel Broadcasting Systems and third nations. Today faithful volunteers have been trained in prayer for this task, waiting for the time when the door to North Korea will be opened to missionaries. Missionary specialists to Communist countries including North Korea are studying and planning strategies to reach Communists for Christ.

The Key Factor:High Quality Leaders

There are many contributing factors in church growth, but none are as important as the quality of ministers. They should be highly qualified for their respective departments. I am sure that our Lord has enabled us to assign good ministers to every department, including missions. Several of our missionaries have continued to work efficiently for more than ten years in foreign countries.

On the tenth anniversary of our church I prayed, "Oh Lord, if every department of the Sunday school would have its own minister, we would need more that fifteen ministers." The present number of our church's ministers, including twenty ordained pastors, is sixty-one. We are planning here-after to appoint ministers as specialists.

I believe that organization is important, but we appoint according to the basic principle that "people are more important than organization."

Expand Facilities According to Growth

A church building should be a place to worship God and to perform our responsibility more effectively. As much water needs a large vessel and every vessel has its purpose, so a worship place and its adjunct buildings should be used according to their respective purposes.

A church's facilities should accommodate its present and projected future growth. Often we have been forced to build a larger church facility every five years or more because of our rapid growth in numbers. Due to our rapid growth, extension of the church building was inevitable within three years. Rapid growth has continued, making the present church building more and more crowded so that five worship services are necessary now.

In 1970 in expectation of this growth, we bought a piece of land of 19,800 square meters for a new church building. On May 25, 1978, we conducted the ground breaking ceremony. And by August 1983 the education building, the Mission Center building and part of the main church building will be completed The entire construction project will be finished in 1986, and the estimated cost is about 15 million dollars.

All the funds for this construction have been supplied through the saints by the grace of our Lord without any help from outside the church. Our conviction to construct the new church building with money given by God Himself makes this one of the largest church buildings in Asia built entirely through the sacrifice of the members themselves.

We believe that this new construction will allow us to receive and educate the new lambs of God at the right time and in the proper place so the church can continue to grow. Our Lord is looking for those who are prepared to lead His lambs to Him. Let us do our best to be so prepared and then God will surely bless us.

The True Nature of the Church

My beloved brothers and sisters! In closing I suggest that we meditate on what is the nature of the Lord's church. What do the words "I will build my church" mean? Let me express my opinion. The church of Jesus Christ is:

1. The spiritual body of Jesus bought by His priceless blood.
2. A spiritual pasture for the chosen people of the kingdom.
3. A spiritual school to educate for worship in the

heavenly kingdom.

4. A training center to disciple crusaders of the cross.
5. A spiritual hospital to heal diseases of the soul.
6. A sanctuary to meet the Lord.
7. A place to receive grace from God.
8. A resting place to find Comfort from God.
9. A refuge for protection by God.
10. A branch office to glorify God.

I have presented the reasons for our church's growth among the middle class people of surburbia in Seoul, Korea. I have tried to show herein the crucial features of our church. I now hope that this explanation may be a helpful model for the growth of other churches in the world. As a reminder, I wish to share with you my favorite Scripture verse, "I love you, Oh Lord, my strength."

Dr. Kim Sun-Do, Senior Minister of the Kwang Lim Methodist Church and President of the Korea Institute for Pastoral Ministry was educated in the Haeju Medical College (B.S.), Methodist Theological Seminary (B. D.), Wesley Theological Seminary in Washington, D. C. (M. R. Ed.) and Fuller Theological Seminary (D. Min.). Dr. Kim is lecturer in seminaries and author of several books including A Dialogue of Hope for the Modern Men and The Root of True Happiness.

Some people think that pastoral care and counseling are possible only on an individual basis. Dr. Kim Sun-Do recognizes the importance of personal contact but also utilizes the pulpit ministry, home visitation accompanied by other church officers, and interpersonal relationships developed in cell groups. In these ways the laity are encouraged, instructed and trained to reach out to others. These ideas will be helpful to pastors of both large and small churches.

16 PASTORAL CARE AND COUNSELING

by Kim Sun-Do

Since the Second World War, pastoral care and counseling have become academic disciplines for research and practice around the world. Consequently, many professional pastoral counseling and care centers have been established in different parts of the world. In Korea, a course dealing with this subject has been offered as part of the seminary curriculum since 1950. Today, all theological schools in Korea are giving special attention to pastoral care and counseling in order to help the church grow quantitatively and qualitatively.

In fact, the Korean church had practiced family visitation long before the Western church launched academic research on pastoral care and counseling. From the beginning of the Western missionary movement in Korea approximately 100 years ago, the Korean church practiced a family visitation program, even though the program had no academic foundation. Family visitation helped the Christians to grow spiritually and to solve many personal problems.

The uniformity of Korean language and culture is an advantage for the Korean church and for pastoral care and counseling. This uniformity facilitates communication and dialogue among the people and contributes to the fast growth of the church in Korea.

When Western missions began working in Korea, the Korean people were facing many political, psychological, and economic difficulties. Added to the threat from Japan and China was the fact that Buddhism and Confucianism had not really given the people peace of mind tranquility. People in Korea began to experience peace and harmony only when the gospel of Christ liberated her people from their sins and brought physical healing to the sick. For Koreans who were suffering under Japanese colonial rule, the gospel was good news, not only because it met their spiritual needs but also because it brought mental and emotional satisfaction. The gospel not only gave the Korean people a future hope. It also gave them courage to go through difficult times, that is, it gave them a sense of belonging, peace of mind, and present satisfaction. Consequently, a new type of relationship developed between the pastor and his congregation because he brought the hope of salvation and God's love to the people. A number of characteristics of pastoral counseling and care in the Korean church are described below.

Pastoral Care and Counseling Through
the Pulpit Ministry

Rev. Emerson Fosdick, formerly a renouned preacher

in America, said that preaching is one way to counsel. Preaching can give comfort and solutions for the spiritual and
mental problems of the Christians and non-Christians alike.
Many Christians in my congregation go to church primarily
not to learn the ethical teachings of Jesus but to receive
comfort, encouragement, peace, and love to face problems in
their daily life. As the pastor, I should communicate comfort-
ing messages from the pulpit so as to meet their needs. Dr.
Howard Climebell believes that the church should be a healing
center for people who have lost the meaning of life and who
are discouraged. Thus, the gospel of Christ can be good
news and a message of hope to heal these people. Dr. Henry
Sloan Coffin, a renouned preacher, mentioned that there
are five different kinds of preaching: expository, doctrinal,
ethical, pastoral, and evangelistic. Therefore, I emphasize that
preaching should not only transmit information but should
also reform and transform the life of the hearers. In preparing a message, I try to evaluate my congregation's life situation and background in order to show how God can meet
their needs. In this way, I try to bring a message of healing,
support, guidance, and reconciliation.

From the history of the Korean church, we learn that
when the people were persecuted by the Japanese during
World War II and by the Communists durng the Korean War
(1950 to 1953), God used preaching to bring comfort, salvation, and hope to them. Consequently, the churches experienced a revival and rapid growth.

In order to preach sermons on pastoral care and counseling, the pastor himself must clearly understand the meaning of pastoral care and counseling. He must have a proper understanding of human relationships and maintain good
rapport with his people. Compassion, empathy, and love should
be the basis for his preaching. Only then will he be able
to help his congregation. A person who has a fuzzy concept
about these things will have an ineffective ministry.

I try to develop a special concern for the individual

problems of my people so as to meet their specific needs in my preaching. Even though I preach to thousands of people in my church every Sunday, I consider my preaching to be like an individual counseling session to solve an individual's problem through the application of the gospel. I observe that my congregation responds to such preaching.

Dr. Emerson Fosdik said that before he stood in the pulpit to preach, he always prayed, "O God! Someone here needs what I have to say. Help me to reach him." Just as the good teacher grasps the content of his subject and understands his pupils, so the preacher must understand the background of his individual members in order to communicate the gospel to them.

I also deal squarely with the consequences of sin in my preaching. At the same time, I always offer God's forgiveness, reconciliation, peace, and joy if they repent. I do not let people go home with fear and a guilty conscience. The pulpit is not the place to condemn and judge. It is a place to offer forgiveness, peace, and love. Consequently, people who experience hardship, suffering, and agony during the week come to church to experience comfort, truth, freedom, and forgiveness.

Home Visitation

One of the strong elements of the Korean church is home visitation. Every spring and autumn, each church conducts a home visitation program. My church members are divided according to different districts. The pastor organizes the home visitation schedule very well and announces it to the congregation well in advance, so that the people will prepare themselves spiritually and psychologically for the pastoral visit.

Along with a district evangelist and three or four other lay leaders in the district, I visit each family to learn about its situation. We have a family worship service together with an appropriate Scripture passage for the family. We listen to the family's problems and then pray, asking the Lord to help them solve their problems.

This home visitation provides an excellent opportunity not only for the pastor, but also for other church leaders to have close contact with each member and to understand their home life. The home visitation often helps the family before their problems become unsolvable. It also provides a pre-counseling opportunity for later counseling sessions. The lay leaders who visit the homes with me testify that the home visits not only help them to understand their fellow members, the visits are also a blessing to their own lives.

Unlike other kinds of work which emphasize organizational structure, the pastoral ministry values person-to-person contacts highly. The ministry can create a deep concern for people and reinforce life-changing Christian fellowship among the members. Church members experience the love of Christ through Christian fellowship. Therefore, home visitation must be centered in the love of Jesus Christ and follow the guidance of the Holy Spirit.

Besides the periodic home visitations twice a year, I also visit families who need immediate attention. This more urgent home visitation not only provides opportunities to bring comfort and joy to the family but also becomes an excellent opportunity for family evangelism. For instance, some of our members experience traffic accidents, tragedies from fire, business failure, delinquent children, various sicknesses, and death. I have the privilege of ministering to these people through home visitation, bringing comfort, guidance, hope, and healing from the Lord. When I do hospital visitation, I usually avoid visting the patients during meal times and rest times. I also try to avoid discussing the nature of medical treatment. Rather, I read Psalm 23 so as to bring the Lord's comfort to the patient, and I pray with him or her. I also pray for the patient's family who may be physically tired and anxiously waiting for quick recovery.

I also visit new members and new comers to our church and those who transfer membership from other churches. I encourage them to be intimate members of our church family. My visit gives them a sense of belonging to the Body of Christ. If a member is transferred to another area and is not visited by a pastor within six months, often the person becomes a backslider. Therefore, we consider the visitation of those who transfer their membership to our church just as important as visiting new believers who want to join the church for the first time. We also have home visitation for those who are deeply discouraged, discontented, and inactive and try to find the cause of these problems so as to help them. If we cannot visit them personally, we will either call them on the telephone or write letters to them.

Pastoral Lay-training Program

It is impossible for the minister to do all the pastoral care by himself in our modern churches. Therefore, the minister has a responsibility to train the laity in order to create a team ministry for the growth of the church. First of all, the minister must discover the various spiritual gifts of the laity in his congregation (Eph. 4:11-16) in order to utilize them for building up the Body of Christ and to provide spiritual blesssings for the lay people themselves.

A church is like an athletic game where the minister plays the role of a coach while the laity are athletes. Unless the coach trains and disciplines the athletes, it will be difficult for them to win the game. One of the main reasons why Christians today do not live a victorious Christian life is because they lack spiritual discipline and obedience to the Lord.

In our church we have a lay training program and during every New Year's week, a lay minister's seminar is set up for all the district lay leaders of our church. We offer laymen courses on Bible study, home visitation, soul winning, pastoral care and counseling, worship, ushers training, etc. This seminar and other workshops for the laity encourage them to dedicate their service to the church for that year.

We also provide serendipity training (group dynamics) in the church. Every Tuesday evening, we have lay training in our church with our district leaders and church staff. For the first sixty minutes, I teach them the content of the Bible study for the following week, and for the next sixty minutes, I teach them methods in personal evangelism, family therapy, pastoral care and counseling, Christian doctrine, and so on. And we also deal with the practical problems of many Christian families.

We spend much time on counseling methodology so that these lay leaders will be able to counsel people in their own districts. The church organizes a special retreat in the countryside to train lay ministers. We also organize family counseling seminars twice a year for married couples in order to help strengthen their marriages.

We also have an all-night prayer meeting every Friday evening from 11:00 p. m. to 5:00 a. m. during which people sing, testify, and pray together for individual requests. If a person in the church is sick, we will pray for him or her. Through this prayer time we express compassion and love for the people in our own church.

Twice every year, in the spring and autumn, the church sets up a lay-leaders training seminar for twenty hours with special lectures on evangelism and church growth so that the laymen will learn and practice the skills and methods of church growth. In the spring, our church also conducts a Bible Knowledge Contest in order to increase the biblical knowledge of believers. Although all members are encouraged to participate in the contest, the lay leaders are especially required to attend for their biblical training.

Every autumn, we have a revival meeting in our church to help stimulate our spiritual life, to renew our dedication to the Lord, and also to stimulate a Wesleyan type of missionary compassion for the lost. This revival meeting provides special opportunity for the Holy Spirit to work, particularly among the lay leaders. Even though they have a knowledge of the Scripture and learn methods of evangelism, if they have not experienced the working of the Holy Spirit, their spiritual lives will not prosper. Therefore, we always emphasize the importance of the filling of the Holy Spirit in the life of a believer. Because of the experiences mentioned above, I am convinced that a major factor in church growth is the mobilizatization of lay leaders through training.

Cell Group Activities

Rev. Eddie Gibbs of Great Britain says that one sign of a healthy church is the multiplication of life cells. He calls this the explosive generation of small groups. Not only the church but other secular organizations emphasize small group dynamics, too. If no small group activity is effectively operating among the church members, church growth will not take place.

Historically, John Wesley started small group activities in the eighteenth century in England and adopted this as the traditional method of training in the Methodist church. Later, other denominations also adopted the cell group method for their churches. Today our church has 650 small groups organized throughout Seoul. And once every week five to six people meet together in different homes to study the Scripture and to pray together. The ideal size of a small group is between five to seven families. If a group grows to more than ten families, then we divide it into two groups.

Modern people in dehumanized urban societies often feel lonely and have lost the taste for life. They need friendship and love from others and a sense of belonging. Cell groups certainly provide an opportunity for believers to meet each other's needs through the love of Christ.

Dr. Halford E. Luccok said, "All the great movements

in Christianity have been based on the training of small groups." Jesus Christ not only spoke to the multitudes, He also selected twelve disciples and trained them to become the founders of churches. By doing so, He laid the foundation of the Christian church in the following generations.

Through small cell group activities, our church has experienced renewal in prayer, Bible study, and fellowship. I will mention here some of the positive results of small group meetings in our church.

Educational purposes

We are able to achieve our educational objectives effectively through small groups. We do this by using small groups to provide biblical training and to discuss matters pertaining to education.

Bible study, prayer, and discussion

The group leaders present biblical content to the people at the weekly small group meetings. They are able to discuss various questions about the lessons, and consequently, a group dynamic is created which promotes the spiritual life of individual Christians and provides opportunities for them to pray for each other.

Opportunities for Christian fellowship

Many urban people who live busy lives do not have much opportunity for fellowship. They obtain fellowship in these small group meetings by eating together, drinking coffee, and discussing matters together. Christian fellowship becomes a vital part of their Christian lives through small groups.

Therapeutic purposes

Through small group meetings, we are able to discover positive and negative characteristics of each member and are able to help each other. If a person is physically ill, we pray for him or her. A number of people in our church have been healed through these intercessory prayers of Christians.

Christian social service

We have been able to teach our people through cell groups how to serve society and to help needy people. The members of our cell groups discuss specific ways to express Christian social concern and participate actively in the distribution of money and materials for needy people in the community. Through this ministry scores of people have come to know Christ as their personal Savior and have joined the church. I, therefore, cannot see how our church could grow apart from the effective small groups operating in our church.

Promote home and foreign missions

Our church has organized a number of mission prayer groups according to the ages, districts, professions, and sex of members in order to promote missions within Korea and in foreign countries. We have altogether thirty-five mission prayer groups in our church: fifteen men's prayer groups, seventeen ladies' prayer groups, and three others according to their profession. These three professional groups are the Luke Missionary Prayer Group for medical doctors, the Philip Missionary Prayer Group for professors, and the Philemon Missionary Prayer Group for businessmen. Different groups pray that our various ministries, such as the rural ministry, medical missions, etc., will be effective means of evangelism. For instance, if the mission fund needs finances, the businessmen in the Philemon Missionary Prayer Group will collect offerings and provide the finances for missionary projects. Each of the thirty-seven missionary groups in our church have approximately forty members. If they grow beyond forty members, we will divide the prayer groups again.

We believe that the church which does not have a missionary burden looses its purpose for existence. When each missionary society finds its own best ways to promote missions within and outside the country, church growth will take place.

I believe that the secret of church growth in Korea rests upon the proper recognition of Jesus Christ as the Head of the church and the unreserved dedication of His people to their Master. Pastoral care and counseling are ways to assist church members and, thus, contribute to the growth of the church.

Dr. Paul Yonggi Cho was born in Korea in 1936 and later converted from Buddhism and miraculously healed of tuberculosis. Ordained in 1961, he is the founding Pastor of the Full Gospel Central Church, the largest church in the world with 325,421 (September, 1983) members. Dr. Cho received the D.D. degree in 1968 from the Bethany Bible College and D. Litt. degree from the California Graduate School of Theology in 1978.

Dr John Hurston was a missionary for 10 years in Liberia West Africa where he was decorated as a Knight Official in the Humane Order of African Redemption. He came to Korea in 1958 and worked with Dr. Cho, serving as Executve Director of Church Growth International. Dr. Hurston is presently director of the American Christian Theological Seminary in Anaheim, California.

A Presbyterian missionary from China introduced the "Nevius Principles" to the Korean church and the Methodist missionaries brought the "Wesleyan Class Meetings." Though these vital principles of church growth are now used widely by most denominations, Dr. Cho's development of the "cell units" captured the attention of church leaders worldwide. This idea is supra-denominational and can be adapted to large or small churches in any culture. Read how this church trains and involves laity in ministry.

I7 MINISTRY THROUGH HOME CELL UNITS

by Paul Yonggi Cho
and
John W. Hurston

There is a popular fable in Korea about a man who visited hell and heaven. When he arrived in hell he noticed that everyone was eating with huge spoons. Each person in hell had one of these spoons, and was constantly striving to dip enough food to feed himself. Since all tried to feed themselves at the same time, there was much confusion, and never did anyone dip enough food to be satisfied. As the man looked around hell he sensed deep dissatisfaction, and a selfishness that resulted in continual hunger.

Then the same man went to heaven. The people in heaven also ate with large spoons, but their manner of eating was different. The people in heaven stood across from each other. One would politely dip his spoon in the food until it was full, then extend the spoon to feed the person across from him. That person would next dip his spoon in the food and feed the person who had just fed him.

As the visitor looked around he noticed that each person smiled. A sense of peace and love filled heaven, and each one was always satisfied. "Ah!" exclaimed the visitor. "Now I understand. Hell is when people selfishly take what is better shared. However, when people desire to give to one another, and cheerfully share what they have, joyously receiving what is given to them--that is different. That giving and receiving is heaven."

Heaven on Earth

We Christians know that there is more involved in heaven than the assessment by the man in the fable. Heaven is a definite place of promise reached by those with saving faith in Jesus Christ. There is, however, a principle of "heavenly" truth in this fable, a principle of unselfishly sharing to meet another's needs, and allowing them to give to us of their resources. This principle is encapsulated in the scripture: "Give unto others what you would have them give unto you."

Throughout the past years of my ministry I have had the opportunity to travel extensively. In my travels I have observed hundreds of churches, and have been able to sense the spiritual climate in many of them. In churches where spiritual prosperity flows throughout the congregation this "heavenly" principle of unselfishly giving and receiving abounds. In churches where the main theme is that of struggle and strife, **many** are concerned primarily with receiving, thus blocking the full flow of God's love through them.

It is not easy to encourage the development of this divine spirit of giving and receiving, for human nature in part rebels against God's precedents. Moreover, many of us pastors are further at fault. We have often allowed a clergy-centricity to evolve in our churches, an attiude that prompts a congregation to remain uninvolved--though distantly concern-ed--pew-sitters. I discovered this reality through a difficult experience in my life, an experience that showed me a chan-nel that could help to make a type of "heaven on earth" a greater possibility in my church.

From Breakdown to Build-Up

My ministry as a pastor began in 1958 with the found-ing of a small tentroof church in a poorer area of Seoul, Korea. Assisted by my future mother-in-law, Jashil Choi, and later by Missionary John Hurston, this church gradually came to a point of growth. Within three years a new church had been built in a downtown area of Seoul, and the congregation was to soon climb to the thousands.

Although the church continued growing, I still main-tained my Bible school concept that the pastor was responsible for doing everything. This responsibility ranged from marrying to burying, from preaching to home visitation, from counseling to baptising. Though I did not realize it at that point, I had developed a congregation of well-intentioned, tithe-giving, regularly attending pew-sitters. I had trained my congregation to eat the Word with large spoons. Unfortunately, in ignorance I had also trained them to be more interested in feeding themselves than in feeding each other.

One Sunday in 1964 the months and years of continual activity overtook me. That particular Sunday morning I preached in three consecutive services; in the afternoon I baptised at least 300 people. During that Sunday evening service while interpreting for a visiting American evangelist, I collapsed on the platform, and was rushed to the emergency room of a nearby hospital. Doctors diagnosed that I had a complete physical breakdown. They strongly recommended that I should only gradually, if ever, return to pastoring.

During the following months of recuperation God showed me a divine alternative in the development of my congregation. God spoke to my heart through the example of Moses in Exodus 18. I realized that, like Moses, I should not be the primary one to be giving in my church. I needed to delegate my ministry and authority to lay leaders, and allow them to more fully comprehend the necessity of giving to and receiving from each other.

In my mind repeatedly rang the phrase, "church in the home." Although we already had scattered home prayer groups, their purpose and potency was only partial. Through the months of recovery I came to understand that God wanted me to put lay leaders in charge of new home groups; these groups needed a teaching and evangelistic thrust aimed at the care of the individuals of each group's community. These groups needed to teach and exemplify the "heavenly" principle of giving and receiving to all those around.

After I grew stronger I shared the concepts God had

placed in my heart with the deacons and deaconesses of my church. Many were quick to say that they felt incapable of such a venture. Others were hasty to point out that this new step would result in my neglecting my rightful job. But I remained firm. God's guidance is never meant to be modified, and He had given me His plan to more fully build up my congregation.

Strangely enough, it was the deaconesses who were first obedient to the call for lay leadership in home groups. The deacons later responded positively. However, before I continue with a history of the home cell units of Central Church, I think that it would be profitable for us to examine some key scriptures. The remainder of this article was written by myself and Dr. John W. Hurston, author of a book on our church's home cell units.

Scriptural Foundations

Lay Leadership and Moses. Leaders need others, under their authority, to share the burdens and time-consuming responsibilities of leadership in order to free leaders for more important tasks. This has long been a recognized reality, a reality evident in the life of so famed a leader as Moses. In the account of Exodus 18:13-27 Jethro, Moses' father-in-law, advised Moses to establish "rulers of thousands, and rulers of hundreds and rulers of tens" (v. 21). This was done for three reasons: 1) in order that Moses would be able to endure (v.23; (2) in order that Moses would be free to be "God-ward" (v. 19); (3) in order that the people would regain peace and harmony (v. 23).

In Numbers 11:11-30 a beautiful account of Moses and some of this layleadership is given. In this account God responds to Moses' cry to lift the heaviness of his burden (vs.11-15). God directs Moses to gather 70 elders, conferring some of the same spirit God had given Moses on this group of elders. It is noteworthy that Moses' leadership is considered to be among the most outstanding in Jewish history and in entire biblical history.

Lay Leadership in the New Testament. Christ Himself had a band of disciples around Him. Much of Christ's effort was aimed at the training of these disciples, as a reading of the Gospels easily reveals. Christ also had what could be termed "lay leaders," with the commissioning of the 70 and the 72.

In Acts 6:1-7 the inception of the appointment of deacons, and lay leadership, can also be seen. Just as in Exodus 18, another level of leadership was established in order that: (1) the Apostles could be free to be "God-ward," giving themselves continually to prayer and the ministry of the Word (v. 4); (2) peace and harmony could be established, especially in response to complaints regarding the neglect of the Greek widows (v. 1). Lay leadership seems to have been a standard in the New Testament from that point onward, with specific qualifications for lay leaders given in both 1 Timothy 3:1-13, and Titus 1:5-9.

From the record of the appointment of the deacons in the Jerusalem church is it evident that the original intent was not to establish an office, but to appoint men to assist the pastors-apostles and to minister to people. It is notable that the noun form of the Greek word for "deacon" was rarely used in the Book of Acts: primarily the verb form *diakoneo* and derivatives. These deacons were selected and ordained (appointed) by the laying on of hands by the apostles (Acts 16:6).

Appointment to Minister. Acts 6:8 through 8:40 shows that the work of these appointed deacons was not limited to serving tables. Some were used by the Holy Spirit for ministry as well. Stephen and Philip, both deacons, taught and preached the Word, with results which confirmed the validity of their ministership.

Tests of Time and Experience. In the chapters of Acts which precede the appointment of deacons it is evident that the church was already full of people serving and ministering. They were "breaking bread from house to house." They were "deaconing" although they had not been appointed by the apostles. The selection of the seven only marked the beginning of a portfolio assignment of specific duties. They had proven their worth as servers. Full of the Holy Spirit's power and wisdom, they had passed the tests of time and experience. Through their appointment they were given authority in their active "deaconing."

The Validity of Deaconesses. Although there is no record of deaconesses in the Jerusalem church, in the churches of Asia women were appointed as well as men. Phoebe is mentioned as a deaconess in the church in Cenchrea (Romans 16:1). The same root word for servant-deacon is used in mentioning other women's names. Priscilla and Aquilla, left by Paul to minister to the church in Ephesus, could be called a deacon and deaconess team (Acts 18:2-3, 18-19). If the appointment of deaconesses is denied in a church, that church suffers from a great disservice.

Worship in the Home. While reading through the Gospel it is surprising how often Christ can be found ministering in the home. Though He usually taught in the temple, Christ met man at his point of need, wherever that need arose.

The fast-growing New Testament Church is our model even today. The following Scriptures taken are from the Book of Acts, for it is there we can see implementation of principles that we need to continue in our present time.

In Acts the word "synagogue" (συνζγωγη) occurs about twenty times, with Christians speaking in the synagogue on behalf of Christ's sake mentioned about eleven times (9:30; 13:5; 13:14; 17:1; 17:10; 17:17; 18:14; 18:19; 18:26; 19:8). "Temple" (ζερον) occurs twenty-five times, three incidents in which Christians taught of Christ in the temple (3:11-12; 5: 21; 5:42). "House" (οικος) occurs at least nineteen times, with there being nine references to times when believers worshiped and / or were taught in a home (2:2; 2:46; 10:24-48; 16:32-34; 16:40; 20:20; 21:8-14; 28:30).

"And daily in the temple, and in every house, they ceased not to teach and preach Jesus Christ" (Acts 5:42). In this verse a blend of teaching both in the formal structure of the synagogue (parallel to our church buildings) and in the informal structure of the home is clearly pointed out. It is interesting that it is in the following seven verses (6:1-7) that the previously mentioned lay leadership evolves. The rapid growth of believers in the early church (6:16) was aided in a great sense not only by teaching done in the formal structure of the synagogue, but also "in every house" (5:2). in which it was previously mentioned that very often they "broke bread... (eating) their meat with gladness and single ness of heart" (Acts 2:46).

The culmination of lay leadership and teaching with worship in the home is evidenced in Acts 7:6, "And the Word of God increased, and the number of disciples multiplied in Jerusalem greatly." The Christians in Jerusalem learned the process of giving to and receiving from each other; and this "heavenly" principle resulted in unprecedented growth.

Historical Tracings: The Home Cell Unit
System at Central Church

The full implementation of a lay leadership which involved heading neighborhood, Christ-centered, home cell units passed through two stages before arriving at its present stage.

In the beginning each lay leader was allowed to teach whatever he or she felt best in the weekly meetings. Some deacons and deaconesses, however, applied their own interpretation of scripture, interpretations that bordered on heresy. For a short while I developed a deep desire to abandon the home groups. But I sensed that God's desire for their continuance remained resolute.

In the second stage cassette tapes of short messages were played during the home meetings. Lay leaders acted more as facilitators, stressing important key points, guiding times of prayer and evangelization, and providing encouragement and advice to home group members. But the taped messages missed an important aspect: the personal touch, the Word made flesh in the speech of the lay leader.

It was then that we moved to the present stage. Home cell group leaders became "carrier teachers," teaching their groups the lesson that they had been taught that week. As senior pastor I teach that lesson on video-tape, a tape that is played for lay leaders to view during the Wednesday training sessions. A month's worth of lessons can be found in the church's monthly magazine *Shinangge*. In this way all are learning the same lesson, and the entire church can grow in the same direction of truth.

Home group leaders are motivated during the teaching shared with them in the Wednesday training sessions; there is also a semi-annual home cell unit leaders' seminar. Group leaders are taught to embellish the lessons they teach with their own insights and experiences, with primary emphasis on powerful practicality.

Home cell unit participation is required of all Central Church's members. It is felt that this two-pronged stress--church and home cell unit participation--results in greater personal and spiritual growth.

Organizational Structure

A sprawling metropolis of nearly nine million people, the capital city of Seoul has been divided into fourteen districts by the Korean Government. Central Church has combined two or three of these fourteen districts into one district, and covers the same geographical territory with eight church districts. Each district is further broken down into seven to twelve sections, each section containing 25 to 95 home cell units.

A district head is appointed over the membership of each district; over each section, a section leader. Neighborhood home cell units are led by a home cell unit leader--usually a deacon or deaconess--and often an assistant leader. Each home cell unit is ideally composed of members from ten households; if the number increases above that, another cell unit begins to form (the apprentice assistant leader then becoming leader of the new group).

Organizatonal Functions

District Head. This man is either an ordained or a licensed minister with ministerial experience reflecting a stable and mature spirituality, capable of pastoring a district. Each district head has a large office in the church, which is shared with his section leaders. Before and after services these offices are used as a place of contact between the district's ministerial staff and the district's members. In addition to daily home vistation, district heads are held responsible for: (1) the section leaders of their districts, and are to meet with them often; (2) counseling the' many delicate problems that arise among the cell units; (3) checking the appointment of each newly suggested home cell unit leader; (4) making monthly reports of units' membership gain or loss; (5) dedicating babies, conducting weddings and funeral services; (6) alternating with other district heads in officiating on Sunday mornings and in preaching during various services; and (7) always being accessible for praying for the sick and for special invitations to home cell unit meetings.

Section Leader. Always a licensed minister, section leaders are carefully chosen by a screening process in an annual meeting of the district heads. A list is made up during this meeting, with final appointment coming from Dr. Paul Yonggi Cho.

The district heads and section leaders comprise the majority of the church's pastoral staff. This staff's day begins officially at 9:00 a. m., with pastoral staff devotions. During this important half hour I focus on preaching a positive message of encouragement and motivation from God's Word. After a time of prayer all divide and meet in their respective district offices for discussion. From 10:00 to 10:30 a. m. the buses leave for home visitation, dropping members of the pastoral staff off at central locations.

Section leaders are responsible for: (1) the home cell leaders and assistant leaders located in their section; (2) visiting the sick daily; (3) visiting new believers (either the section leader or one of the lay leaders visits those who made a decision for Christ the preceding week); (4) heading monthly cell unit leaders' meetings; (5) conducting requested home cell unit meeting; (6) counseling with cell unit leaders over the many delicate problems that arise; and (7) giving a list of members recommended for home cell unit leadership.

Home Cell Unit Leader. It is on this level that lay leadership begins. The home cell unit leader is chosen on the basis of the visible expression of faith in his or her life. This is reflected in such areas as: consistent attendance at church and at home cell meetings, faithfulness in tithing, and enthusiasm and wisdom in his or her Christian walk. It is interesting that the qualification which is given top priority is that a prospective leader must have received the Holy Spirit. After having been recommended by a section leader, Dr. Cho officially confirms the home cell unit leader's appointment by giving him a cell unit leader's certificate.

A home cell unit leader's responsibilities are: 1) to care for the members of that particular home cell unit; (2) to attend one of the weekly training sessions; (3) to head the weekly home cell unit meetings, where they give that week's Bible study, and lead in a time of prayer; (4) to be instrumental, along with cell unit members, in evangelization; (5) to make a weekly written report of the previous meeting handing in the offering taken during that meeting; (6) to faithfully attend Sunday and Wednesday services; and (7) if possible, to participate in the semi-annual leaders' training conference.

A little more than two out of three of the home cell unit leaders are deacons and deaconesses. There was a time when all leaders were deacons or deaconesses. However, demand has changed this pattern. At present a person initially is a home cell unit leader, later becoming a deacon or deaconess during one of the regular installment services.

Assistant cell leaders are considered potential cell leaders, and are encouraged to receive all the apprenticeship training possible. Assistant leaders often join in the semi-annual training seminars.

The Home Cell Unit. Headed by a unit leader, helped by an assistant leader, the home cell unit meets weekly in various members' homes.The home cell unit functions to: (1) build faith into the lives of its members through the teaching of the Bible and the sharing of positive experiences in Christ; (2) allow for faith to flow and grow through prayer for each other's needs and burdens; (3) be an outreach for non-Christians: after each meeting members often go out together to visit non-Christians and invite them to attend Sunday services and home cell unit meetings; (4) build strong bonds of Christian fellowship and friendship among those who otherwise might find themselves lost in the wake of a fast-growing congregation: and (5) to teach the "heavenly" principle of giving and receiving to those involved.

Growth-Producing Elements

The home cell units at Central Church have resulted in greater spiritual growth in the lives of those who participate, and in increasing numerical growth of the membership of Central Church. Though there are many growth-producing elements in the home cell unit system, we will focus only on nine; these aspects are also discussed in a book written about Central Church's system, *"Caught in the Web"* (Hurston, 1978).

Close Fellowship. Close fellowship is necessary for divinely directed giving and receiving. Church attendance can provide a needed source of inspiration and challenge. Nothing, however can replace the closeness of consistent committed fellowship.Home-cell unit members not only meet weekly, but throughout the week often visit, pray and care for each other. If properly directed,this results in deepening spiritual growth and attracts non-Christians to commitment.

Ready Access to an Informed Pastoral Staff. A common complaint I hear among many ministers is that they feel that they are over-burdened with work. They say that there is no possible way that they can adequately care for the people in their congregation as they should. These ministers are correct: no one man, no matter how dedicated, can give each member of the church the care he needs.

That is why ministry as well as authority should be delegated. We have 316 on our pastoral staff (September 1983), with a delegated portfolio. But even they are not enough. For this reason we rely heavily on the lay leaders of our 19,380 home cell units. These home cell unit leaders live in the same communities as their cell unit members, and intimately know and understand each person.

Each week these lay leaders report to their respective section leaders, who in turn report to their district heads. This call to responsibility is reflected not only in weekly and monthly reports, but also in carefully kept home cell unit leaders' handbooks and section leaders' notebooks. The diffusion of information so time-consuming to pastors is primarily handled on a laity level, resulting in an informed pastoral staff readily accessible to minister to those who need their attention.

Systematic Bible Study in the Home. The Word-centeredness present in the ministry from the pulpit is also found in the cell unit meetings. This teaching provides a Scriptural base upon which people can build their lives. Systematic Bible study in the warm atmosphere of the home serves to give members further Bible training needed in the process of their maturing spirituality.

Faith Active and Contemporary in the Community as Well as in the Church. Because the entire home cell unit system is geographically divided each cell unit is established in one individual neighborhood. The truths gleaned from teaching and preaching are applied on a practical basis to the needs of the community. Each neighbor's problems are made the subject of prayer, and active faith is released for God to bring full solution.

Prayer Specific to the Needs of the People. Closely intertwined with the preceeding growth-producing element, prayer is a potent power when properly implemented. In the intimate associations of the home cell unit vague requests become specific petitions. Any sickness or problem is matter of prayer by the entire unit, and prayer is continued until health is restored, problems solved, and faith vibrant and alive. Those with persistent problems are encouraged to spend time in prayer and fasting at the Prayer Mountain, often accompanied by a home cell unit leader.

Opportunity for Laity to be Directly Involved in Evangelism. One district head said that he urges members to: "Keep their ears open in the market place (comparable to the Western supermarket), or anywhere else they might be. If they hear of someone sick or with a problem, that becomes a chance for them to visit those people in their homes, and share with them the Christ who can heal and solve problems." Taught basic scriptural principles in evangelization, members of the home cell units are motivated to search for the receptive. This emphasis on personal evangelism has had four primary effects: 1) the development of love and compassion in the hearts of active cell unit members; 2) a continual growth of faith; 3) a continual increase and multiplication of the home cell units; 4) the realization that each person is a part of the royal priesthood of our Lord.

The Creation of a Spiritual Climate. Many people are shy, or hesitant in expression, in a public meeting. However, when among friends, with their patient encouragement and understanding in the warm atmosphere of a home, it becomes easy to pray, and to yield to the Holy Spirit. Central Church believes strongly that in this New Testament age every individual believer can, and should be, baptized in the Holy Spirit. The home cell unit helps create a climate in which baptism in the Holy Spirit is a comfortable possibility.

Also involved is the creation of a climate in which participants are open to the operation of spiritual gifts. Special emphasis is on the gifts of healing, miracles and faith. The usage of these gifts is directed and carefully watched, so that they will not be used promiscuously, or for the gratification of the individual, but rather for the edification of the Body. In the warm setting of the home--where unanimity in the Body is constanty striven for, and appreciation of those in leadership is cultivated--it is easy to correct abuses, resulting in greater maturity for all those involved.

This climate also avails participants of the opportunity to intimately experience the fact that they themselves are part of the Body of Christ. The uniqueness of each individual, and the function of every member, can progressively clearly be defined as the home cell unit meets from week to week. During these weekly meetings they are studying the Word together, praying together, and learning to "share each other's burdens" (Galatians 6:2). Members are ever reminded that they are part of the Body of Christ, and that in the Body each individual has a place and function. It is within the home cell units in the member's own community that he or she can most closely and realistically experience his or her portion and purpose in the Body.

The Mobilization of Woman Power. The powerful resource of the women in the church is rarely tapped for full utilization. Many of the women in Central Church are married housewives some with limited spare time and great insight into the people of their communities--valuable commodities when put into the Hands of the Master.

Members of each cell unit are allowed to decide the time and day of the week that they will meet, as long as it does not conflict with the church's scheduled services. Usually women of the community meet during the morning or mid-afternoon on a mid-week day, when the children are in school, and the men are at work. The working men have much less spare time, and they usually meet on Friday or Saturday evening.

Women cell unit leaders have shown themselves to be diligent workers. While their husbands are at work they constantly visit, share, witness, pray and minister to those in their community. Women cell unit leaders focus on the other wives in the neighborhoods, and with their gentle touch have brought many into the Kingdom of our Lord.

Reinforcement of the Types of Giving Already Practiced in the Church. At Central Church the principles of financial giving and tithing are preached, and near the end of each service offering bags are passed. Never in the church's history have "pressure offerings" been allowed. Giving is a voluntary act on the part of the people, one manifestation of a giving spirit that permeates all aspects of church life.

Often when members come to a cell unit meeting for prayer for healing or some other difficult need, they will bring a thanksgiving offering. This serves as a symbol of the faith they have in the Lord to meet their needs, and to also continue to bestow His blessings on them. All regular offerings received at the home cell unit are brought to the church, later to be turned into the church's financial office.

The Making of a Member

The extrovert, evangelistic thrust and attention to nurture in the home cell units is credited as being responsible for much of Central Church's membership growth. With a message of positive hope and power in a caring God, non-Christians are drawn to commitment. In one article concerning the phenomenal growth at Central Church it was written: "Such growth is all the more remarkable in that 75% of it comes from the world (non-Christian), and only about 25% from transfers from other congregations or denominations" (The Biggest Little Church in the World" *Church Growth Bulletin,* Vol. XIII, No. 1, 1976, p. 83).

The making of a member at Central Church often begins in the home cell unit level, where a person is made the subject of prayer, and their needs are given special attention. The non-Christian is soon invited to attend a Sunday morning service, with bus or taxi fare paid for by the accompanying Christian friend or friends. Near the close of four out of five of the Sunday morning services there is a time when all who want to become Christians are asked to stand. While standing they are given decision cards to fill out, and return to an offering bag when it is passed.

After information from these decision cards is recorded, it is given to the district heads who preside over those particular areas. The name and address of each person who filled in a faith decision card is then passed down through the channels to the home cell unit leader nearest that individual. The new Christian is then visited in his or her home, or sometimes telephoned, within a week after a decision card is filled out.

During these visits home devotions are usually held. Many times these new converts decide that they want to join Central Church as a member. First an application for membership is submitted; this application is held for a period of three months. During those three months the applicant is visited at least twice in his or her home. If, at the end of three months, the applicant has shown faithfulness and a continuing desire to become a member, information from the application is transferred to a permanent form. At that point the new convert officially becomes a member; if not already water-baptized, he or she is urged to do so during the next water baptismal service. The new member then becomes an even more vital part of his or her home cell unit, an integral and crucial part of church life at Central Church.

Starting Home Groups:
Some Guidelines

Starting home groups in a church is a challenging goal. The drive to initiate home groups must issue from the pastor's heart, and be a Spirit-born desire. If initiated by any other leadership except that of the senior pastor's, and born of just well-intended human desire, the home groups will falter, never to develop their full potential. Organization is an important aspect, especially when used to allow the correct channeling of God-given ministries and gifts. This organization, however, must be flexible and creative: organization is applied to serve man's needs, not the reverse. You must also adapt the concepts of home groups to your specific culture and situation. There are a few units in our church that meet in factories during the lunch hour; others meet in restaurants.

Rebellious lay leadership is frequently a concern. When any in Central Church hear of a rebellious lay leader, that leader is first confronted privately, discussion centering on the importance of unity and the need for all leaders to be an example in obedience. Often that rebellious lay leader will be suffering from a personal problem that wise counseling will help to resolve. If the rebellion continues then the leader is accompanied by another leader to the Prayer Mountain for a time of fasting and prayer; it is unusual for rebellion to continue after this. However, if it does, then that leader is allowed to separate from the church, with any members who wish to follow. The principle involved is this: a pastor's main concern should not be in controlling his home group leaders, but rather with providing practical Scriptural teaching material. And the importance of motivation and personal encouragement can scarcely be overstimated.

One must remember to develop extroverted home groups, groups reaching out to give to non-Christians and to Christians. Constantly instill the principle of giving and receiving into your home groups. Establishing home groups is more of a process than a product, a process that can bring more heaven onto earth and into your church!

Rev. Kwak Jae-Ki is General Secretary of the Rural Life Department of the General Assembly of the Presbyterian Church of Korea. A graduate of the University of Dubuque (B. A.) and from the Theological Seminary, University of Dubuque and Presbyterian Theological Seminary in Seoul, he was ordained in 1968. Participation in several international seminars on community development and organization of credit unions have helped him learn how to mobilze human resource in rural areas.

Much attention is given these days to urban development socially, economically, spiritually, etc. The massive population shifts require this. However the rural people cannot be forgotten. The insights offered by Rev. Kwak will be especially helpful to those living in countries where the rural church still struggles because of inadequate finances and untrained leadership. Principles suggested here will give hope!

I8 DEVELOPMENT OF COOPERATIVES FOR RURAL CHURCH SUPPORT

by Kwak Jae-Ki

A church is a living body. A living body will either grow or die. A church is not merely an assembly of people. The church is a union of the Holy Spirit and God's people. A healthy church will grow naturally. If not, something must be wrong. If the church does not grow, she needs immediate examination to find out the problem. If the cause is found, it must be removed so that the church may continue to grow.

Reciprocal Relationships Between
Rural and City Churches

The rural churches in Korea are like a seed bed for rice. The Korean farmer sows, waters, and fertilizes. The Bible says that one sows and another reaps. This saying is certainly true in Korea's churches. As a result of the emphasis on rice industry in the 1970's, many rural youth left their homes to work in industrial plants in the city. Consequently, urban churches grow rapidly in church membership. God requires us to be faithful to our duty like sowers sowing rice in the rice fields. Christians in rural churches should not complain. They should keep silent, work hard, sweat, and sacrifice themselves in their field of labor, while at the same time expecting a great crop in the harvest. Often it is the urban churches which reap the crops from the seeds that the churches have sown. Urban churches may reap 30 fold, 60 fold or 100 fold. Thus, it is true as the Bible says, one sows and another reaps for God's glory.

Self-support of a rural church can lead to the establishment of new rural churches. We have 4,000 congregations now under the General Assembly, of which 65 percent (2,660 churches) are located in rural areas. Most of these are not self-supporting churches. Once they become self-supporting churches, both economically and spiritually, they come to a turning point where they can begin to work toward establishing a new church.

By contrast 1,400 churches are located in the urban areas, and for the most part, they are self-supporting churches. They have 35 percent of all our churches, and they are responsible to share burdens of the rural churches. The following is the result of the growth of our church: 6 percent Christian in 1966, 16 percent Christian in 1977, 21 percent Christian in 1980, and 25 percent Christian in 1981. In order to make disciples for Jesus Christ, we must plant the seed of the gospel in the hearts of children, youth, men, and women. The sooner the faith can be sown in the hearts of younger children and youth the better for the truth endures forever. We must also take care of people's physical as well as spiritual life.

Factors in Planting Rural Churches

Survey and Plan

If you are assigned to a rural village with pastoral responsibility, what do you do first? You have to know the people and the village situation. In order to achieve the above two goals, you have to make an initial survey. Accurate numbers and right understanding of the situation can be obtained through a correct survey. This can provide more accurate information about the people and the village situation. Statistics can reveal various interesting facts, such as, what are the needs of the people and what are the people's goals in life. Analysis is very important. The statistics should be evaluated precisely so that you can set long term plans for the village ministry. A detailed plan gives direction to the people.

The following four elements must be considered seriously: (1) All decisions must be made by as many people as possible; (2) Discover the urgent needs of the people relating to their lives, income, and benefits; (3) Prepare a simple short term program which can be carried out by many participants; and (4) Evaluate the results of the work, whether it is a success or failure. Describe in detail the successes and failures so the undesirable elements can be taken into consideration by the planner. Make an evaluation every six months or at least once a year.

Cultivate Yourself Constantly

The key of church growth is the pastor. He must be the type of person whom the village people can *trust,* and he must have a sense of *calling* and *responsibility.* A responsible person is one who practices what he preaches. In other words, he does what he says. This kind of person can be trusted because his words and actions are consistent.

As a leader or minister, he must cultivate himself constantly. Self-training helps him to grow continuously. He should train himself both mentally and physically. If we neglect our own education, we are going to stop growing in faith, love, and knowledge. We must keep in mind that we are leaders both in the church and in the community. So we must pray and exercise ourselves spiritually and physically. Our self-training should involve active participation in training seminars, conferences, and discussions.

As leaders or pastors of churches, we must also educate, organize, and mobilize the people and set goals and provide direction. A good leader organizes, motivates, and participates. You can do some things, but not all things. We must train our people to help us to do as much as possible so we can multiply ourselves.

A sensitive pastor sets a high goal in life and walks forward in the right direction so that his people may move and work accordingly; and he is also faithful in training younger leaders.

Arrange for Adequate Living Expenses and Salary

The income of ministers belongs to policies set by the presbytery and by higher administrative levels such as the General Assembly. A great gap exists between the salaries of urban and rural ministers. Urban ministers get much higher salaries which cover the living expenses of their families and the cost of their children's education. But rural ministers get much lower salaries, which do not meet their expenses or pay for their children's education. Consequently, good rural ministers tend to move to the cities where they get better pay. As a result, the villages are constantly losing good ministers. The same is true of lay leaders in the villages because people in the villages receive much lower income in money and crops.

We hired a minister to serve two community churches but it has not worked well for two reasons. First, one of the churches tends to monopolize the minister. And second, the great distance between the two churches hinders his work. So our General Assembly has issued a directive to all the thirty-five presbyteries to standardise the salaries of both urban and rural ministers based on the lower rural salary scale. This policy is carried out by the presbytery within the region. A shortage in a minister's salary is supplemented by urban churches who raise the extra money. This is very succesful in some presbyteries. We have been pleased with such results.

The following are some reasons why ministers evade rural pastoral responsibilities:

1. Insufficient pay to cover family expenses
2. Children's education is a heavy burden
3. Lack of medical care
4. Lack of library facilities
5. Poor communication systems
6. Lack of modern facilities
7. Unavailability of pension plans and insurance

Organize for Mission

The primary duty of a church is missions. The pastor is to organize and mobilize according to his people's talents and lead them into mission activities. So administration, information, and logistics must be focused on the mission of God. Personal cards must be prepared, information collected, and operation and logistical support must be implemented in order to achieve success.

For an effective operation of a mission, the following facts must be taken into consideration.

1) Relevance--determine the needs of the people

2) Effectiveness of the mission depends on the mission organization

3) Basis of mission is the Bible

4) Mission is the ultimate goal of education, administration, and financial support

5) Education must be available for the common people- ladies, children, and peasants

6) Tithing is the financial basis for missions. All people must share the burden and responsibility for missionary activities.

Emphasize Unity in Christ

We are linked with one another horizontally, and we are under the direction of God vertically. It does not make any difference to God and should not make any difference in the body of Christ whether we serve a rural or urban church. We are all in the same mission with a common faith and one heart. We emphasize unity in order to consolidate our efforts in mission.

At the same time, we must assume individual responsibility in mission. This can be done through the "doubling movement"; that is, one Christian converts at least one non-Christian each a year. We have made a survey of the whole country to discover the location of churches and the Christian population density. The results of this survey shows us where we need to start new frontier churches and how to recruit those who will invest and work. We now have 4,000 congregations with 1,200,000 members in the Presby-terian(Tong Hap) denomination. If we continue to grow at the present rate, we will surely be able to reach our goal of mission: 1,500,000 members in 5,000 congregations by 1984.

In the entire country, we have now 7,500,000 Christians in over 25,000 congregations, not including 1,200,000 Roman Catholics. This means that 25 percent of the population is Christian. So we emphasize in our mission call that individual members must be Christian witnesses and actively participate in the various mission programs. The Lord requires each believer to give his or her energy, money, talents, and time as needed.

Encourage Community Development

A church is located in the community and the community is located in the church in a broad sense. The relationship between the two is inseparable. An effective church, therefore, will be a counseling center, a cradle of spiritual growth, and a base for community life. Church and community need to co-operate with each other to promote community development and welfare.

Inevitably, the pastor of a church has to play dual roles: pastor and community leader. Consequently, he has to pay attention to the needs of both and to a development and welfare program for the church and community as a whole.

He has to take the following elements into consideration. First, the *quantity* and *quality* of community *development*. Agriculture is a basic industry, supplying food for the entire population. The second and third stages of industry can be built on the foundation of agriculture. This is true especially in Asian countries, such as the Philippines and Japan. If agriculture is failing, the rest of industry is insecure.

The second element to take into consideration is the *security* of the community. Community security, especially in rural villages is very weak socially, and, yet it is very strong in its conservative attitude. Most of the youth in rural villages have gone to the industrial cities. Those who remain in the villages are the middle-aged and old folks who lack creative ideas, second and third stage industrial skills, and spiritual education. The pastor is the key person who gives assurance and assumes responsibility for the rural community.

The third element which we need to take into consideration is *balanced development*. We know that economic, social, and intellectual gaps exist between rural and urban areas. Seoul has 9,000,000 people and Pusan has 3,000,000 people. These two cities together have 12,000,000 people, which is over 30 percent of the entire population of Korea. And these people own more than 70 percent of the nation's wealth while the remaining 70 percent of the people own only 30 precent of the nation's wealth. This reveals a great economic difference between them. Fair distribution of the nation's wealth is indispensible.

In the 1960's the Korean government emphasized the growth of national industry at the expense of the farmers. In the 1970's, the emphasis was on community development, and in the 1980's, the present government of Korea has the goal of ideal social welfare. This goal, I believe, never can be achieved unless the people's spiritual condition is improved prior to improving economical growth.

Church leaders must assume this responsibility; that is, they must provide spiritual education and discipline. We see the rise in social crimes today. Without a spiritual revival in the nation, we can never have an ideal society and social justice. Political and economic power do not solve social and spiritual problems. We must remember what the Lord said: "Men shall not live by bread alone, but by every word that proceeds from the mouth of God."

The fourth element we need to consider is the *strategy* for community development. A main theme for development must be chosen for our communiity, just as for our nation. Possible themes could be growth, self-reliance, welfare, or security in accordance with community's urgent needs in the near future. To implement these themes in community development, various means can be used, such as adult education, land reform, family planning, leadership development, information gathering, life style improvement, credit unions, rice bank programs, etc.

Develop the Whole Person

The pragmatic, balanced development of both physical

and spiritual life should be emphasized. The church once emphasized individual salvation too strongly at the expense of the believer's present life in this world. To provide the proper balance, the church needs to emphasize more human rights, human dignity, and the human being as a whole person which includes the physical, social, and spiritual aspects of man. Human rights are very important, for we remember what Jesus said: the soul of a human is worth more than the whole world (Mark 8:36).

Education should be emphasized in the following areas: discipline for righteousness, tithing, stewardship, and doubling the membership of the church, medical insurance, pension programs, and social welfare programs in order to meet the needs of men and women today.

Though we rejoice in growth of the urban city churches, we cannot neglect those in rural areas. I firmly believe that these principles will enable us to win our entire nation to Christ.

PART FOUR

LEADERSHIP TRAINING

Dr. Kang Shin-Myung is president of the Soong Jun University president of the Seoul Presbyterian Theological Seminary and pastor emeritus of the Saemoonan Presbyterian Church. He graduated from the Soong Sil College and Presbyterian Theological Seminary in Pyung Yang and from the Princeton Seminary (Th. M.). Later he received an honorary Th. D. from Sterling College. He is also director of the World University Service in Seoul and is president of the Korean Christian Leaders Association.

Why does Korea have so many seminaries and Bible schools where thousands of men and women prepare to become Christian leaders? Why do Korean parents pray that their sons will become pastors when most Asian Christians desire their sons to become successful businessmen? Dr. Kang, a pastor and educator, tells how Korean pastors gain and lose their dignity. Biblical teachings blend with certain aspects of Confucianism to produce Christian leaders serving in 22,000 churches and in various Christian organizations. Dr. Kang's insight focuses upon another "secret" of Korean church growth.

19 THE DIGNITY OF KOREAN PASTORS

by Kang Shin-Myung

Korea, which had been rejecting any contact with foreign countries, opened diplomatic relationships with Japan and the United States of America at the end of the nineteenth century. Soon foreign missionaries entered Korea lawfully and began evangelistic activities carefully but freely. The uniqueness of Korea's evangelism is the fact that missionaries entered here with Korean Bibles, and they met Korean Christians who had their own Bibles.

In 1885 Rev. Horace G. Underwood from the Northern

Presbyterian Church and Rev. Henry G. Appenzeller from the Northern Methodist Church in the United States came to Korea with Bibles. Mr. Lee Soo-Jung had translated this version of the Bible into Korean in cooperation with missionaries while he was studying in Japan.

Rev. Horace Underwood did evangelistic work in Seoul mosty, but made evangelistic tours to Hwanghae Do through Pyung An-Do. Messers Suh Kyung-Jo, Su Sang-Yoon, and Baek Hong-Joon were led to the Lord and baptized by Rev. John Mackintyre from the Scottish Presbyterian Church. These Korean Christians translated Bibles into Korean with the help of Mr. John Ross in Manchuria and distributed the printed gospels as they witnessed for Jesus in their hometown of Eui Joo City. They tried to pierce the nearby boundary between Manchuria and Korea, risking their own lives since the gospel was not allowed to be spread in Korea. This explains why Mr. Underwood met Christians when he came to Korea who had their own Bibles.

This kind of evangelism became traditional in the Korean church. Once a person came to trust Jesus through the gospel of salvation, he began witnessing from the moment he believed. Although he was not trained at Bible school or in the theological seminary, he had a deep compassion for dying souls and witnessed for Jesus with great joy and assurance of salvation in his heart.

Such a movement coincided with the Nevius method which was introduced later. Presbyterian missionaries in Korea adopted and encouraged this method; thus the Korean churches grew rapidly. The Nevius method means self-propagation, self-support, and self-government by the church.

In Korea when one comes to know the Lord Jesus, he leads his family, friends, and fellow workers to Jesus. Every member of our church in the countryside where I grew up diligently visited non-Christian neighbors' houses at least once a week to win lost souls to Christ. Once a month or several days a year some members visited homes regularly in the villages two or three kilometers away from our church. I saw them finally establish some churches there.

Sunday mornings after an early breakfast when I was about ten years of age two or three of my friends and I walked to a neighboring village two kilometers away to bring many children of our age to church. After faithfully coming for several weeks, the children decided to come to church by themselves. Almost all the church members did this kind of personal witnessing. When the number of new converts increased, churches were established by those church members who voluntarily won people to Christ.

As these churches grew, they invited pastors to lead their churches. Early pastors had studied Chinese litera-ture. They became evangelists after studying the Bible and church history at Bible schools in the countryside and after taking a written test. Churches established in this manner were run independently according to their own policy.

Church members used democratic procedures to select deacons and elders and to invite their pastors. When early churches were run in this way, all the church members proud-ly took part in the church activities although they didn't use the word "democracy." The members loved their church dearly because of this participatory democracy. They hurried-ly returned home even if it were late on Saturday evening to take part in Sunday worship service the next day at their own church. They valued the church in which they worship-ed God more than their own homes.

Some pastors and scholars criticize the self-supporting policy of the Presbyterian church to which I belong. Jesus said, "For where your treasure is, there will your heart be also" (Matthew 6:21, NIV). Church members grow to love their church dearly when they offer material possessions to the church. I have never seen a church grow and prosper that was built and its pastor supported by sources outside the church itself.

However, I have seen many a small church grow

numbers when it was built with offerings from the church members. Members love such churches with all their hearts and are full of thanks and joy whenever they come to church. But when pastors are sent to churches through help from outside, both the invited pastors and church members feel as if the pastors are guests. Consequently, close contact between the pastor and the members is lacking.

Churches in the countryside or in the mountains which followed the policy of self-support had many difficulties. Although they had built their own church, the members were unable to maintain it or to support their pastor financially; so two churches had to share one pastor and had to adjust the time of their Sunday worship services and Sunday schools. However, each member thought of his church as his own, and he greatly loved his church. Members had a strong sense of stewardship. The pastor was the leader and shepherd who taught his people the Word of God and how to live according to the Scriptures.

The early Korean church enlightened the community because the pastors played a major role as community leaders. The pastors were highly respected and people consulted with them about all the community problems. Pastors were consulted even more when they had a good academic background. Pastors were respected as leaders in the community for two reasons. One reason is that pastors devoted all their efforts to evangelize and to serve the community even though they received a small salary. They worked hard even though they could become materially successful in society with their experience, knowledge, and ability.

The other reason is that church members tried to supply the pastor's needs according to the church's policy of self-support. For instance, when church members gathered Chinese cabbages, they selected the best ones and gave them to their pastors. They willingly and joyfully gave the best chestnuts, dates, persimmons, and pears in the harvest season. As a result, even people outside of Christ began to respect the pastors because they were so highly respected by the Christians.

When Christianity was first introduced to Korea, many problems arose because it banned ancestral worship, calling it idolatry according to the tradition of Confucianism. However, as the Korean people gradually came to understand Christian doctrine, the church understood the difference between idolatry and ancestral worship. Instead of worshiping ancestors, a Christian ceremony has been developed to show respect to their ancestors; consequently, the conflict between Christianity and Confucianism slowly diminished.

The idea of respecting king, teacher, and father is so strongly emphasized in Confucianism that even pastors are given great authority and respect in society. Teachers in society and fathers in the homes have almost the same dignity and exercise almost the same authority as the king of a country. It is natural that kings and fathers exercise authority over their subjects. However, the teacher's authority exists only while he is instructing his students. Although a teacher may be very good, he cannot exercise this authority apart from the teaching situation. In countries like Korea, Japan, and China, pastors are called teachers and are highly respected as spiritual leaders. Most of them have a good education and serve as good leaders in society as well as helping believers grow in the Christian faith.

As the prophets in the Old Testament proclaimed, "thus saith Jehovah," and "the Spirit of the Lord came to me saying, thus saith the Lord," so pastors have authority because they speak with God's words. They speak like prophets of old who always proclaimed the Word of God and boldly told the people what was right and wrong. Nobody respects preachers who flatter people and refuse to tell them what is wrong with them.

However, pastors who are called by God and have a strong sense of responsibility toward that call deliver God's message boldly without any reservation. They speak boldly even though they speak to men of power and high authority as did Elijah or John the Baptist. These God-empowered pastors certainly have an authority no one can question.

The Korean church emphasized and practiced the Puritan, separated life from its early history to the fall of the Japanese empire. Accordingly pastors were the center of the Christian movement. They were like commanders-in-chief. Now, in the eyes of this present generation, it seems as if they were somewhat extreme law-keepers. They recognized the authority of God's Word and tried to live faithfully according to it; their instruction to church members was based on the Word of God. The question with these pastors was not, "Who is doing it?" but "What does the Bible say?" They diligently studied the Scriptures and helped Christians to live according to its teachings.

The reason why pastors today have the authority they do in the Korean church is because they accepted Christianity along with Western culture and taught not only church members but also people outside the church. Pastors were respected for their nobility of character and their ability to instruct people concerning the meaning of life. They spoke as men of God who dealt with all matters according to the Word of God.

After World War II, Korea was liberated from the Japanese rule. The American army stayed in the South while the Soviet army advanced into North Korea. Much turmoil and disorder tore apart the political world. Degenerate ideas from foreign countries began to flood into Korea. In the face of such moral collapse church leaders should have worked hard to stem the tide of decay. But some pastors and lay leaders plunged into politics to gain personal fame instead of standing firm for the truth. Thus, the image of ministers was marred and the authority of church leaders was undermined. Politically, Korea was divided into two sections--South, and North.

Soon the Korean war broke out. This tragic war left

many widows, orphans, and a large number of aged people with no one to care for them. Many widows' homes, babies' homes, orphanages, and senior citizens' homes were organized and supported by overseas voluntary agencies such as World Vision, Christian Children's Fund, Compassion, and the Holt Adoption Agency.

Among the superintendents of these institutions were Korean ministers, elders, deacons, and deaconesses who embezzled support money and used it for their own benefit. Some of them even used the money for their election campaigns in order to become members of the National Assembly. This matter became a public scandal. As a result, the authority of church leaders fell into even more disrepute. Furthermore, many pastors neglected their mission as prophets within the church and stooped to slandering and backbiting each other rather than uniting together. Thus, the Korean churches were divided.

When Korea produced her first seven pastors in 1907, the Northern and Southern Presbyterian churches in the United States, the Canadian Presbyterian Church, and the Australian Presbyterian Church formed one Presbyterian church in Korea. These denominations united together to form one unique Presbyterian denomination in Korea which cooperated in evangelism with the Methodist church. However, authorities say that Korea now has more than forty different Presbyterian denominations, including some which we have never heard about. Because of this confusion and division in the churches, the quality of church leadership has declined and the authority of the pastors has decreased. When such conditions exist, the church can no longer be salt and light in the world.

However, we report with much joy that the churches in Korea now have begun joint evangelistic meetings, Easter sunrise services, commemorative services for the March first independence movement in 1919 and for Independence Day on August 15. Since the 1970's the Korean churches have again begun to do marvelous works and the authority of ministers is being recovered. The authority of pastors will be completely recovered when they do their best to fulfil their responsibility as prophets. This is a privilege granted to pastors which God has not entrusted even to angels.

Mrs. Chou Sun-Ae is dean of The Graduate School and professor of Christian Education in the Presbyterian Theological Seminary, Seoul, Korea, She graduated from the Presbyterian Theological Seminary, the New York Theological Seminary (M. R. E.) and the Graduate School of Education in the New York University. In addition to teaching, she also serves as chairperson for the curriculum committee of the General Assembly for the Department of Christian Education.

Anyone who doubts the value of education, especially education of women, will find the observations of Professor Chou to be enlightening and stimulating. The Christian attitude toward women is much superior to that of other religions. Emphasizing Christian education and providing opportunities are "secrets" for mobilizing the gifts and abilities of women who represent over half of the Christian community in Korea.

20 KOREAN CHURCH GROWTH AND CHRISTIAN EDUCATION

by Chou Sun-Ae

Before Christianity entered Korea, education was generally based on the teachings of Confucius. Shamanism was prevalent until the fifth century and then Buddhism controlled the nation for a thousand years. Meanwhile, Confucianism was introduced to Korea and spread throughout the nation from the fifteenth century. Even today Shamanism, Buddhism, and Confucianism still influence the way Korean people think. When Protestantism was introduced during the late 1800's, Korea had a feudalistic society with a background of Confucianism. This learning of moral teachings was based primarily on obedient behavior to Confucius' ethical instructions. The middle class worshipped according to Confucianism, but Confucian education was not emphasized.

Confucius will be greatly condemned for one thing in particular on the Day when the Lord comes again. This is because Confucius had no regard for women and thought children were the possession of the adults. Education of women meant teaching them how to obey their husbands, do the housework well, and serve their husband's parents. Teaching women to read was unthinkable. Therefore, women could never know the teachings of Confucius nor did they need to know them.

Shamanism was very close to women, and accordingly, they served the devil in all their household affairs. In this respect, Korea was a heathen country where ignorance and darkness prevailed. The evangelistic work of the American missionaries sowed the words of life and truth in the hearts of the Korean people. Just as good weather gives abundant harvest, so God's grace and love made the Korean church grow. If you ask me why Korean churches grew so fast, I would say that it was because of education and the grace of God. In other words, the rapid growth of the Korean church today can be traced primarily to Christian education.

Many factors have influenced the growth of the Korean church. For our purposes we will examine some of them, namely, an awakening to Western civilization and Christian education, mission education, revival meetings, Bible clubs, Christian schools, and leadership training.

An Awakening to Western Civilization and Christian Education

I do not think that the results of evangelization always depends upon the work of the missionary; they depend rather upon the hearts of the people and the work of God. I am not saying that the condition of the Korean people's hearts was much better than the efforts of missionaries, but that God had prepared the hearts of the Korean people, and they were thirsty for the gospel of Christ.

When the missionaries first came, Korea was in political turmoil nationally and internationally. Leaders in society were divided into many different parties, and they did not agree on political affairs. The Korean people did not know which way they should go and were suffering from political difficulties. In the meantime, a group of leaders were awakened to the new Western civilization. They traveled to the United States, Europe, Japan, and many other countries. These leaders came to know Jesus, and they encouraged fellow Koreans with a new vision of nationalism, political independence, and human rights.

This awakening to a new civilization was understood as a movement to save our nation and its people. This awakening was encouraged by the spirit of patriotism in the Christian faith. Churches initiated and promoted this awakening to Western civilization and the Christian spirit fostered the idea of political independence and patriotism.

For example, a report in 1895 by missionaries with the Northern Presbyterian Mission (U. S. A.) stated: "One of the most interesting phenomenon of the Korean church is patriotism. They hoist their national flags on their houses or on the churches." Koreans, who were in a dilemma, because of the political decay of their nation turned to the Christian faith because it gave them both political and spiritual hope. And when they came to know the true way of living in Christ, they encouraged all Koreans to accept Jesus, the hope of the Korean people.

A Christian magazine of that day said, "Only seek the substance of things hoped for, to be civilized by studying the Bible and to be a rich country by studying physics, mechanics, math and chemistry. . . . We pray earnestly that Chosun (Korea) will be rapidly developed as churches spread through-

out Korea . . . ." Therefore, the spread of Christianity enlightened all Koreans and saved them from their dilemma. In fact, many people, when they were blessed with life
eternal, began to work for the salvation of the nation
through Christian education.

They established many private Christian schools. Christian education was never more keenly needed than in those
days. Christians voluntarily and strongly promoted education.
Korean Christians felt it was their responsibility to give
Christian education to all their fellow countrymen for they
strongly believed it was the only way for our nation to
live. This was why they tried to impart Christian education
to Koreans and to implant a spirit of independence and freedom in their hearts by fighting to the end against the oppression of the Japanese.

Christians thought the best way to enlighten the
unlearned masses was to establish schools, so they began
many primary and secondary schools throughout the nation
to meet this great need. They wanted to assure their nation's
political independence by educating the unlearned masses.
This concept not only motivated the early Korean church, it
also motivates the use of Christian education today to establish
a righteous, democratic society as a defense against Communism. Christian educators believe that the distorted values
promoted by secular, scientific, and materialistic civilization
and industrialization can only by corrected by Christian education, and educators are working hard to accomplish this.
Churches also diligently provide Christian education, assured
of the fact that only as men are renewed by the power of
the Word of God can a new society be established.

Mission Education

Those who have encountered Jesus Christ and have
tasted the life in Him have the responsiblity to witness to
others. Korean churches started to teach every Christian to

witness for Jesus from the very beginning. They encouraged adults to lead adults, children to lead their friends, and women to lead women to Christ. Therefore, personal evangelism was an important subject at church or at Christian schools. To be catechized by a church, a person had to lead at least one other person to Christ before membership was granted. Quite a few women evangelists or "Bible women" would carry their Bibles and / or distribute pocket gospels and witness through home visitation. Korean churches encouraged their members to have a strong sense of responsibility and taught them how to lead others to Christ.

This excellent practice is still alive in Korean churches and is now called the "Training Witnesses Program." This program helps church members have an assurance of their own salvation and teaches them to lead non-Christians to Christ and to practice personal evangelism as they witness two by two. Also all the church members distribute tracts during Christmas or Easter season. Recently a program was begun called "Laymen's Mission Training" for those who are leaving Korea to be employed overseas. All of these programs are the pride of the Korean church and follow the good tradition of the early Korean church.

Bible Study

Bible study has been a main factor in Korea's church growth. Originally Confucianism was a religion which emphasized ethics or statutes. Because of this influence, Koreans are very much interested in learning. I think that Korea is still one of the few countries in the world which is so enthusiastic about education.

When the Good News was introduced to our country, the Korean people who had such zeal to learn plunged into studying the Bible. The women studied Korean Bibles and the men studied Chinese Bibles. Churches had many Bible study groups, not only on Sundays, but also during the weekdays. A special period of time was set aside for systematic Bible study once or twice a year when farmers were not busy. Men and women were separated and studied the basics of the Old Testament, the four Gospels, Epistles, and catechism for a week or two. They started each day with dawn prayer meetings, studied the Bible and personal evangelism in the mornings, went out to witness in the afternoons, and had evangelistic meetings in the evenings.

As they diligently read, memorized and discussed the Scriptures, Christians were motivated to lead others to Christ. This movement started around 1920 and it was said that about 65 percent of all church members took part in these Bible studies. This interest in Bible study has encouraged the development of many different types of Bible study groups. Today several Bible study groups meet in the churches and small Bible studies are conducted during the weekdays. This Bible study movement was primarily for adults.

Bible Clubs

Study groups were started for the young people from poor families by Dr. Francis Kinsler, a Presbyterian missionary, about fifty years ago. These students did not have the opportunity to study at schools because of the poverty of their families. The study groups taught them primary school courses along with Christian education. They learned to have services by themselves and were trained to be Christian leaders and to participate in voluntary work. This is called the "Bible Club Movement" which has about 600,000 graduates. Many of these graduates are now leaders in the churches. The Bible Club Movement is still very active.

Christian Schools

Originally evangelism and education were combined in Korea. The Korean church educated Christians to be good witnesses for Jesus and the church evangelized people through education. Missionaries emphasized education from the beginning and enlightened the masses of unlearned people. They especially worked to educate illiterate women for they thought that educating women was a shortcut to the evangelization of the nation. Aware of a woman's special role and activities in the family, they focused on Christian education for women. Women could easily reach their children, husbands, and relatives. Therefore, missionaries established many Christian schools for women and many Christian institutes where married women and middle-aged women learn. Christian women voluntarily tried to find their rights by taking a part in public affairs as they do in the West today.

Until the 1950's most of Korea's leaders were graduates of Christian schools, because the number and quality of Christian schools exceeded those of public schools. Korean churches continue to show great interest in evangelization through education. From the beginning groups of laymen were divided into smaller groups to study the Bible, personal evangelism, Christian education, and better ways of living. In addition to this, deacons, evangelists, and pastors were divided into groups to study the Bible twice a year. These studies played an important role in supplying Christian leaders.

Later, these Bible studies developed into short-term Bible schools. One-month or three-month Bible schools were held in each province during the less busy farming season. Bible schools played a major role in developing a high quality of lay leaders and pastors.

However, due to their relatively low level of education, graduates of these short-term Bible schools could not lead the masses. Therefore, advanced Bible schools were established to help short-term Bible school graduates and high school graduates. Schools of this nature were established in each district by each elders' association and grew to a large number from the year 1910 through 1950. These short-term

Bible schools and advanced Bible schools were organized with men and women in separate school buildings.

A seminary was established in 1901 to train pastors. Presently, the number of students at the Presbyterian Theological Seminary (Tong Hap) is about 1,400. In addition, other Presbyterian denominations have four big seminaries. Other large seminaries plus many smaller seminaries graduate thousands each year. Besides training pastors, seminaries train many people to be Sunday school teachers, kindergarten teachers, and summer Bible school teachers. Presently, we need more programs for raising the quality of our laymen.

We also have many educational programs for women teachers. One such program is the Christian Women Leaders' Association attached to the theological seminary. Pastors' wives, women evangelists, and lay women study every Monday from 10:30 a. m. to 5:30 p. m. except during the vacation. These classes cultivate middle-aged women's potential for the evangelization of all Korean women. This type of women leaders' education can be developed in local churches using church facilities.

I think the responsibility of the Women Leaders' Training Center is enormous because I believe that when housewives are alive, the family will live. And when women and the family are alive, the whole nation can live as during the time of the early Korean church. It is true that God gives both men and women important responsibilites. However, I feel Korean women can and should contribute to the evangelization of the whole world in a greater way. When Korea becomes the center of world evanglization to carry out this great task, the role of women will be great because two-thirds of Korean church members are women.

Most Korean women are not employed, and they have much more free time to invest in winning others to Christ. Especially, they can witness for Christ to their children, families, relatives, and friends. They can use their church facilities in serving the Lord during the weekdays. Women's education, especially the Christian education for middle-aged women, has great potential now because the standard of women's education is higher than ever and most women have financial power.

Confucian and Buddhist education was a tragedy for Korea. It brought the Korean people under the power of darkness. By contrast, we can see how Christian education has contributed to the enlightenment of Korea. The command of our Lord, "Teach them to observe all things," should be deeply implanted in the minds of the Korean people. When every Christian helps teach and exhorts others according to the teachings of Jesus Christ, Koreans will be evangelized and will play an important role in the evangelization of the whole world. God desires to make Christ known to the world. We should, therefore, follow the example of Paul who said: "Whom we preach, warning every man, and teaching every man in all wisdom, that we may present every man perfect in Christ Jesus: Whereunto I also labour, striving according to his working, which worketh in me mightily" (Col. 1:28-29).

Dr. Chung · Chin-Hwang, · president of the Korea Baptist 'Theological Seminary, is a graduate of the Korea Baptist Theological Seminary (B. D.), Asia Baptist Graduate Theological Seminary in the Philippines (Th. M.), and the Southwest Baptist University (S. T. D.). He also studied in the Golden Gate Baptist Theological Seminary and the Tel Aviv University in Israel.

People usually understand "church growth" in quantitative terms with an increase in church members. But an equally valid meaning is qualitative growth, as Christians become mature in ɩ their faith and stewardship . responsibilities. Dr. Chung gives a careful analysis of parachurch organizations that God is using to help laymen know their Bible and to thus witness to their peers. If quantity growth and quality growth were illustrated by two wings on a bird, which would be considered more important?

21 BIBLE STUDIES AND LAYMEN'S WITNESS

by Chung Chin-Hwang

Mobilization of Laymen--The Key to Church Growth

In recent times, the term church growth is being heard quite frequently. Many pastors and theologians have begun to pay attention to the dynamics and methods of church growth. Throughout the world the church in Korea is well-known for its marvelous growth. The church in Korea is continuing to grow both in quantity and quality. The increase in the number of new believers and the intensification of the spiritual level of Korean Christians and their degree of dedication to the Lord and to His gospel are noticeable especially during recent decades. In this chapter we will discuss the role of laymen's witness and Bible studies because many theologians and pastors point to lay mobilization and involvement as the key to church growth.

The priesthood of all believers was undoubtedly one of the theological foundations of the Reformation. Robert L. Saucy, professor at Talbot Theological Seminary, explains the concept of the priesthood of believers in his book *The Church in God's Program:* "This not only has reference to the direct access of each member of the church to God through Christ the High Priest, but it also speaks of the ministry which every member of the church bears." So the mobilization, preparation, and utilization of each believer is very important.

> And He gave some as apostles, and some as prophets, and some as evangelists, and some as pastors and teachers, for the equipping of the saints for the work of service, to the building up of the body of Christ. (Ephesians 4:11-12, NASB)

The mobilization of laymen has a crucial connection with the objective of the Lord which is the salvation of the people of the whole world. The Lord's strategy to get His message to the whole world can be characterized as "multiplication strategy" or "disciple-building strategy." This method involves training faithful men as genuine and productive disciples of Christ who will continue the disciple-making process.

The same kind of strategy is found in the apostle Paul's ministry, revealed distinctly in 2 Timothy 2:2, "The things which you have heard from me in the presence of many witnesses, these entrust to faithful men, who will be able to teach others also" (NASB). One can easily see a spiritual chain reaction in this verse as follows: Paul trained Timothy who trained faithful men who, in turn, trained others. This chain reaction made it possible for the gospel to spread rapidly and widely soon after the ascension of Christ.

Unfortunately, this multiplication strategy disappeared from the church between the second and the fifth centuries A. D. According to Carl W. Wilson, president of the Worldwide Discipleship Association, Inc., "The decline of the disciple-building ministry and the emergence of a separation between the church leadership (clergy) and the people (laity) are directly related." Church historian, Philip Schaff, also says that "the separation of clergy from laity began in the third century and became rigid and complete by the end of the fourth century."

It is no exaggeration to say that it is impossible to make the church grow in quantity or quality without the active contribution of laymen. We must realize that *every* member of the church is asked to dedicate himself to the Kingdom of God and its proclamation. *Every* Christian is in the "royal priesthood" (1 Peter 2:9). *Every* Christian is a "priest unto God" (Revelation 1:6) and is to give himself as a "living sacrifice" (Romans 12:1).

Fortunately, an awakening to the imperative need for disciple making and spiritual multiplication has recently arisen as a worldwide phenomenon in church and para-church organizations. Some theologians call this phenomenon the "Modern Discipleship Movement" or the recovery of the lost art of disciple making.

The disciple-building or disciple-making process has tremendous effects on church growth. The core of the process is multiplication through spiritual generations, many examples of which are found in the Bible. In 2 Timothy 2:2 we see Paul as the first generation in spirtual multiplication,

Timothy as the second generation, faithful men as the third generation, and others as the fourth generation.

When a pastor applies the multiplication strategy to his ministry with diligence, he will mobilize his people, the laymen, to effectively witness for Christ and to follow up new converts. Since this method is Christ's strategy to conquer the world, we have no alternative method.

Jesus gave His Great Commission (Matthew 28:18-20) just before His ascension. In this passage He clarified His strategy to make disciples so as to multiply continually. Three major verbs, *going, baptizing,* and *teaching* reveal the process of multiplication. It is a continuous process by which men who are converted to Christ relate themselves to each other and become responsible, reproducing church members.

No Christian can be excluded from carrying out the Great Commission of the Lord. Therefore, every church member should be mobilized in order to fulfill his commission through Christ's strategy of evangelism.

Even though a pastor delivers dynamic sermons to his people, preaching alone would never match the rapidness in church growth achieved by the multiplication method. In other words, the key to church growth is mobilization of laymen.

In mobilizing the laymen, Bible studies and witnessing are vital component parts like the two sides of a coin. Bible studies and witnessing are inseparable because each one mutually reinforces the other. We have noted that *going, baptizing,* and *teaching* are important factors in making disciples. We could say that going and baptizing are the witnessing process; and teaching is the follow-up process which mainly consists of Bible studies. Continuous church growth requires both processes (witnessing and follow-up) simultaneously because they are inter-related and inter-dependent.

We must pay attention to the fact that every spiritual revival or awakening, and even the Reformaton, was accompanied by Bible studies under designated leaders or bands of anonymous laymen, or both.

The activation of laymen begins with and is accelerated by Bible studies. No person can expect church growth without the laymen being involved in Bible studies.

A Brief History of Bible Studies and Laymen's Witness

When we look at the one hundred year history of the the Korean Protestant church, the revival movement in 1907 stands out prominently. The revival was triggered by Bible study meetings usually called *Sa Kyoung Hoe,* a term which means a conference for searching the Scriptures. The revival movement gave the Korean church a vivid and vigorous experience of Christian faith, and it became the basic color of the Korean church. But it is needful to make clear that the Bible studies which were conducted at the *Sa Kyoung Hoe* were, in most cases, lecture type studies. Therefore, strictly speaking, it is difficult to define the *Sa Kyoung Hoe* as a laymen's Bible study. Currently, the Christian Business Men's Committee would qualify for the designation of laymen's Bible study and will be considered later.

Recently a new sort of Bible study by the laymen themselves has taken root in Korea. This type of Bible study came into being not through the churches but through several student mission groups such as Campus Crusade for Christ (CCC), Navigators, University Bible Fellowship (UBF), Korea Inter-Varsity Christian Fellowship (IVCF), JOY Mission, Youth for Christ (YFC), and Student Bible Fellowship (SBF). All of these organizations began their ministries between 1950 and 1980.

We can classify the student mission organizations into two categories according to origin; those formed by Korean Christians, and those introduced from other lands. The first grouping consists of JOY Mission (1958); University Bible Fellowship (1961); and Student Bible Fellowship (1976). The second grouping is made up of Campus Crusade for Christ

(1958); Korea Inter-Varsity Christian Fellowship (1959); Youth for Christ (1961); and the Navigators (1966). These groups are student-centered, interdenominational, strongly Bible study oriented, and enthusiastically evangelistic with a keen world vision for lost souls. Bible studies usually consist of small discussion groups in which all members participate. Members are also trained to engage in active witness for Christ.

The learning and training activities of the mission groups have come to be known to Korean churches especially through the three mass crusades which were held in 1973, 1974, and 1980. The first was the 1973 Billy Graham Crusade with one million people at the largest meeting. The next was Explo '74, a discipleship training conference that drew 1.5 million to one meeting. The last was the '80 World Evangelization Crusade to which God brought at least two million people nightly. In preparing and conducting these crusades, Campus Crusade for Christ and the Navigators took responsibility of training counselors to deal with the seekers. Training counselors for the Billy Graham Crusade was entrusted to the Navigators. Campus Crusade for Christ was responsible for Explo '74 when about 323,400 persons received intensive discipleship training. During the '80 crusade, to which CCC was committed, more than 13,000 pastors, assistant pastors, and evangelists attended the special conferences. As a result of these mass crusades many Korean pastors and Christian laymen experienced the power of the multiplication strategy and realized the urgent need to mobilize the laymen.

Student Mission Groups

Let us examine the methods and activities of the student mission groups which have awakened and helped the Korean churches to recognize the necessity of the laymen's ministry for church growth.

JOY Mission

JOY Youth Club was formed in 1958 by those who felt the need of evangelism among high school students. In 1966 the name was changed to JOY Club to include all age groups. In 1976 the name was changed again to JOY Mission with the hope of fulfilling Christ's Great Commission.

The fundamental purpose of this student group is to train and adequately equip persons on the campuses and also in business offices for world mission. JOY Mission concentrates its energy in the ministry of multiplication by means of small Bible study groups meeting weekly. Studies have a fixed curriclum arranged in seven steps. The first step is an evangelistic study; the object of which is to win the lost. The second step is a follow-up course designed to help new converts learn basic Christian life activities such as quiet time, victorious living over sin, Scripture memorization, personal evangelism, and a fruitful church life. The third step is a basic Bible study -basic doctrines and Bible study methods. The fourth step is training as a witness focusing on personality and life attitudes. The fifth step is Leadership Training 1: principles of discipleship training and the discovery of spiritual gifts. The sixth step is Leadership Training 2: skill in the use of the Bible and a grasp of the Scriptures as a whole. The seventh step is Leadership Training 3: world vision and independent discipleship training. JOY Mission has published profitable Bible study materials such as *The Meaning of the New Life, Beginning of the New Life, Studies on Romans,* and *Personality of a True Christian.*

University Bible Fellowship (UBF)

The University Bible Fellowship began activities in Korea in 1961 and became a nationwide organization by 1968. By 1974 the organization had expanded worldwide with branches in the U. S. A., Germany, Bangladesh, Switzerland, France, Spain, Italy, Japan, Canada, Guatemala, Brazil, Chile, Lybia, and others.

The regional director is called a shepherd. Graduate leaders and student leaders under him conduct Bible studies. The UBF divides the year into two semesters, spring and fall. Each semester, the members of this group study the Bible book by book based on the level of their spiritual understanding. The Bible study material, *Daily Food,* has a twofold emphasis: help in regular Bible study and encouragement toward a meaningful devotional life.

During the summer and winter vacations University Bible Fellowship conducts spiritual conferences. Usually the summer conferences are evangelistic in nature and the winter ones major on leadership development. Weekend conferences are held whenever there is a felt need. University Bible Fellowship's rigorous and enthusiastic Bible study approach challenges the Korean churches.

Student Bible Fellowship (SBF)

The Student Bible Fellowship separated from the University Bible Fellowship in 1976 because of different viewpoints concerning local churches. The SBF desired to have a good relationship with local churches while the UBF wanted to continue as an interdenominational mission group. Most of the staff personnel of this organization have had a theological education. Some graduate leaders have started new churches while student leaders are responsible for student evangelism.

Organization, Bible study methods, vision, and other educational activities are quite similar to the UBF. Sending trained student leaders into local churches is one remarkable contribution of this group.

Campus Crusade for Christ (CCC)

Campus Crusade for Christ was introduced to Korea in 1958. Since that time it has grown rapidly in number and influence and has become the largest Christian student movement in Korea. CCC began its ministry as an interdenominational Christian student movement, designed to present the claims of our Savior to the major segment of the collegiate world which has little or no active, vital contact with the Lord Jesus and His church.

The Campus Crusade for Christ organization is convinced that the key to reaching the collegians is to mobilize and train students who, in turn will win, build, and send others for Christ as a multiplication effort. The mission also has developed an effective ministry among laymen and pastors, challenging and training them to become part of a spiritual revolution. Lay Institutes for Evangelism teach laymen how to help others know Jesus Christ personally as Lord and Savior, how to live in the power of the Spirit, how to introduce others to Jesus Christ, how to live by faith, how to be part of a strategy to help fulfill the Great Commision in our time, and how to engage in spiritual multiplication.

An important practical method of multiplication is the Korean concept of *Soon;* the literal meaning of *Soon* is *rod* or *shoot* as found in Isaiah 11:1. The word *Soon* is a genuine Korean word which contains some vital hints regarding the principles of spiritual multiplication; that is, the word connotes the possibility of sprouting leaves, flowers, and of bearing fruit. The sprouted rod has the ability to bud other rods which will have the same potential. *Soon* leaders on campuses form active *Soon* groups for the purpose of training other *Soon* leaders to carry on the multiplication process.

Campus Crusade for Christ has contributed much to the Korean churches but most particularly in the matter of training reproductive laymen. In Korea at present CCC has about 130 full-time staff members, more then 10,000 college student members, and about 180,000 college graduates. More than 1,000,000 persons have been trained by the Leadership Training Institute.

This mission group has excellent Bible study materials. In addition, the *Ten Steps Study Books* designed to follow up new believers and many other small booklets have been published which are very useful as aids to spiritual growth.

Inter-Varsity Christian Fellowship (IVCF)

Inter-Varsity Christian Fellowship, introduced in 1959, has student evangelism as its objective. Evangelical faith, worldwide linkage, and literature work are the foundational activities of IVCF. It has two major fellowships--the campus fellowship and the graduate Christian fellowship. Campus groups are called chapters. The chapter staff worker takes the responsibility of helping each member on the campus. This group has published the following helpful Bible study materials which are available to laymen: *One-to-One, The Way of Living, Invitation to Happiness,* and *Being Willing to Suffer for the Gospel.* Participation in church training programs, ministry in local churches by the staff workers, and publication and distribution of Christian literature are some of the contributions IVCF has made to the local churches.

The Navigators

The Navigators began its Korean ministry in 1966 as an international and interdenominational Christian mission. The aim of the Navigators is to make disciples all around the world, thus helping to fulfill the Great Commission which the Lord gave in Matthew 28:19-20.

This organization is convinced that the multiplicative process shown in 2 Timothy 2:2 is the only way the Great Commission of our Lord can ultimately be fulfilled. Disciple making is central to its ministry. The Navigators emphasize the spiritual quality of every member. The group is well known for its carefully prepared Bible study materials such as *Studies in Christian Living* (ten volumes in booklet form); and *Design For Discipleship* (six volumes). In addition, the *Topical Memory System* is quite valuable in helping laymen memorize the Scriptures. This mission has awakened Korean churches to the imperative of Bible study and spiritual reproduction through the ministry of laymen.

Youth for Christ (YFC)

Youth for Christ focuses on leading teenagers to Christ. The objective of this group is evangelization on the campuses through Christian fellowships. Youth for Christ has three ways of achieving this objective. The first is leading teenagers to Christ and to the church. The second is helping new converts to grow in their Christian experience. The third is encouraging young Christians to dedicate themselves fully to Christ and to become active witnesses for Him.

Youth for Christ has two kinds of meetings; one is for witnessing to the unbelievers, and the other is for training its members. They call the former "Impact" and the latter "Insight." "Impact" is an informal meeting led by the staff of the club. "Insight" is a meeting to help every member grow in Christ and to equip young Christians as workers in the spread of the gospel. The group has 3, 200 members. More than 21,000 high school student members have graduated.

Christian Business Men's Committee (CBMC)

In addition to the student-centered agencies, the Christian Business Men's Committees should be considered. This organization came to Korea in 1952 with the purpose of appealing to the businessman rather than the student. The objective is to evangelize men of the business world through activities such as prayer meetings, mealtime prayer meetings, and follow-up which is called "Operation Timothy." Financial support is provided for such church activities as the early morning interdenominational Easter prayer meetings and the development of a unified hymnal.

Weekly prayer meetings are conducted for the purpose of helping members through prayer, testimony, and Bible study. The Bible studies focus primarily on the application of the truth to daily living rather than on doctrinal teachings.

The mealtime outreach meeting is a strategy to lead

unbelievers in the business world to Christ. Outreach luncheons, banquets, and conferences are held to which each member invites a fellow businessman in order to provide an opportunity for him to hear the gospel.

The follow-up program is for the purpose of encouraging members to attain a higher spiritual level and a deeper committment to Christ. Through this program the CBMC seeks to enlarge its membership.

Besides these activities, the committee has a Mayor's prayer breakfast from time to time which emphasizes prayer for governing authorities and makes possible a witness for Christ to them (See Romans 13:1-2).

Laymen's witness groups and their Bible studies are attracting the attention of most church denominations in Korea. Some churches have adopted the Bible study methods and follow-up activities of the mission groups in their Sunday schools, and have begun to enjoy the effectiveness of the program.

Since the level of education, economics, culture, and other aspects of the Korean society is developing rapidly, it is urgent to adjust the pattern of church ministry to meet the challenge of a changing society. Changes in the patterns of church ministry began in the mission groups working among students and laymen. The trend toward lay ministry is not limited to Korea, but is a worldwide phenomenon. One indication of this fact is that the Southwestern Baptist Theological Seminary in the United States, which is the largest in the whole world, has a course on the subject "Discipleship Evangelism" in which the modern discipleship movement is studied along with the philosophy and strategy of disciple making.

Until now, the modern discipleship movement has been conducted mainly outside the churches; hopefully, it will be incorporated into the life of the local churches for greater growth and fulfillment of the commission of our Lord. As the mobilization of laymen is a major key to church growth, pastors and theologians should not hesitate to study the disciple-making strategy and adopt it in their church programs. Seminary students should be taught and trained in the discipleship process.

The prospect of church growth in Korea will be even more exciting when more churches use discipleship approaches in carrying out the Great Commission.

PART FIVE

DANGERS AND OPPORTUNITIES

Dr. Son Bong-Ho is Professor and Chairman of the Philosophy Department of the Hankuk University of Foreign Studies, Adjunct Professor of Christian Philosophy at ACTS (Asian Center for Theological Studies and Mission) and Preacher for the Seoul Yungdong Presbyterian Church. A graduate of Seoul National University (B. D.) and the Free University of Amsterdam (Ph. D.) he has a unique understanding of Korean church growth. He has published Science and Person, A Study on the Idea of Philosophy as Rigorous Science in Kant and Husserl, *1972.* Modern Spirit and Christian Intellect *(in Korean), 1978 and several articles.*

Though a prophet's message of warning is needed, such words are usually not popular. Even the people of God prefer the praises of men. Dr. Son rejoices in the growth of the Korean church, yet alerts readers to dangers of an overemphasis upon quantitative church growth. What growth results from Shamanism's influence and what is the work of the Holy Spirit? New and important insights are suggested.

22 SOME DANGERS OF RAPID GROWTH

by Son Bong-Ho

The numerical growth of the Korean churches is phenomenal by any estimation. No conscious Christian could be unhappy or unthankful for such growth. This is because the Bible speaks in a positive sense about numerical growth, as when believers grew in number after Pentecost (Acts 2:47). Quantitative church growth is an indispensable requirement for countries like Korea where the majority of the population is still unevangelized. If a church does not aim at increasing her membership as a major goal, she is not healthy. Like other Christians, both within and outside Korea, I am grateful to

God for the numerical strength of the Korean church, and I am proud of serving a church which is also growing rapidly.

A positive attitude toward the growth of Korean chur- ches is held by this writer in spite of its weaknesses. My criticisms, therefore, are by no means intended to discourage Korean Christians from further efforts in evangelism or to keep Christians in other countries from learning from Korea's example. I would be the last to complain about the present growth. On the contrary, I write this criticism in the hope that growth may continue in a better and healthier way. My intention is to "spur a galloping horse."

The negative aspects of rapid growth are, indeed, very real and alarming; they are not just imagined or anticipated. They are realities and their bitter fruits are beginning to be reaped. Unless fundamental self–criticism and reformation take place very soon, I seriously fear that the Korean churches might lose all that they have gained or that Christianity in Korea may be so distorted that all our labors may be lost.

Criticism and reprimand are never pleasant tasks, especi- ally when the people are so visibly God-blessed. It is much easier to go along with the jubilant crowd than to sit back pointing accusing fingers. But someone must assume this unpleasant, yet necessary, task. However, mine is not a lone voice in Korean Christianity today. I am simply voicing the growing concerns of many mature Christians.

The negative aspects of Korean church growth include two main types: one arises from the excessive zeal to increase church membership at any cost; the other is the direct conse- quence of large churches. Though these problems are related to each other, I shall deal with them separately for the sake of clarity.

Quantitative Growth by Any Means

The British philosopher, David Hume, once remarked, "If we take in our hand any volumn of divinity or school metaphysics, for instance, let us ask, 'Does it contain any abstract reasoning concerning quantity or number?' 'No.' 'Does it contain any experimental reasoning concerning matter of fact and existence?' 'No.' Commit it to the flames: for it can contain nothing but sophistry and illusion." The modern materalistic world is obeying Hume without reservation. Anything which cannot be expressed in numbers or cannot be subjected to experiment is disregarded and abandoned as unimportant and peripheral. Any quality which cannot be quantified has little chance of being mentioned in a scientific treatise. And any aspect of life which is not treated by science is considered unessential. Values are also quantified and, in this materialistic world, expressed in terms of money.

Unfortunately, Christians, and even Korean Christians who know little about Hume, too readily accept his philosophy. Without clear awareness of what they are doing, most Korean Christians, like the rest of the population, regard numbers as the essential expression of reality. Churches with rapid membership growth are looked upon as obviously good churches. Pastors who build up large congregations are considered able. The strength of churches is estimated according to the number in attendance at Sunday services and the size of their yearly offerings. Charts and graphs appear in every church office; and statistics are published in the weekly bulletins of most congregations. Gradually, but unconsciously, the numerical growth of the Jerusalem church (Acts 2:47) is magnified out of proportion to other factors, while God's wrath upon David's census in 2 Samuel 24 is conveniently forgotten.

The Neo-Pythagoreanism, * as I call the worship of numbers in modern society, has been recently reinforced by the introduction of the theological pseudo science called church growth which is developed and propagated by the Fuller

---

* The Pythagoreans believed in the mystical significance of numbers.

Theological Seminary School of World Mission in Pasadena, California. In spite of some positive contributions it has made in other parts of the world, church growth theology has done more harm than good to Korean churches in general. This theology is characterized by its naivete or fatal lack of a critical attitude toward the materialism of modern culture. This materialism is the anti-Christ of today. When an emphasis on numbers is introduced without any understanding of its materialistic cultural background, Korean pastors are unaware of the philosophy they are absorbing. Consequently, the witness of their churches to modern culture is weakened. The fact that Robert H. Schuller of the Crystal Cathedral near Los Angeles, California, is becoming a hero to many Korean pastors suggests the degree of preoccupation of Korean Christianity with numbers. Numbers takes precedence over the purity of church discipline and teachings. Numbers are even used to represent the quality of faith.

The Neo-Pythagoreanism of Korean Christianity, coupled with a national spirit of competitiveness and success consciousness, is putting heavy pressure on church leaders. If membership does not increase and if the offerings are not as large as ambitiously planned, the pastor should be ready to leave. According to the general understanding of Korean Christians, all other spiritual factors, such as prayer, Bible knowledge, maturity, consistent Christian living, love, etc., should be expressed in terms of increased membership and offerings. Quantitative growth then represents everything good about a church.

It is, therefore, understandable that most pastors try to increase membership by every means possible. Of course, witnessing for Christ and bringing more souls into Christ's fold is required not only of pastors but of every Christian. By God's grace, Korean churches have a fine tradition of diligent evangelism which should be kept alive. But when the motivation is not pure and the methods are not fair or biblical, evangelism may defeat its own purpose. This kind of evangelism may obliterate the identity of the Christian gospel and eventually prevent further witnessing. This is precisely what I fear most. I will, therefore, discuss some of the dangerous practices of many Korean churches which are, nevertheless, very effective in increasing the physical strength of the church. These practices must be discontinued.

Shamanizing Christianity. Churches, such as those in Korea, can never grow without the active intervention of the Holy Spirit. This fact, however, does not preclude our analyzing from a human standpoint possible reasons why Korean churches are growing. These reasons are also analyzed in other sections of this book.

One such reason is the Shamanistic background of Korean culture which plays an important role in the present growth of Korean churches. Shamanism is the oldest religion in Korea, brought to the peninsula by the first settlers. As one of the most primitive natural religions of the world, Shamanism has almost no ethical teachings. Innumerable demons are believed to bless and curse men according to the demon's whims. Neither blessings nor curses are morally deserved. The demons are believed to be manipulated by Shamans using special occult techniques and offerings which amount to briberies. Both the blessings and curses are entirely worldly. Blessings include wealth, health, power and honor. Curses include disease, poverty, failure in business, etc. Shamans teach little about the next world.

Shamanism's impact upon the Korean mind and culture is as profound as it is old. The Korean value hierarchy, social practices, family life, and political life all reflect the influence of Shamanism. Even though it has been pushed aside throughout Korean history by Buddhism, Confucianism, and Christianity, Shaminism's resilience has been remarkable. Buddhism and Confucianism have been Shamanized to a certain degree and Christianity has also been influenced. Shamanism's penetration has speeded up recently, especially because of the churches' drive for numerical growth.

Some Shamanistic elements are very effectively used by the Christian churches, mostly without fully realizing their origin, in order to attract more people. Most apparent is the excessive emphasis in sermons on the believers' earthly blessings. The Full Gospel Central Church in Seoul, which claims over three hundred thousand members, for instance, uses as a church slogan 3 John verse 2: "Beloved, I wish above all things that thou mayest prosper and be in health, even as thy soul prospereth." The church teaches that all believers will be rich in possessions, healthy in body, and prosperous in spiritual life. They call this "the triple meter faith." Faith healing by laying hands on the sick is much practiced. People pray for material blessings shamelessly while at the same time giving offerings, sometimes in large amounts. The church, in spite of much criticism and some irregularities, is growing day by day. It is already the largest single congregetion in the world and perhaps the richest.

The visible example of success of the Full Gospel Central Church has made enormous impact upon the Korean churches. Numerous pastors attempt to imitate Rev. Cho Yong-Gi, the pastor of the Full Gospel Central Church, but they lack his charisma. They are experiencing moderate success as far as the increase of membership and offerings are concerned.

With little emphasis on Christian social responsibilities or daily Christian living, they loudly promise earthly blessings as rewards of faith, prayer, and sacrifices in forms of offerings and services to the church. Prayer with fasting, speaking in tongues, and visible signs of the second birth are excessively stressed. As a result, many Christians who do not have the gift of tongues or an ecstatic experience of the second birth fall into doubt and end up in mental clinics. The majority of the Korean churches, mostly Presbyterian, Methodist, and Korean Evangelical, remain rather sound, but very few remain totally unaffected by this Shamanistic mysticism. The main temptation is to emphasize the promise of earthly blessings in order to attract the Shamanistically attuned Korean populace.

As a strategy of mission, Shamanism may legitimately be used as a point of contact. The Scriptures certainly teach that believers may expect earthly as well as spiritual blessings from God. Furthermore, the doctrine of grace is the cornerstone of the Christian gospel. Believers, therefore, can without hesitation pray for wealth, health, and deserved honor on the earth. In order to attract the attention of the Shamanistically oriented Koreans, we can legitimately tell them that God is the source of all blessings including worldly ones. This, however, should be done with care and moderation.

Earthly blessings, though not excluded, are not the only blessings promised to believers, nor are they the most important ones. Having accepted Jesus Christ as Savior, new believers should learn that "It is more blessed to give than to receive" (Acts 20:35). Blessing in giving is something which is entirely unknown in Shamanism and is increasingly being neglected in many Korean churches.

Sacrifice and Social Responsibility Neglected

New believers should be trained to recognize the great value of spiritual blessings which sometimes demand the sacrifice of earthly possessions, honors, health, and pleasure. Sacrifice and selflessness are not sufficiently emphasized in the Korean churches for fear of losing members. It is widely known that Korean Christians are giving very much, perhaps more than Christians in many other parts of the world, but not everyone is giving out of a pure heart. Many give in order to receive more, based on the Shaministic practice of bribing demons.

In the spiritual world, evils travel in groups. Once a Shaministic practice gains entry, various other Shamanistic influences quickly rush into churches. Pastors are, for example, looked upon and treated almost as Shamans by many new believers rather than as spiritual leaders who teach them the Word of God.

Believers obey their pastors, but believers do not respect their pastors as much as they fear them. A considerable portion of Korean Christians are more interested in their pastor's prayers for them than their sermons. Many seem to think that the minister's prayer is more efficacious than that of a lay believer. This attitude puts pastors in a special position far above the elders in the Presbyterian church in which the ministers and elders officially hold the same authority. In other words, the priestly function of a minister is emphasized far more than that of prophet. This is a clear contradiction of one of the basic principles of the Protestant Reformation.

Unfortunately, many pastors are consciously fostering such an image of themselves in order to enjoy higher authority than the elders. Pastors overemphasize the efficacy of pastoral prayers and the rights of baptism and benediction so as to get more power. Gradually, but unconsciously, laymen give cultic respect rather than personal respect to pastors, and laymen listen to, obey, and fear pastors simply because they are ordained. Certain elements of magic may be feared and practices of simony can arise in this atmosphere.

The preaching of the gospel has two general aspects: witnessing for Christ to unbelievers and transforming individuals and culture by edification. In order to communicate the transforming message of the gospel, the churches must use the language and cultural elements of the society in which the gospel is preached. At the same time, the churches should make it very clear how the gospel is different from the teachings and practices of other religions.

Unless communiction and edification are balanced, the churches do not fulfill their task properly. In Korea the communication of the gospel is overemphasized and edification and the transformation of culture and society are neglected.

The time has come for Korean churches to re-examine themselves in order to correct the unbalanced emphasis on numerical growth and the Shamanization of Christianity.

Capitalistic competition for increased membership. Having been under Confucian influence for many centuries, Korean society is highly competitive. This competitive spirit can be seen everywhere: in entrance examinations to universities, in selecting high government officials, in getting jobs, etc. The capitalistic mentality was in Korea long before Western capitalism was introduced. Several state-owned companies, for example, which were losing money began to make profits as soon as they were turned over to private hands.

A similar competitive spirit is visible even in church growth. Churches with the Episcopalian type of government where authority and power are held by officials at the top have not grown rapidly. But Presbyterian churches which are loosely controlled by the presbyteries and where the layman has more authority and power are flourishing. There is nothing wrong with competition, However, excessive competition has its negative side. And in the case of church growth, its damaging effects can be spiritually devastating. Several of these negative aspects need to be pointed out.

One of the worst practices is sheep snatching. In order to increase church membership and the size of offerings, many churches accept members from other congregations without asking for any letter of recommendation. Furthermore, most churches do not issue a letter of recommendation unless members who ask for it leave the city. Gradually, the practice of officially issuing a letter of transfer is dying out in Korean Christianity. Thus, any member being disciplined by one church can join another congregation and participate in the Lord's Supper without any problem. This practice makes all church discipline useless, and so discipline is disappearing from the churches. To discipline a member means to lose a member, thus, few church sessions are willing to practice discipline. The purity of the church is being seriously endangered for the sake of numerical growth. Now Christians wander from church to church, especially in large cities like Seoul, in search of a congregation to their liking. Many ministers are eager to catch as many of these wanderers as possible and make every effort not to lose anyone.

In a situation like this, one can see how unreliable church membership statistics are. Many "floating" believers are counted twice or three times because they may register in one church without bothering to withdraw from the other. Each church is unconsciouly tempted to magnify the number of members, and this sometimes blinds the eyes of the one who counts. Consequently, statistics based on the reports of local churches are not entirely trustworthy.

"A battle of all against all" is going on in Korean church life now. This war has almost no rules of the game. Resolutions of general assemblies on this matter are scarce and not well obeyed even if they are made. Korea is one of the few countries in the world which has no law regulating religious affairs. The government cannot interfere in this matter. In large cities like Seoul, one can see two church buildings of the same denomination adjacent to each other and more than a dozen church signs in one apartment complex.

Once a newspaper reported that in one building in Seoul more than ten new congregations were competing with each other. For several historic reasons the unbelieving Korean society holds a rather tolerant attitude toward Christianity. But unethical practices and excessive competition in the churches invite criticism from non-Christians.

The normlessness of Korean churches also results in a large number of theological seminaries. The majority of these seminaries are not qualified to provide theological education and are usually not accredited by the government. Recently the government, after long hesitation and deliberation, forced some of these seminaries to close. But more than one hundred of them, mainly in Seoul, are still operating illegally, thus defying the government's perfectly justified order. These unaccredited theological schools, run by a few ambitious clergymen or small denominations or fractions of large denominations, have been producing unqualified graduates. These graduates are becoming one of the main sources of disorder, even though their vigorous evangelism has certainly contributed to the number of church members as well as to the number of congregations. Because of poor education, such men usually cannot find any posts within existing congregations and are thus forced to start frontier churches requiring much hardship and diligent work. In many cases they have caused more harm than good by lowering the quality of faith and by disrupting interchurch relationships.

The free competiton of all against all produces one result which is looked upon as the worst consequence of the capitalistic economic system: the rich become richer and the poor become still poorer. The rich churches attract good pastors, and good pastors attract more people, so that the church becomes still larger, while the poor churches and the churches in the countryside usually have to be satisfied with less qualified or less able ministers and thereby become still poorer. Not only good preachers but also beautiful, large buildings, glittering interior decorations, well-practiced and expensively robed church choirs, costly musical instruments, and well-organized home visitation attract some people. Excessive money is often spent on unessential things while much needed works of mercy and mission are neglected. Proportionally little money or interest is given to the church's social concerns, while too much is spent for church buildings and decorations.

Korean pastors, especially of large city churches, are highly paid, perhaps higher than anywhere else in the world. The minister of a medium sized congregation of about 600 members in Seoul is on an average paid almost twice as much as a university professor if all his fringe benefits are counted. I personally am in favor of pastors being well paid.

The problem lies in the enormous difference between what the large church pays as compared to the small church; and what the city pastor receives as compared to the rural pastor. No real effort has been made so far to close the gap. This capitalistic way of payment increases the stress on many already overworked Korean pastors.

Because one soul is important to the Kingdom of God, the church of Christ has every responsibility to increase the number of sheep in the fold. Nourishing believers with good food and leading the sheep along correct paths should be emphasized equally. Furthermore, the church's first concern should be the enlargement of the Kingdom of God, not the growth of the local church. Any efforts to add members should focus on unbelievers and not on the sheep of other folds.

The capitalistic competition for the growth of one's own congregation has blinded the eyes of believers from seeing their other responsibilities. Their competitive spirit is one of the reasons why Korean churches have such great difficulty cooperating in worthwhile efforts. Even in mission efforts, more missionaries are sent out by local congregations than by mission societies or by denominations.

Problems Following Rapid Growth

In the preceeding, I have tried to analyze some of the main problems arising from excessive zeal to increase church membership. In the following, I will deal with some of the problems resulting from the rapid growth of the Korean churches. In this section I can be relatively brief because the social and religious background in Korea has been sketched earlier. Again, I would like to make very clear that I do not wish to complain about the rapid growth. My purpose is to indicate the problems so that we may be aware of them and solve them -- and to warn other churches which want to follow the Korean example so that they can avoid our mistakes. The following problems are visible at the moment in the Korean churches.

Shortage of qualified leaders. One of the inevitable consequences of the rapid growth of the churches is the shortage of qualified church leaders. Korea must have more ministers and theologians, and the demand for them is greater than can be met. Training costs time and money. The leaders of today were trained when we had a relatively small number of Christians and the churches were poor. Among the many who were trained years ago, a considerable number stayed in the United States and in other Western countries. There are several hundred Korean churches in America with memberships running from ten to several hundred. These churches claim a large portion of the Christian leaders who could work much more effectively in Korea.

An acute shortage of theologians is especially felt. Many theological seminaries do not have even one qualified teacher. Thousands of Christian groups ask for good leaders who can guide them in their Bible studies and advise them concerning journalism, arts, literature, music, etc. Able Christian workers are in demand but the supply is insufficient.

With God's blessing, some agencies in Korea are now investing in the training of future Christian leaders. Several scholarships have been set up to educate able young people both in and outside Korea. But we will have to wait for some time before we taste the fruits. Fortunately, the number of candidates for Christian work is increasing and the mumber of applicants to theological colleges and seminaries is growing every year. Meanwhile, however, the present shortage will continue with long-term consequences.

Image of Christianity as immature. Until recently the Korean people have either not thought much about Christianity or have a favorable attitude toward it; but now they are watching the Christians. Suddenly, the church has become an important factor in our society so that nobody can easily ignore it. The mass media are giving us more attention, and the government is becoming ever more cautious in dealing with church affairs. Some people feel a bit threatened by the enormous numbers and social influence of the church. In any case, the Korean people are forming their own image of Christianity.

Unfortunately, their image of Christianity is now based on the immature state of the Korean churches. The immaturity of the churches is almost inevitable because the quantitative growth has been so fast. Like a mentally retarded youth, the body has outgrown the mind. Korean churches are not prepared to use their power and influence responsibly, and their immaturity is being observed by Korean society. It will take time and the conscious effort of Korean Christians to change the image which society has formed of the church.

The problem of uncommitted Christians. When Christians were a small minority, every single believer was precious. This is still the case with many small churches, especially in frontier churches and in the countryside.

In congregations with more than a thousand members, a growing number of people are becoming anonymous, unnoticed, uncared for, and uncommitted. They float from church to church searching for sermons, services, and pastors of their liking. To avoid having to make a commitment, they hide themselves in the crowd. These people, therefore, go only to big churches where they can remain unexposed. Such is hardly an ideal believer. Tragically, the number of such uncommitted believers increases as churches grow.

Epilogue

I have so far compiled a list of evils in relation to the numerical growth of Korean churches. The list is, of course, far from complete, but sufficient to provide some balance to the rosy picture generally painted. In spite of all these shortcomings, I love Korean churches and thank God for their growth.

Dr. Han Kyung-Chik is pastor emeritus of the Young Nak Presbyterian Church in Seoul, Korea. A graduate of Soong Sil (Union Christian) College in Pyung Yang, he received his B. S. degree from the Emporia College (Kansas), B. D. from Princeton Seminary, and the Doctor of Divinity from Emporia in 1948. Born in North Korea, he came south following liberation in 1945. He began the Young Nak Church with 27 members and now it has a constituency of over 60,000. Dr. Han has served as a board member for many institutions and is respected around the world for his vision for evangelism, mission, education and social concern.

Dr. Han Kyung-Chik is eminently qualified to write this concluding chapter. The positive and negative aspects of the Korean church are honestly and humbly presented. Paul's statement that we have this treasure in earthen vessels (2 Cor. 4 : 7) applies to the Korean church also. However, let us not dwell on the weaknesses of men, but upon the love, power and mercies of God.

23 THE PRESENT AND FUTURE OF THE KOREAN CHURCH

by Han Kyung-Chik

Soon we will celebrate the 100th year of Protestantism in our country. I feel that it is wise at this time to look back upon the past of our church and to make new plans for the future, correctly evaluating the present situation. As we look back upon our church we cannot but thank God for how He has blessed the Korean church in a special way among the many churches throughout the world. In Korea, church progress and growth are amazing. Korea has over seven million Christians today. It is surely by God's grace and mercy that Korean churches are so greatly blessed. The Lord in His great providence must intend to reach the world through the Korean church.

However, one sad fact is that North Korea has no visible church, although I believe underground churches are there. Before Korea was divided by the Thirty-eighth Parallel in 1945, Christianity was prevalent throughout the North. Between 1945 and 1953 a great number of pastors and Christians were martyred and all churches were closed. Naturally, when I now speak of Korean churches, I mean South Korean churches. Although many Christians were put to death in North Korea, a large number fled to the South which is the land of freedom. Those people greatly influenced the growth of our churches after Korea was liberated from Japan and was divided at the Thirty-eighth Parallel. When North Korean Christians fled south, they established a great number of churches, not only in the cities but also in the countryside where they settled. Sons and daughters whose parents had been martyred traveled throughout South Korea proclaiming Jesus for whom their parents had so willingly bled to death.

Those anti-Communists who were caught by the North Korean Communists and forced to join the Communist army became war prisoners in the South during the Korean War. However, they were freed to live in the South by the wise decision of the late President Syngman Rhee. Hundreds of those people submitted to God completely, and they serve Him as pastors and elders in our society now. It is true that God blessed the Korean people in the midst of our national tragedy.

Positive Aspects of the Korean Church Today

We are aware that the Korean church has both good points and weaknesses. First, let me present an analysis of the positive aspects.

Church growth

The Korean church is growing rapidly, for which we are most thankful. Several countries in the world have more than one hundred years of Christian missions, but their churches are not growing as they should for many reasons. These churches scarcely influence their countries. I do not want to discuss those countries, but I am sure you know of them.

By contrast, Korean churches have produced seven and a half million Christians in less than one hundred years of Protestantism. This figure represents about 20 percent of South Korea's population. I do not know the exact number of churches here, but I would judge it must be about 25,000. It is true that churches in Korea grew first in cities. This is often the case when we read world church history. In the New Testament church, the Apostle Paul's policy was to witness in the big cities and to establish churches there. Then other churches were established in the small cities and in the countryside because of the evangelistic activities of big city churches. Therefore, I believe it is natural for Korean churches to center in and around the big cities as this is the fastest way to evangelize the whole nation.

Several factors caused the Korean church to become a growing church. We can never forget the devoted efforts of early missionaries. They had a sound Christian faith based on the Bible and great zeal to reach the ends of the world with the gospel. After they established Korean churches, they encouraged them to become self-supporting and taught them the principles of stewardship and to support their own pastors. If possible, they tried to stand in the background. This allowed Korean Christian leaders to teach their church members, to govern their churches democratically, to encourage their fellowmen to witness with zeal and eagerness, and to teach the right concept of giving. We owe much to the early missionaries in Korea.

Christian witness

The Korean church is very diligent in witnessing. Churches the world over are active in witnessing, but I think that few churches are so eagerly engaged in witnessing as are our Korean churches. For instance, Korean pastors emphasize personal evangelism from the pulpit so that members will bring newcomers every Sunday. When a Korean church is established, it forms a Women's Witnessing Committee within a year or two and then it forms a Men's Witnessing Committee. With their united loving efforts, they send evangelists to start many new churches in areas which previously had no churches. This outreach is also seen in other countries of the world, but we are thankful that Korean churches are so diligent in this respect.

I also observe that many Korean Christians witness at work. For instance, soldiers witness to fellow soldiers. At hospitals, Christian doctors and nurses try to win people to Christ. Christian teachers and students try to evangelize their non-Christian schools. Christian groups meet in government offices, courts, schools, hospitals, factories, companies, and many other places. These groups meet for Christian fellowship, to witness to others, and to serve others through group activities.

One of the characteristics of the Korean church is the establishing of unusual churches such as the Entertainers Church. Many entertainers have repented of their sins and trusted Jesus. How diligent they are to win others to Christ! And they do it well. Athletes have organized Christian Athletes' Meetings and a Hallelujah Football Team has been organized. They are active in witnessing to fellow athletes. Christian taxi drivers also gather to fellowship together and to preach the gospel. Surely it is because the Korean church is so diligent in witnessing for Jesus that it has grown so rapidly. We should continue this spirit of witnessing.

Prayer

The Korean church is diligent in praying. The active

witnessing just described, above did not happen acciden-
tally. First, it is the result of God's grace, and second,
the Korean church is always diligent in praying. Churches in other countries have Wednesday prayer meetings, such
as in the United States. Some churches in the northern part
of the States have Sunday evening services, though this is more
common in the South. Many have only Sunday morning
worship at 11:00 a. m. However, the congregations in
Korean churches are as big on Wednesday as on Sunday.
And they have power in prayer. The Korean church is famous
for its dawn prayer meeting. Christians gather at 5:00 a. m.
and pray earnestly. On Fridays, they pray through the night.
They also have area prayer meetings on Fridays.

In Korean church history, we had prayer retreats or nunneries. Around the time of the Reformation, the early nunneries
were very much corrupted under the leadership of the Roman Catholic
Church. In Protestant churches, nunneries and monasteries were
abolished. However, many prayer retreat centers have been established in Korea and on the outskirts of Seoul. I do not go
to prayer retreats very often, but whenever I take part in
pastors' seminars, from five hundred to ten thousand pastors
and youth gather together. We are much blessed through
prayer. It is through prayer that Korean churches grow so
fast. The Holy Spirit fills our hearts whenever we pray, and
we bear fruit naturally in our lives and in witnessing as well.
When people are blessed through much prayer, they diligently
win others to Christ. This spirit of prayer is the joy of our
Korean church, and I am so thankful for it.

Hymn singing

Korean Christians sing hymns diligently with all their
hearts. Not only Christian leaders, but also regular church
members sing hymns well. Foreigners visiting Korean churches
say, "The entire congregation is such a good choir." Regardless
as to whether a Korean church is big or small, it always has
a choir. Churches have kindergarten choirs, primary school

children's choirs, middle school students' choirs, and high school choirs. These choirs learn music diligently, and they do it well. They have a zeal to learn hymns and therefore sing well.

After I retired from my church, I visited many small churches. Although a church is very small, they will have a choir and sing well. My heart is full of joy while listening to them. When I visited churches established by Koreans in Japan, the United States, and South America, I found that they also have excellent choirs. In fact, the Korean church contributed much to the Korea Music Society. People often think that famous musicians are non-Christians, but in Korea almost all famous musicians are Christians. How thankful I am for this! We Christians have joy and thanks in our hearts and want to sing praises to God. I feel the Lord has blessed us Koreans with a love for music. We read in ancient Chinese history that Koreans are mentioned as people who sing well. Surely, Korean churches have contributed much good music to Korean society.

Church building

The Korean church is diligent in building churches. I have watched how Korean churches grow. Today, churches are started in the apartment buildings, but churches used to be started in a tent. Then the church would meet in a small wooden house and then in a brick house. This is surely one of the good points of the Korean church. Once I visited an old church in another country where Christianity had been introduced a long time ago. I asked the church members there, "Who provided money to build the chapel?" I learned that their church and other churches were built with the help of missionaries. Hearing this, my heart was full of thanks for Korean Christians who build their own churches.

Korean churches have also been diligently helping to build chapels for the army. There are quite a few chapels in divisions and battalions and this contributes a great deal to the evangelization of the army. This, too, is God's grace, and I cannot but thank the Lord for it.

Financial support

Korean church members give tithes of their income wholeheartedly. I do not know what percent of Korean Christians give tithes. Probably the rate is still small, but I know quite a few Christians do tithe. Besides tithing, they give offerings on many special occasions. There are several kinds of offerings in the Korean church: weekly offering, monthly offering, and special offering for church construction, evangelism, and for needy people.

They serve actively in many ways. There are many Christians in Korea who are willing to build their own church, to evangelize with their own money, and to serve the Lord, not depending upon the foreign missionaries. However, Korean churches should make more effort in this respect. More Christians should give tithes. Realizing that we are God's stewards in dealing with money, more Christians should give more than one-tenth of their income. A young businessman came to me and said, "I give more than one-fifth of my income now, but I am praying and waiting for the day when I can give nine-tenths to the Lord and live on one-tenth." How thankful I am to know his heart!

Christian education

The Korean church is very much interested in education. We are indebted to the loving efforts of early missionaries. When they came to Korea to evangelize, they first built schools and then churches. I often repeat the following story: When I attended Soong Shil College in Pyung Yang City, I happened to take part in Dr. Samuel A. Moffett's sixty-first birthday service. I have forgotten all the stories told during the service, but I still vividly remember that Dr. Moffett founded around 250 churches in Pyung An Nam Do and the same number of Christian primary schools. What an excellent idea it was to establish schools and to train the workers for our country.

I realize that churches need schools to grow. The Korean church received this fine inheritance and has now founded quite a few middle schools, high schools, junior colleges, and colleges. The churches have also established many theological seminaries. How good it is to teach and to establish as many Bible schools as possible for this purpose. Now Korean churches are making an effort to teach old people and groups of housewives to use their abilities so as to serve their community in an effective way. Such schools are called Old People's Colleges and Housewives' Colleges. However, I feel that a greater effort must be made in the area of education. I know several churches which have large congregations and rich elders and deacons who are able to invest in education but have neglected it. The Korean church has made strong educational efforts compared with other countries of the world where Christianity was introduced. Accordingly, Korean Christians have high academic abilities and Korea has almost no illiterate people. Certainly Korea owes much to the churches for their zeal in education.

Volunteer service

The Korean churches are active in promoting volunteer service. Soon after the Korean War many orphanages, widows' homes, children's homes, and old people's homes were started. As far as I can remember, about three-fourths of the owners or administrators were Christians. Before Korea was liberated from Japanese rule, Christians ran all the orphanages. Now the government has many schools for the blind but these schools were run by churches during the Japanese rule. Christians started many schools for young widows in Pyung Yang. I visited an institute for handicapped people in the same city.

Christians are the ones who serve the most on all levels of our society. They do many charitable works such as helping the needy and income laborers. Today, industrial evangelism is sometimes criticized, but evangelism is an expression of the Christian spirit to help laborers in many ways, and it is something we must do. The Korean church should continue this good tradition and make even greater efforts in this field. How Christlike it would be if our Korean church would look after the most needy, the most unfortunate, those who are in trouble, and the deserted.

Medical work

How thankful I am that the early missionaries established hospitals. So much good has been accomplished through Severance Hospital in Seoul, Hee Yul Hospital in Pyung Yang, and Dong San Presbyterian Hospital in Taegu. No one can deny this important fact.

About twenty years ago I visited Cameroon and was surprised to learn that only two medical doctors practiced medicine in the entire country. Why? Because Cameroon does not have any medical schools. Cameroon was under French rule, and to become a medical doctor one had to study in France. Although missionaries entered Cameroon many years ago, and although many churches were started, they did not establish any schools above high school level and never thought, of course, of starting a medical school.

I do thank God for the early missionaries' foresight in founding medical schools in Korea. I hope and pray that the Korean church will make greater efforts to do more medical work. Severance Hospital has a fine ministry in Seoul, but I hope it will open many more branch hospitals in the countryside. I hope that Christian doctors will establish many more medical centers instead of opening private hospitals. If these Christian doctors would do their medical work through rural churches, the churches will grow faster.

Cultural contribution

The Korean church has contributed much to our culture. The Korean Bible and hymnals which were published and used by Christians contributed much to the development of Korean literacy and writing. Thus, illiteracy disappeared among Christians and this strengthened Korean society by increasing the literacy rate. I hope that Korean society will use the Korean alphabet exclusively so people won't spend so much time learning the difficult Chinese characters. How convenient it would be if one could learn everything in easy Korean! We Korean Christians should make more efforts in this respect.

One of the first institutions Christian leaders founded was the Korean Bible Society which has made a tremendous contribution. The Korean church also contributed to the publication of many books. I am thankful many Christians here own publishing companies and publish a great number of books. Now each denomination is aware of the importance of mass media and has its own weekly publication. The Christian Broadcasting System, the Far East Broadcasting System, and the Far East Broadcasting Company are effective tools to spread the gospel and to improve Korean culture as well.

National impact

Lastly, I must mention how the Korean church has contributed politically and socially to the nation. When Korea was attacked by Japan, Christians were the first ones who suffered. It is true that people with different religions took part in the March First Independence Movement in 1919, but Christians were persecuted and suffered the most. I was told that more than half of the thirty-three people who signed the Declaration of Independence were Christians.

I have no intention to discuss it in detail, but Christians contributed a great deal to establishing the Korean government after liberation from Japan. I don't think it was just a coincidence that our first president, Mr. Syngman Rhee, and our second president, Mr. Yoon Po-Sun, both were Christians. We see through all this how Christianity serves our nation and people and what benefits Christianity brought to us as a result. We need more wisdom and unselfish, sacrificial patriotism for our country. We should pray earnestly, work harder, and be willing to give our lives to achieve true democracy in this land. We desire that freedom, equality, and a high respect of human rights will be practiced and enjoyed by all people and that our nation will prosper.

Negative Aspects of the Korean Church Today

So far I have enumerated the church's good points; now I am going to mention the negative side, or some weak points of the Korean church. I think that the glorified church--the Body of Christ--has no weak points, but the visible church has many weak points. We must look closely at these problems and seek to correct them.

Fightings and divisions

Korean churches have many fights and divisions. Nobody can deny it. Sometimes, however, divisions are not purely negative. When one church is divided, sometimes both churches in the division prosper because God's grace works even through human weakness. Fightings and divisions certainly affect the growth of churches.

The following story was told by a missionary who evangelized in the countryside. He visited the New Village Movement leader of an exemplary farm village and asked,"Why don't you have a church since you have a meeting hall, a library, public bath, and all the necessary cultural facilities?" The leader said, "I also feel that it would be good if we had a church in our village, but I have a problem. As far as I know, there is much fighting and quarreling in the church. Our village is peaceful, and I worried for fear that the villagers would fight if we established church." My face blushed with shame to hear this story from the missionary. We must repent and realize that these fightings and divisions within the churches are much criticized in our society.

Korean Christians do not seem to know the real meaning of a church. They think it is simply a group of people-it is not. The church is the Body of Christ. Each one of us is a member of Christ's Body, and we cannot divide it. It is a weak point for the Korean church to be divided into so many denominations. We must work hard to keep unity and peace between the mother church and her branch churches. We Christians should be a good example in our own denomination and in whatever we do interdenominationally. It is such a shame that we Christians do not give an example of unity to our society in this crucial time. We must preserve and develop a democracy based on peace and unity so as to protect our nation from Communist attack. We must not blame some other person for our disunity. Each should repent of his or her sin and try to keep peace in the church and denomination. We should "gird the loins of our mind" with an ecumenical spirit. I feel that the Korean church grieves the heart of Christ in this respect.

Theological training

Korea has too many theological seminaries. It is good to establish schools, but so many seminaries teaching different doctrines cause confusion. I believe that a small country like Korea needs only one denominination and one seminary. However, we now have too many seminaries in our country. I feel that we so-called leaders and senior pastors should repent and realize our responsibility to solve this matter.

Self- preoccupation

Korean believers are preoccupied with their mother church. Our natural tendency is to be faithful to those closest to us. We must be faithful in our homes and in our church for if we do not take care of our own church, what else can we do? However, when all our work is centered in our own church, we neglect the work of our denomination as a whole.

It is more difficult to cooperate in a meeting of Presbyterian pastors and elders than to cooperate in the church where I serve. It is far more difficult to cooperate in a general assembly meeting than to cooperate in the Presbyterian pastors' and elders' meeting. Words cannot express how difficult it is to cooperate interdenominationally with all Korean churches; but we must realize that the church is one and that Christ is one. We must unite in the Holy Spirit according to the words of the Bible. I am sure the situation can be corrected if church leaders would think deeply about it and lead and teach members to work together.

The National Council of Churches (N. C. C.) was the representative of all Korean churches after the liberation from Japan and all Korean church leaders used to cooperate with that organization. But now only six denominations belong to the N. C. C., representing much less than half of all Korean church members. The majority is still outside the council. How difficult it is for us to work interdenominationally! Of course the N. C. C. itself has some responsibility for this and should admit this fact.

We should do some things together with all the churches in Korea, such as the Easter service, social service, and voluntary service for our nation. I must confess that this lack of a united spirit is surely one of our weak points. We leaders should repent deeply and lead our churches in an ecumenical spirit

Unsound mysticism

Korean Christians have tremendous zeal and pray earnestly, but are sometimes swayed by unsound mysticism. True, we must pray earnestly, but we must not neglect our other responsibilities. One day a husband came to me and complained that has wife did not take care of their home but had gone to the prayer retreat center and had spent more than one month praying there.

We must correctly understand the Bible. When God says, "Pray without ceasing," He does not mean we should pray and not work. We believers should have the habit of praying in a special place every day plus always praying in our hearts. Our hearts should always be in communion with Christ. He should be in fellowship with us and we with Him. Staying for weeks in prayer retreat centers to the neglect of responsibilities in the home and in business is surely not the Bible's teaching.

According to the Bible, the worship service should be orderly and reverent, and we should glorify God through it. I was told that church members in certain churches clap their hands from the beginning of the service to the end and they pray so loudly that little babies are terrified and cry. Dear Christians! Don't misunderstand speaking in *other* tongues. I do not deny other tongues. However, so many people eagerly yearn for this experience (see 1 Cor. 14:19). Our churches must pray for the sick. God heals the sick, of course, but we must remember that the church is not a hospital. Retreat centers are not hospitals either.

The Bible commands us to not turn aside to the right hand or to the left, because people tend to be swayed by emotions and excitement. This is not biblical. We should learn how to lead a harmonious Christian life, and not turn aside to extremes on the right hand or on the left.

Some Bible scholars claim that shamanism or witchcraft is penetrating deeply into Korean churches. In the midst of such an extreme situation, immoral behavior does happen and some churches are characterized as groups of pagans by our society. We are ashamed that many pagan groups have risen in Korea even though our church is praised throughout the world as a fast-growing church.

Though it is true that God blesses Christians with material blessings, church leaders should not encourage people to ask God for material and worldly blessings. God promises the salvation of our souls when we trust Jesus according to the truth of the Bible. God does not promise that we will be rich and powerful. We may, in fact, be persecuted, troubled, misunderstood, and sometimes put into prison as we try to live according to the will of God. We must realize that we will not always be blessed with good health and success in our business when we believe Christ. Rather we should be ready to be persecuted for the sake of righteousness as we try to live a holy life before God. Therefore, we must teach Christians according to the truth of the Bible, instructing them in sound doctrine and in the proper ways in which to worship our Lord.

Self-righteousness

The Korean church indulges in self-righteousness. We need correct theology and faith to live the Christian life. We must conserve the truth of the Bible. We should hold to orthodox theology which interprets the truth of the Bible correctly; we should not turn aside from this. The words "conservatism" and "orthodoxy" are often heard in the Korean church. And everyone claims that they are either conservative or orthodox. A certain denomination even claims that it is conservative-orthodox.

We should realize that Korean Christians are self-righteous when they claim to be conservative and orthodox, because they often divide churches. Because of this matter of conservatism and orthodoxy, one of the big denominations in Korea split and then split again in a month. Another new seminary was established and it, too, was divided. In fact, those who claim that they are the most conservative and orthodox sometimes turn aside from the truth. We must understand the real meaning of biblical theology and should not continue to be self-righteousness. Those who are church leaders and theologians should repent deeply. We should preserve the conservative faith, but we must not indulge in this divisive kind of conservatism and orthodoxy.

Faith without works

The Korean church needs to have works and not only faith. One of the the weak points of the Korean church is that Korean Christians do not practice Christian ethics. This saying is often heard within and outside of the church: "They seem to praise God and pray diligently, but the way they actually do is different." Christian ethics should accompany our Christian profession.

Once I asked a school teacher who had worked at one school for a long time, "What is the difference between Christian students and non- Christian students?" He said, "They can sing hymns well." I also asked, "Are Christian students more honest in everyday life or more diligent or do they have higher morals in everyday life?" He said, "I cannot tell any difference." My face blushed to hear this. I wonder how much we really do God's will when we say "Lord, Lord" but fail to live as Jesus taught in His sermon on the mount. Don't misunderstand me. In Protestantism we are saved through faith, not through works. However, if we have saving faith, we will bear good fruit, that is, good works. Something must be wrong with our faith if our works do not agree with Christian ethics. Saying, "Lord, Lord" with our mouth and denying Him with our actions is wrong. In fact, we should emphasize the virtues of truth, meekness, and humility. How true, humble, and meek are we Christians? We must repent and reflect upon our lives deeply.

Let me tell you another story. Two churches were established in a city far, far from Seoul. The names of the churches are The First Church and The Central Church. If the city had only one church, it could be called The First Church. Then when another church began later it could be called The Second Church. In Shim Eui Joo in North Korea where I lived, the churches were named The First Church, The Second Church, The Third Church, etc., according to the order of their establishment. If a church is situated in the the center of the city and it had a big congregation, it would be called The Central Church. However, pastors like to name their churches The First Church or The Central Church even when there are many churches around them. This practice is far from Jesus' teaching. It comes from pride.

Wherever I go, I find the name Korean Presbyterian Church. I was told that even those who are not Presbyterian church members establish churches and call them Presbyterian churches. Pastors who do this are not ethical and must deeply repent. All of us should repent. There are many more weak points in our Korean church, but nobody can deny the things illustrated here. Of course I don't think I am excluded from it. I am also one of the violators. Confessing my own sins, I would like to lead the Korean church rightly even though the past has some wrongs.

The Korean Church in the Future

In conclusion, I would like to discuss the future course of our Korean church.

Biblical faith

The Korean church should keep a sound biblical faith. Liberalism and neo-orthodoxy have crept in. If one follows after a social ideology or a faith that centers on the ideas of a certain person without biblical basis, his faith is going in the wrong direction. If the Korean church wants to be blessed continually, it must follow what we call the "conservative faith" which is based on the Bible. Biblical sermons are always best. We can talk about social problems at times, but Korean churches can only be blessed when Christian leaders direct their church members toward a biblical faith and a biblical theology.

Presbyterian theology

I tell Presbyterian church members that we must establish a theology of the Presbyterian church. I am not saying this out of self-righteousness. I believe Calvinism is a sound theology centered on the Bible. We should not be narrow minded, on the one hand, but we should not, on the other hand, turn aside from the truth to the right hand or to the left. We must establish our own traditional, historial Presbyterian theology and help church members to lead Christian lives based upon it. Then I am sure that the Korean church will be blessed and prosper continuously.

Godly living

We must lead a godly life like that of the Puritans. When I studied in the United States a long time ago, young people would laugh when the ideas of Puritans were mentioned. Of course, many years have passed since Puritan days. They said, "The Puritan life is an old story now. It has nothing to do with us in modern days." Young people today say the same thing, but I don't agree. Of course Puritans who lived in England made lots of mistakes and were rejected. However, their principles encouraged purity, love, meekness, humility, and truth which are based on the Bible. We Christians should show an exemplary life in this society by leading a clean Puritan life. We need such a life style so badly today when morality is corrupted and degrading influences of Western society are rushing into this country with such speed. We should lead an exemplary Puritan life to correct the wrongs in our society.

The Korean church today needs to emphasize the restrained use of liquor. This problem was not serious years ago in the Korean churches. But recently I have met several pastors who think it would not be wrong to drink a glass of liquor. If this practice wrongly influences Korean Christians' lives, how can we be the salt and light in our society? Today people are advised not to smoke because it causes cancer. Sadly, the Korean church is rather silent about smoking and also about drinking. What a poisonous influence it is on our families and on our society when we drink and smoke. The

Apostle Paul said, "I will never eat meat, lest I cause my brother to fall" (1 Corinthians 8:13). Following Paul's example, we must abstain from every appearance of evil and pastors need to emphasize abstinence in their messages from the pulpit.

Christians who work in political, social, economical, and cultural fields of our society should conduct, regardless of their position, exemplary lives before others. As all of you well know, Jimmy Carter was the president of the United States. However, he led an exemplary life while he was president. If he could do it, why shouldn't you do it whatever high position you may have in this country? Let's all sincerely reflect upon this.

Undeviating purpose

Several times the Bible speaks of not turning aside to the right hand or to the left, a practice especially important for us in Korea. It is said that the Christian faith has three elements: knowledge, emotion, and will. We know God with our mind; we feel the presence of the Holy Spirit when we pray or when we hear people testify about their salvation; we use our will to live in the will of God. We should not turn aside by using only our mind and knowledge as we trust the Lord. I was told that someone said, "He is a theologian, but not a Christian." We should not relate to the Lord that way.

Some people go the wrong way by being too excited emotionally. Some people feel that they are blessed only when somebody lays his hand upon their heart. Some people think they must look at a sparkling light when they pray. We should not lean to one side or the other. People should emphasize living right and doing good works. It is well to do good works, but we lose power to live right when we turn aside to doing only good works. Trying to live right with our own effort is an idea taught in Confucianism. If we depend upon our strength, we will fail. Why are we human beings weak? Because of our corrupt sinful nature. Therefore, we need faith and we must receive power to do right things through prayer. We should lead a good Christian life and not turn aside to the right hand or to the left.

United in spirit

The Korean church should be united in a sound ecumenical spirit. Some people think the ecumenical movement is worldly. They do not know the real meaning of it. Ecumenical means that we are members of God's universal church, so we should respect others and cooperate with one another in love although our theology and our form of worship may be different.

Though many readers of this book may have a different opinion. I personally believe that all Korean churches should join the National Council of Churches. I am sure that what the N. C. C. accomplishes is poor, but you can join and try to make improvements. Don't criticize from the outside. There are many things which should be done by the united efforts of all Korean churches and Christians around the world. Therefore we need the N. C. C. for Korean churches and the W. C. C. for the whole Christian world. It is not wrong for Korean churches to join the N. C. C. or for the N. C. C. to join the W. C. C. Many mistakes may be made by these organizations, but people who think right should join the organizations in order to correct the mistakes. We Christians should not disappoint our fellow Koreans who sincerely want national unity and peace through our lack of a spirit of unity. We should be good examples to our fellow Koreans by uniting and cooperating with one another.

Voluntarily active

I earnestly wish that Korean churches would serve more actively in evangelism, education, and voluntary service. The church does not exist for its own benefit, but for the benefit of the whole world. It should actively take part in voluntary social work and build Christian schools. To build our country rightly and firmly, those who have sound ideas should enter all the different areas of our society. We must meet poor laborers to learn about their personal matters and see if they have some difficulties in their lives. Churches should play the role of servant rather than the role of master. Jesus said, "The Son of Man came not to be ministered unto, but to minister, and to give his life a ransom for many." Jesus came to this world to save men not only spiritually, but also culturally and materially. To save men wholly, social and economic matters are involved.

Aggressively evangelistic

Evangelism is our first responsibility. We must learn to effectively evangelize our nation. The Korean church should work in the three main fishing grounds--the army, schools, and factories. These are golden fishing places as there are so many soldiers in the army, students in the schools, and laborers and businessmen in the factories. I think all Korean churches should concentrate on evangelizing in these three places.

I believe evangelizing the military is the shortcut to the evangelization of the entire nation as all young men must join the army, navy, or air force. Naturally, when we reach soldiers with the gospel, the whole nation will be evangelized faster. Forty-five percent of the soldiers are now believers. This means that the army chaplains have made great efforts to win soldiers to Christ.

We must help the evangelistic work of army chaplains and sometimes help with their living expenses. I always emphasize distributing hymnals to the army. There are two kinds of hymnals. One is a small hymnal which each soldier can carry in his pocket and the other is a larger hymnal used in the army chapels. Since 200,000 soldiers are enlisted and 200,000 soldiers are discharged from the army every year, we must provide 200,000 new pocket hymnals every year. Also, the army chapels need 50,000 larger hymnals. A pocket hymnal costs 100 won (14 cents) and the larger hymnal costs 500 won (70 cents). If Korean civilian pastors cooperated a little bit more, these hymnals could be easily supplied.

If the majority of Koreans in South Korea come to know and obey Christ, Korea will become a prosperous, dem ocratic country where freedom and equality are enjoyed and human rights are respected. Then Christianity will be Korea's spiritual and mental foundation. This is our national purpose. We have been hoping and praying for this. When the ma- jority of South Koreans are evangelized, Korean churches can reach Southeast Asia, Europe, and the rest of the Third World with the gospel of Christ.

When the South is fully evangelized, unification of South and North Korea will be an easier matter. Both sides speak of unification but the intent of North Korea's unification is different. Kim Il-Sung, the dictator of North Korea, wants to unite South Korea under Communism. It is absolutely use- less to attempt to communicate with this man.

The Korean church's idea of unification is to establish a free democratic country where a representative government is practiced with true freedom and equality and human rights are respected. This is the basic spirit of democracy. Therefore, peaceful unification would be impossible under Communism as the ideology of South and North Korea is quite different. We want North Korea to be a nation like ours. If we want peaceful unification, we must evangelize our fellow North Koreans. We must pray diligently so that they will repent of their sins and come to know the Lord.

We have many ways to witness for Jesus. Nobody can block the sound waves or evangelism through tracts and liter- ature. Evangelism through crew men on ships is needed, too. We have many ways to reach our fellowmen in North Korea with the gospel of Christ. We must evangelize them so as to cause North Korea's evil ideology and system to collapse. Then the faith and ideology of our fellowmen in North Korea will be the same as ours.

My dear fellow Christians, the reason why God has

placed us in this land at this time is to evangelize our nation first, then North Korea, and then the whole world. On this special occasion of the 100th anniversary of Protestantism in Korea, we must respond to God's great commission in a new way and recommit ourselves to the Lord with a new devotion, greater effort, and willing spirit of sacrifice to fulfill this great task.

INDEX